BID 173

Divorce and Remarriage:
International Studies

The *Journal of Divorce & Remarriage* series:
(formerly *Journal of Divorce* series)*

Impact of Divorce on the Extended Family, edited by Esther Oshiver Fisher*

Therapists, Lawyers, and Divorcing Spouses, edited by Esther Oshiver Fisher and Mitchell Salem Fisher*

Divorce Mediation: Perspectives on the Field, edited by Craig A. Everett*

The Divorce Process: A Handbook for Clinicians, edited by Craig A. Everett*

Minority and Ethnic Issues in the Divorce Process, edited by Craig A. Everett*

Children of Divorce: Developmental and Clinical Issues, edited by Craig A. Everett*

Women and Divorce/Men and Divorce: Gender Differences in Separation, Divorce, and Remarriage, edited by Sandra S. Volgy

Marital Instability and Divorce Outcomes: Issues for Therapists and Educators, edited by Craig A. Everett

The Consequences of Divorce: Economic and Custodial Impact on Children and Adults, edited by Craig A. Everett

Divorce and the Next Generation: Effects on Young Adults' Patterns of Intimacy and Expectations for Marriage, edited by Craig A. Everett

The Stepfamily Puzzle: Intergenerational Influences, edited by Craig A. Everett

The Economics of Divorce: The Effects on Parents and Children, edited by Craig A. Everett

Understanding Stepfamilies: Their Structure and Dynamics, edited by Craig A. Everett

Divorce and Remarriage: International Studies, edited by Craig A. Everett

These books were published simultaneously as special thematic issues of the *Journal of Divorce & Remarriage* and are available bound separately. For further information, call 1-800-HAWORTH (outside US/Canada: 607-722-5857), Fax 1-800-895-0582 (outside US/Canada: 607-771-0012) or e-mail getinfo@haworth.com

Divorce and Remarriage: International Studies

Craig A. Everett, PhD
Editor

The Haworth Press, Inc.
New York • London

Divorce and Remarriage: International Studies has also been published as *Journal of Divorce & Remarriage*, Volume 26, Numbers 3/4 1997.

The development, preparation, and publication of this work has been undertaken with great care. However, the publisher, employees, editors, and agents of The Haworth Press and all imprints of The Haworth Press, Inc., including The Haworth Medical Press and Pharmaceutical Products Press, are not responsible for any errors contained herein or for consequences that may ensue from use of materials or information contained in this work. Opinions expressed by the author(s) are not necessarily those of The Haworth Press, Inc.

Cover design by Thomas J. Mayshock, Jr.

The Haworth Press, Inc., 10 Alice Street, Binghamton, NY 13904-1580 USA

Library of Congress Cataloging-in-Publication Data

Divorce and remarriage : international studies / Craig A. Everett, editor.
     p. cm.
     "Has also been published as Journal of divorce & remarriage, v. 26, nos. 3/4, 1997"–T.p. verso.
     Includes bibliographical references and index.
     ISBN 0-7890-0319-8 (alk. paper)
     1. Divorce. 2. Remarriage. I. Everett, Craig A.

HQ814.D63 1997   97-5224
306.89–dc21   CIP

INDEXING & ABSTRACTING

Contributions to this publication are selectively indexed or abstracted in print, electronic, online, or CD-ROM version(s) of the reference tools and information services listed below. This list is current as of the copyright date of this publication. See the end of this section for additional notes.

- *Abstracts of Research in Pastoral Care & Counseling*, Loyola College, 7135 Minstrel Way, Suite 101, Columbia, MD 21045
- *Applied Social Sciences Index & Abstracts (ASSIA) (Online: ASSI via Data-Star) (CD-Rom: ASSIA Plus)*, Bowker-Saur Limited, Maypole House, Maypole Road, East Grinstead, West Sussex RH19 1HH, England
- *CNPIEC Reference Guide: Chinese National Directory of Foreign Periodicals*, P.O. Box 88, Beijing, People's Republic of China
- *Current Contents . . . . see: Institute for Scientific Information*
- *Expanded Academic Index*, Information Access Company, 362 Lakeside Drive, Forest City, CA 94404
- *Family Life Educator "Abstracts Section,"* ETR Associates, P.O. Box 1830, Santa Cruz, CA 95061-1830
- *Family Studies Database (online and CD/ROM)*, National Information Services Corporation, 306 East Baltimore Pike, 2nd Floor, Media, PA 19063
- *Guide to Social Science & Religion in Periodical Literature*, National Periodical Library, P.O. Box 3278, Clearwater, FL 34630
- *Index to Periodical Articles Related to Law*, University of Texas, 727 East 26th Street, Austin TX 78705
- *Institute for Scientific Information,* 3501 Market Street, Philadelphia, Pennsylvania 19104. Coverage in:
    a) Social Science Citation Index (SSCI): print, online, CD-ROM
    b) Research Alerts (current awareness service)
    c) Social SciSearch (magnetic tape)
    d) Current Contents/Social & Behavioral Sciences (weekly current awareness service)
- *INTERNET ACCESS (& additional networks) Bulletin Board for Libraries ("BUBL"), coverage of information resources on INTERNET, JANET, and other networks.*
    - JANET X.29: UK.AC.BATH.BUBL or 00006012101300
    - TELNET: BUBL.BATH.AC.UK or 138.38.32.45 login 'bubl'
    - Gopher: BUBL.BATH.AC.UK (138.32.32.45). Port 7070
    - World Wide Web: http: / / www.bubl.bath.ac.uk./BUBL/ home.html
    - NISSWAIS: telnetniss.ac. uk (for the NISS gateway)
    The Andersonian Library, Curran Building, 101 St. James Road, Glasgow G4 ONS, Scotland

(continued)

- *MasterFILE*: updated database from EBSCO Publishing, 83 Pine Street, Peabody, MA 01960

- *Mental Health Abstracts (online through DIALOG)*, IFI/Plenum Data Company, 3202 Kirkwood Highway, Wilmington, DE 19808

- *Periodical Abstracts, Research II* (broad coverage indexing & abstracting database from University Microfilms International (UMI), 300 North Zeeb Road, P.O. Box 1346, Ann Arbor, MI 48106-1346), UMI Data Courier, P.O. Box 32770, Louisville, KY 40232-2770

- *Periodical Abstracts Select* (abstracting & indexing service covering most frequently requested journals in general reference, plus journals requested in libraries serving undergraduate programs, available from University Microfilms International (UMI), 300 North Zeeb Road, P.O. Box 1346, Ann Arbor, MI 48106-1346), UMI Data Courier, Attn: Library Services, Box 34660, Louisville, KY 40232

- *Population Index,* Princeton University Office Population, 21 Prospect Avenue, Princeton, NJ 08544-2091

- *Psychological Abstracts (PsycINFO)*, American Psychological Association, P.O. Box 91600, Washington, DC 20090-1600

- *Published International Literature On Traumatic Stress (The PILOTS Database),* National Center for Post-Traumatic Stress Disorder (116D), VA Medical Center, White River Junction, VT 05009

- *Sage Family Studies Abstracts (SFSA)*, Sage Publications, Inc., 2455 Teller Road, Newbury Park, CA 91320

- *Social Planning/Policy & Development Abstracts (SOPODA)*, Sociological Abstracts, Inc., P.O. Box 22206, San Diego, CA 92192-0206

- *Social Science Citation Index. . . . see: Institute for Scientific Information*

- *Social Work Abstracts*, National Association of Social Workers, 750 First Street NW, 8th Floor, Washington, DC 20002

- *Sociological Abstracts (SA)*, Sociological Abstracts, Inc., P.O. Box 22206, San Diego, CA 92192-0206

- *Studies on Women Abstracts*, Carfax Publishing Company, P.O. Box 25, Abingdon, Oxfordshire OX14 3UE, United Kingdom

- *Violence and Abuse Abstracts: A Review of Current Literature on Interpersonal Violence (VAA),* Sage Publications, Inc., 2455 Teller Road, Newbury Park, CA 91320

SPECIAL BIBLIOGRAPHIC NOTES

*related to special journal issues (separates)
and indexing/abstracting*

☐ indexing/abstracting services in this list will also cover material in any "separate" that is co-published simultaneously with Haworth's special thematic journal issue or DocuSerial. Indexing/abstracting usually covers material at the article/chapter level.

☐ monographic co-editions are intended for either non-subscribers or libraries which intend to purchase a second copy for their circulating collections.

☐ monographic co-editions are reported to all jobbers/wholesalers/approval plans. The source journal is listed as the "series" to assist the prevention of duplicate purchasing in the same manner utilized for books-in-series.

☐ to facilitate user/access services all indexing/abstracting services are encouraged to utilize the co-indexing entry note indicated at the bottom of the first page of each article/chapter/contribution.

☐ this is intended to assist a library user of any reference tool (whether print, electronic, online, or CD-ROM) to locate the monographic version if the library has purchased this version but not a subscription to the source journal.

☐ individual articles/chapters in any Haworth publication are also available through the Haworth Document Delivery Services (HDDS).

Divorce and Remarriage: International Studies

CONTENTS

ABOUT THE EDITOR

Craig A. Everett, PhD, is a marriage and family therapist in private practice in Tucson, Arizona, and Director of the Arizona Institute of Family Therapy. In addition to his 20 years of experience in clinical practice, he was formerly President of the American Association for Marriage and Family Therapy. Dr. Everett's previous positions include Director of Family Therapy Training and Associate Professor at both Florida State University and Auburn University. He has been the Editor of the *Journal of Divorce & Remarriage* (formerly the *Journal of Divorce*) since 1983 and is an editorial board member of six professional journals.

Introduction

This collection has been evolving over nearly an 18 month period. The goal has been to bring together under one cover a broad variety of divorce-related studies from international authors. It was not possible to assemble these manuscripts under specific themes. However, despite the diversity, there is a richness of perspectives, methods and orientations to inform the reader.

Some of the articles will focus specifically on certain unique aspects of the divorce process within specific cultures such as Australia, Hungary, Japan and The Netherlands. Other articles will focus on more specific divorce dynamics and variables as studied within international cultures such as the Icelandic study of parental custodial patterns, the study of stress and social support on single parent families in Hong Kong, and the British study of infant-mother attachment.

I want to thank these international authors for their patience in delaying publication of their manuscripts until this volume was ready for production.

Craig A. Everett, PhD
Editor

[Haworth co-indexing entry note]: "Introduction." Everett, Craig A. Co-published simultaneously in *Journal of Divorce & Remarriage* (The Haworth Press, Inc.) Vol. 26, No. 3/4, 1997, p. 1; and: *Divorce and Remarriage: International Studies* (ed: Craig A. Everett) The Haworth Press, Inc., 1997, p. 1. Single or multiple copies of this article are available for a fee from The Haworth Document Delivery Service [1-800-342-9678, 9:00 a.m. - 5:00 p.m. (EST). E-mail address: getinfo@haworth.com].

Divorce Australian Style:
A Demographic Analysis

Gordon A. Carmichael
Andrew Webster
Peter McDonald

SUMMARY. A recent administrative decision having seriously disrupted the database from which divorce trends and patterns in Australia can be monitored, the time is opportune to take stock of the country's divorce experience. This is done by examining marriage duration-specific proportions divorcing and cumulative rates of divorce calculated

Dr. Carmichael is a Fellow in Demography and Dr. McDonald is Professor of Demography, Research School of Social Sciences, Australian National University; Mr. Webster is Research Officer, Demography Section, Australian Bureau of Statistics. The willingness of the Australian Bureau of Statistics to allow data prepared by Mr. Webster to be incorporated into this paper is gratefully acknowledged.

Address correspondence to Gordon A. Carmichael, Demography Program, Research School of Social Sciences, Australian National University, Canberra ACT 0200, Australia.

[Haworth co-indexing entry note]: "Divorce Australian Style: A Demographic Analysis." Carmichael, Gordon A., Andrew Webster and Peter McDonald. Co-published simultaneously in *Journal of Divorce & Remarriage* (The Haworth Press, Inc.) Vol. 26, No. 3/4, 1997, pp. 3-37; and: *Divorce and Remarriage: International Studies* (ed: Craig A. Everett) The Haworth Press, Inc., 1997, pp. 3-37. Single or multiple copies of this article are available for a fee from The Haworth Document Delivery Service [1-800-342-9678, 9:00 a.m. - 5:00 p.m. (EST). E-mail address: getinfo@haworth.com].

for annual synthetic and real first marriage, remarriage and total marriage cohorts. The response to the advent of 'no-fault' divorce in 1976 is demonstrated, and the subsequent emergence of new equilibria in cross-sectional levels of divorce to given marriage durations which seem to render them good predictors of the eventual experience of contemporary marriage cohorts is traced. While remarriages following divorce always have been more dissolution-prone than first marriages, the latter are shown to have dramatically narrowed the gap following the re-evaluation of normative sanctions against divorce which both led to and was stimulated by 'no-fault' legislation. Reasons for the much higher divorce rates in Australia in the last two decades are discussed, as is the failure of the adoption of objectively sounder mate selection and marriage timing practices since the early 1970s to more noticeably impact on divorce rates. *[Article copies available for a fee from The Haworth Document Delivery Service: 1-800-342-9678. E-mail address: getinfo@haworth.com]*

INTRODUCTION

The Family Court of Australia, in recently revising the form on which it transmits case by case divorce data to the Australian Bureau of Statistics, has deleted the items 'Marital status of wife at marriage' and 'Marital status of husband at marriage'. Overnight, a capacity dating from 1961 to routinely monitor both the extent to which *first* marriages end in divorce and differentials in the propensity to divorce among first marriages, remarriages following widowhood and remarriages following divorce was lost. With this serious data limitation effective from 1995, the time is opportune to take stock of Australia's divorce experience. This paper does so by drawing on both unpublished work undertaken some years ago by the first and third authors and an updating and extension of that work to 1994 for which the second author was responsible.

In broad terms the likelihood of a marriage ending in divorce in Australia has risen from around 10 percent in the 1950s and early 1960s to around 40 percent in the 1980s and 1990s. After briefly tracing the history of Australian divorce legislation, this phenomenon is explored through the presentation and discussion of trends in several more refined measures of the incidence of divorce. Explanation of detailed features of these trends is largely integrated with description, but a separate discussion section summarizes the main findings from the data, reviews the broader forces underpinning the higher divorce rates of the past two decades, and extends the analysis of particular findings. Measures of divorce examined are marriage duration-specific and cumulative rates of divorce for both real and annual synthetic marriage cohorts. They are calculated both for entire cohorts and for cohorts of first marriages and remarriages following widowhood and divorce, analyses mostly being refined by sex and at some points also by age at marriage. Entire cohort figures cover 1938-39 to 1989-90 (July-June) real marriage cohorts and 1946-94 synthetic cohorts; those for first marriage and remarriage cohorts cover 1960-61 to 1989-90 real cohorts and 1961-94 synthetic cohorts. Refinement by age at marriage is possible only from 1975-76 in the case of real marriage cohorts and 1977 in the case of synthetic cohorts.

The 'reduced events' approach to the analysis of demographic processes is employed. It is applicable to processes (such as fertility, nuptiality and divorce) which 'do not exclude members of [a] cohort from [future] observation' (Wunsch and Termote, 1978, p. 45) (as, for example, mortality and emigration do). At its core in a study of divorce is a matrix of annual ratios of divorces at each single-year duration of marriage to the *initial* size of the relevant marriage cohort; in other words, becoming divorced does *not* remove an individual from the denominator of ratio calculations at longer marriage durations. However, other processes, labelled 'disturbances' by Wunsch and Termote (external migration and mortality), which alter the sizes of marriage cohorts over time by physically augmenting them or removing cohort members from further observation do require duration by duration adjustment of ratio denominators. The matrix of divorce ratios produced yields the cumulative experiences of synthetic marriage cohorts summing vertically from marriage duration 0 years, and of real marriage cohorts summing diagonally, the latter (but not the former) being likely to approximate well results a life table analysis would yield. The adjustments made for 'disturbances' mean that reported cumulative rates of divorce by exact marriage duration *i* years measure likelihoods of having divorced assuming both parties remained alive *i* years after marrying.[1]

DIVORCE LEGISLATION

Before 1961, legislation governing divorce in Australia was the preserve of State (or, prior to 1901, Colonial) parliaments. Divorce laws first were enacted in South Australia, Tasmania, Victoria, Western Australia, Queensland and New South Wales in 1858, 1860, 1861, 1863, 1864 and 1873 respectively. All were modelled on England's *Divorce Act* of 1857, which instituted matrimonial wrongdoing as the fundamental principle determining when divorce should be permitted and specifically provided for it only on the grounds of a wife's adultery, a husband's adultery combined with incest, bigamy, serious cruelty or desertion for two years, and a husband's being guilty of rape, sodomy or bestiality. An attempt in the original Victorian bill to add desertion for four years and simple adultery by the husband was refused Royal Assent.

The range of matrimonial offenses accepted as grounds for divorce later widened in all States, although there was no uniformity in the timing of changes to laws, in criteria used to establish particular offenses, or in the specific offenses ultimately recognized (Joske, 1952). Among offenses added over the years in one or more jurisdictions were simple adultery by the husband, desertion, habitual drunkenness, habitual failure to support one's wife, habitual cruelty, habitual neglect of domestic duties, imprisonment for serious crime, repeated imprisonment, conviction for the attempted murder of or serious assault upon one's spouse, incurable insanity, failure to comply with a Decree for the Restitution of Conjugal Rights, being pregnant to another man or responsible for another woman's pregnancy at marriage, and habitual failure to pay maintenance. The first semblance of 'no-fault' divorce came with the admission of separation for five years as a ground in Western Australia in the late 1940s. Into the 1950s adultery and desertion were everywhere by far the most frequently cited grounds for divorce, but the specifics of State laws varied appreciably.

The *Matrimonial Causes Act 1959* established, from 1961, a single, uniform divorce law for Australia. Previously the only Federal involvement in divorce had been to specify who had jurisdiction in cases of uncertainty (e.g., cases involving deserted brides of American servicemen after World War 2 (Moore, 1981)). Essentially the new Act perpetuated existing grounds for divorce but set standard criteria for determining that each had been established. It also extended Australia-wide the possibility of divorce once separated for five years. Adultery and desertion, however, remained the favoured grounds, separation ranking a distant third. Though more dignified, the lengthy qualifying period discouraged its use, as did its being seen as for those unable to prove misconduct by an estranged spouse. One could divorce (and remarry) much more quickly if able to establish adultery or desertion for two years.

The *Matrimonial Causes Act* governed divorce proceedings for 15 years, but by the early 1970s pressure was building for legislation which did away with fault and would impart to the divorce process 'the maximum fairness, and the minimum bitterness, distress and humiliation' (Stewart and Harrison, 1982, p. 1). The *Family Law Act 1975* came into force in January 1976, introducing irretrievable breakdown of a marriage as evidenced by separation for one year as the sole ground for divorce and establishing a separate Family Court. A major short-term increase in the number of divorces and heated criticism of legislators for liberalizing the divorce process to the point of encouraging its use were inevitable. Subsequent amendments to the Act have sought to streamline Family Court operations, have modified provisions for dealing with ancillary matters of custody, access, maintenance and division of property, and have attempted to promote counselling and mediation, but have not altered the single ground for divorce.

DIVORCE TRENDS

Late last century the divorce rate in Australia was negligible–closer to zero than to one divorce per 1000 married women. By the early 1940s it had risen to just over two per 1000, and it then climbed rapidly to five per 1000 in 1947 as hurried wartime marriages and marriages undermined by wartime separations and trauma foundered. Thereafter the divorce rate fell, reaching 2.8 per 1000 in 1961. It then rose again to 4.2 in 1971 and 7.4 in 1975, before soaring to 18.8 in 1976 with the advent of 'no-fault' divorce under the *Family Law Act*. Much of this increase was a short-term response to a reduction in waiting periods between separation and becoming eligible to file for divorce; in 1976 56 percent of *Family Law Act* divorces (outstanding *Matrimonial Causes Act* cases also were finalized in that year) involved petitioners separated for more than 2 years when filing for divorce, whereas by 1978 the figure was only 33 percent. Over the next three years the divorce rate fell, reaching 11.2 per 1000 married women in 1979. It recovered to 12.5 in 1982, then declined again to 10.6 in 1986 and 1987 before rising hesitantly to 10.9 in 1990 and more strongly to 12.1 in 1993. Essentially, though, the era of the *Family Law Act* has seen a new plateau in the incidence of divorce become established in Australia.

Rates of Divorce for Synthetic and Real Marriage Cohorts

Figure 1, showing cumulative divorce rates per 1000 marriages to selected exact marriage durations for 1946-94 synthetic marriage cohorts, confirms this observation.[2] These rates indicate what levels of divorce by the nominated marriage durations would be in (real) marriage cohorts that happened to experience the marriage duration-specific ratios of divorce observed cross-sectionally in each calendar year. Early synthetic cohorts show evidence of the decline in divorce from its immediate post-war peak. By the mid-1960s 3-4 percent of married couples could expect to divorce

FIGURE 1. Cumulative Divorce Rates (per 1000 marriages) to Successive
Exact Marriage Durations: Synthetic Marriage Cohorts 1946-1994

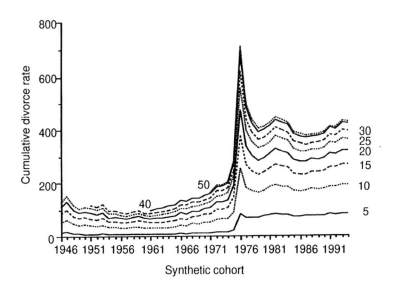

within 10 years, 8-9 percent within 20 years and 10 percent within 30
years. Rates of divorce then began to climb, the trend accelerating in the
lead-up to the *Family Law Act*. This is an important point given a tendency
to blame the Act for the rise in divorce. By 1975 chances of divorcing
within 10, 20 and 30 years stood at 9, 19 and 25 percent, double and more
the levels of a decade earlier. The *Family Law Act* did not suddenly
materialize in January 1976; the debate surrounding it probably affected
the social acceptability of divorce earlier than this. But such major legislation is not initiated in the absence of demand, and the massive early
response to it confirms that demand.

Cumulative divorce rates for 1976 implied that 25, 47 and 62 percent of
marriages would end in divorce within 10, 20 and 30 years, and 71 percent would be dissolved within 50 years. There is no foreseeable prospect
of any actual marriage cohort being so dismembered, but during 1978-94
the synthetic cohort evidence placed the risks of divorcing within 10, 20,
30 and 50 years on average at 18, 30, 37 and 41 percent. Moreover, the fact
that Figure 1 shows relative stability at about these levels throughout the
period suggests that these synthetic cohort risks of divorce approximate

well the likely experience of real marriage cohorts formed during that time. Stable synthetic cohort demographic experience over an extended period implies similar real cohort experience.

Prior to the *Family Law Act* the percentage divorcing at marriage durations 0-4 years ranked below figures for all but the longest marriage duration interval recognized in Figure 2. Since 1978, however, only the 5-9 years duration interval has accounted for more divorces than the 0-4 years interval. Shorter post-separation waits before being eligible to file for divorce largely explain the change, but two other unique features of the 0-4 years trend line also bear noting: it does not fall throughout 1977-79; and during 1977-94 it remains close to its 1976 peak value. The new Act allowed marriages which failed to meet expectations early on to be quickly formally abandoned. A marked widening of the first birth interval during 1961-76, underpinned by new contraceptive technology and greatly reduced bridal pregnancy as abortion became more accessible after 1971, was conducive to such a trend (Ruzicka and Choi, 1981; Refshauge, 1982; Carmichael, 1995b), as was a large increase in the proportion of marriages

FIGURE 2. Percentages Divorcing at Nominated Marriage Durations: Synthetic Marriage Cohorts 1946-1994

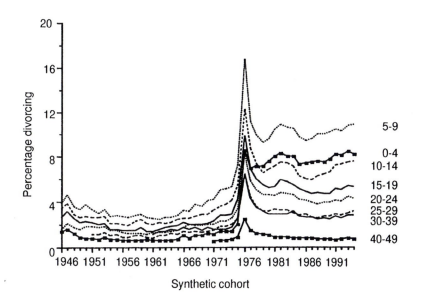

which were remarriages following divorce. Whereas during 1966-70, 9.9 percent of marriages involved at least one divorcee, during 1971-75, 1976-80, 1981-85, 1986-90 and 1990-94 12.9, 28.1, 30.3, 30.8 and 30.9 percent did so. There is reason to expect divorcees to be especially intolerant of disharmony early in a new marriage.

Also notable from Figure 2 is evidence that the 1979-82 divorce resurgence mainly involved marriages of shorter (0-14 years) durations, perhaps indicating that couples with younger children adjusted more slowly to the new legal environment. Shorter duration intervals, but especially 5-9 and 10-14 years, were also significant, though not the only, contributors to the decline in divorce through the mid-1980s. One explanation for this decline focuses on the essentially period, or cross-sectional, nature of the increase in divorce after 1975, while another highlights the more cautious approach to marriage, and especially the huge decline in 'shotgun' marriage, that developed from the early 1970s (Carmichael, 1987, 1988). The former reality saw a simultaneous 'cleaning out' of backlogs of unfulfilling marriages at all marriage durations, eventually leaving, it seems reasonable to suppose, inherently more stable residues of still intact marriages which became a force for decline in the divorce rate. That declines occurred at most marriage durations (Figure 2) gives credibility to this argument. That they were steeper at shorter marriage durations is supportive of an influence of greater caution in the marriage market.

These declines did not persist, however. Through the late 1980s and the 1990s the balance of forces for change in the divorce rate altered again. Despite greater circumspection in the marriage market, more frequent testing of relationships through premarital cohabitation (Australian Bureau of Statistics, 1993,1995) and falling rates of formal remarriage after divorce (Australian Bureau of Statistics, 1995; McDonald, 1995), forces for greater personal autonomy in intimate relationships (McDonald, 1988) held net sway. They may have been supplemented by a build-up in the proportion of marriages in which at least one partner had prior experience of divorce, by rapidly escalating mortgage interest rates and the ensuing recession which from 1989 generated high unemployment, and by initiatives to improve compliance with and consistency between Family Court maintenance orders (Harrison et al., 1990). Figure 2 shows that this latest upturn in the cross-sectional incidence of divorce phased in earlier and more emphatically at shorter marriage durations. Perhaps younger couples led the way in setting still higher standards of expected personal fulfillment within marriage, although it is also pertinent that until 1991, post-*Family Law Act* remarriages following divorce all were of less than 15 years duration and that the issue of child maintenance was most pressing at these durations.

Figure 3 shows cumulative rates of divorce for financial year real marriage cohorts. It reveals that while recent synthetic cohort rates have pointed to lifetime risks of divorcing exceeding 40 percent, as of 1994 no actual marriage cohort had yet been depleted by as much as 30 percent. Higher depletion levels are, however, inevitable. Divorce trajectories for recent marriage cohorts (Figure 4) are so steep it is inconceivable levels will not rise well above 30 percent. Marriage cohorts of the early 1940s, affected by the *Family Law Act* only beyond marriage duration 35 years, lost about 15 percent of their members to divorce. Those of the 1960s and early 1970s, formed over a period when ages at marriage were historically low (McDonald, 1974; Carmichael, 1987, 1988) and marriage often was accompanied, if not precipitated, by pregnancy (Refshauge, 1982; Carmichael, 1995b), were by the mid-1990s closing on a dissolution rate twice as high, and likely to significantly exceed it in the future. The indication from Figure 3 is that new equilibrium levels of divorce by given wedding

FIGURE 3. Cumulative Divorce Rates (per 1000 marriages) to Successive Exact Marriage Durations: Real Marriage Cohorts 1938-39 to 1989-90

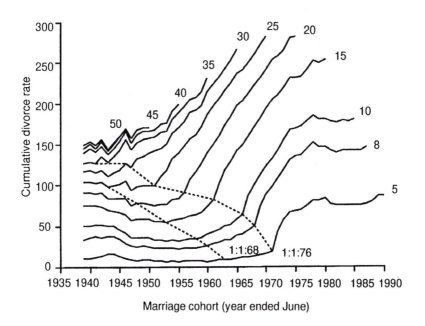

FIGURE 4. Cumulative Divorce Trajectories for Selected Real Marriage Cohorts and the 1994 Synthetic Marriage Cohort

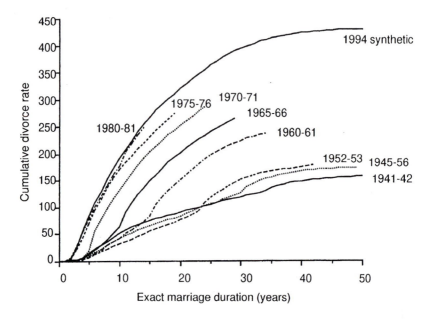

anniversaries are being established by marriage cohorts formed during and after the late 1970s–essentially those whose entire divorce experience has been governed by the *Family Law Act*. Thus the typical rate of dissolution within five years has stabilized at 7-8 percent and that within 10 years at around 18 percent, with tentative signs that the figure to duration 15 years will be about 25 percent. These real cohort figures match closely recent synthetic cohort rates of dissolution to the same marriage durations, again suggesting that the latter provide a very reliable indication of the extent to which marriage cohorts of the last 15-20 years ultimately will be affected by divorce.

The already noted period nature of the upsurge in divorce is clear from Figure 3, which features time lines identifying the dates 1:1:68 and 1:1:76. The former marks the approximate date from which cohort rates of divorce began to rise; the latter coincides with the introduction of the *Family Law Act* and a marked steepening of most trend lines. Were further evidence needed that the *Family Law Act* ushered in higher divorce rates at all marriage durations it is provided by real cohort marriage duration-specific divorce rates (not shown), all of which rose sharply for cohorts passing through each duration interval when the Act came into force. That save at duration 0-4 years all subsequently fell again attests to the backlog of unhappy marriages that were cleared. The exception reflects the substantial removal of the previous legal impediment to early divorce.

Figure 4 also affirms the period nature of the post-*Family Law Act* upsurge in divorce. Divorce trajectories for marriage cohorts formed between 1941-42 and 1970-71 steepen noticeably beyond marriage durations reached as of 1976. It further supports, as well, the proposition that recent synthetic cohort divorce trajectories match closely those of real marriage cohorts whose attrition to divorce has occurred exclusively under the *Family Law Act*. The 1994 synthetic cohort trajectory and that of the 1980-81 marriage cohort track one another closely, and there seems every prospect that the former will prove a good predictor of that portion of the latter yet to be determined.

Divorce Rates for First Marriage and Remarriage Cohorts

How have divorce trends for persons in first marriages and in remarriages following widowhood and divorce compared? Tables 1 and 2 show synthetic cohort cumulative rates of divorce after 10, 20, 30 and 50 years for females and males in these groups during 1961-94.[3] Basic trends have been not dissimilar. Divorce levels increased steadily, if a little irregularly, through the 1960s and early 1970s, leapt in 1975 and 1976, then fell steeply again. For first marriage cohorts these declines lasted until 1979, but for remarriage cohorts they lasted a year or two longer. First marriage cohorts also mirror entire cohorts in that rates of divorce declined again after 1982, before beginning to rise once more after 1986 or 1987. The pattern is similar for remarried divorcees, except that the most recent upturns began a year or two later. For remarried widows and widowers, peak rates during the 1980s were recorded in 1983 or 1984, and the latest upturns also were delayed, commencing in 1989 or 1990.

The more interesting aspects of Tables 1 and 2 are relative rates of divorce by prior marital status and changes therein. Through the 1960s divorce rates for those in first marriages and for remarried widows and widowers were similar, although the former began to exceed the latter in the early 1970s. Apparently remarried widows and widowers hesitated over joining the pre-*Family Law Act* rise in divorce, being older and consequently undoubtedly more conservative in such matters. Throughout 1961-75, however, divorce rates for remarried divorcees were clearly the highest. Subsequently a different pattern has emerged. Rates have remained higher for remarried divorcees than for those in first marriages, but

TABLE 1. Estimated Cumulative Divorce Rates (per 1000 marriages not terminated by death) to Selected Exact Marriage Durations: Female Synthetic First Marriage and Remarriage Cohorts 1961-1994

| | Exact marriage duration and marital status before marriage | | | | | | | | | | | |
| | 10 years | | | 20 years | | | 30 years | | | 50 years | | |
Cohort	NM	W	D	NM	W	D	NM	W	D	NM	W	D
1961	29	33	58	62	62	120	83	81	154			
1962	28	34	56	64	72	125	87	99	145			
1963	30	35	59	67	70	117	90	86	153			
1964	30	29	51	69	76	119	94	97	163			
1965	33	37	64	74	73	134	100	89	173			
1966	39	42	74	84	88	151	114	125	202			
1967	37	32	72	80	84	150	112	114	195			
1968	44	53	75	90	94	148	122	123	199			
1969	45	49	66	91	84	150	123	115	190			
1970	52	42	74	100	85	148	134	118	192			
1971	52	42	74	105	86	158	139	112	204	161	119	249
1972	64	49	80	125	94	172	166	124	220	189	140	240
1973	65	41	84	127	90	174	168	117	221	191	134	234
1974	66	50	86	135	103	177	179	132	233	203	158	273
1975	91	68	120	186	134	235	242	171	299	276	191	350
1976	249	215	324	464	381	631	608	497	781	695	593	857
1977	178	153	219	331	262	427	431	322	532	489	366	570
1978	168	139	199	299	231	375	382	291	470	429	349	512
1979	160	139	186	278	220	337	353	276	410	395	315	455
1980	172	117	185	291	200	320	366	241	401	404	292	437
1981	183	118	198	306	189	345	382	237	412	420	264	445
1982	190	126	221	322	193	367	402	232	435	439	254	470
1983	184	135	211	314	214	362	392	249	420	430	269	454
1984	181	133	213	306	203	349	382	242	413	420	275	445
1985	167	128	191	279	192	320	349	227	384	383	246	424
1986	163	128	194	271	196	322	341	225	381	374	247	406
1987	167	112	188	272	167	318	337	191	369	369	205	402
1988	172	110	191	280	181	321	343	211	369	373	234	395
1989	172	102	186	281	156	315	348	178	366	379	196	394
1990	177	107	192	286	158	325	352	181	371	383	189	401
1991	187	115	197	308	173	335	378	200	394	411	213	413
1992	182	116	199	304	182	335	372	214	390	404	233	414
1993	190	137	208	318	210	351	392	250	410	428	270	437
1994	188	131	213	314	196	357	388	227	420	421	250	440

Source: Carmichael and McDonald (1986); Webster (1995).

NM = Never married; W = Widowed; D = Divorced; figures to exact marriage duration 50 years only available from 1971 because data set commences with the 1921 real marriage cohort.

TABLE 2. Estimated Cumulative Divorce Rates (per 1000 marriages not terminated by death) to Selected Exact Marriage Durations: Male Synthetic First Marriage and Remarriage Cohorts 1961-1994

| | Exact marriage duration and marital status before marriage | | | | | | | | | | | |
| | 10 years | | | 20 years | | | 30 years | | | 50 years | | |
Cohort	NM	W	D	NM	W	D	NM	W	D	NM	W	D
1961	30	26	52	63	51	103	85	70	145			
1962	29	33	53	65	63	117	89	81	152			
1963	31	34	62	67	70	122	91	87	157			
1964	31	31	51	70	63	114	96	83	159			
1965	34	35	60	75	71	126	102	87	162			
1966	41	40	68	86	76	143	118	101	193			
1967	37	39	69	82	81	144	114	100	200			
1968	45	54	74	92	91	151	124	110	203			
1969	45	45	76	93	77	146	125	101	186			
1970	51	49	75	102	80	150	135	110	195			
1971	52	45	74	106	88	164	141	109	207	163	127	228
1972	62	49	87	127	89	180	168	108	227	191	122	274
1973	64	51	96	129	100	185	170	115	234	193	123	271
1974	66	48	86	137	88	178	182	109	225	208	117	265
1975	91	73	116	188	141	227	246	179	287	281	219	330
1976	250	233	322	471	393	618	619	484	782	709	538	881
1977	181	146	220	338	239	414	442	296	523	502	338	579
1978	170	140	197	305	221	367	393	284	465	441	314	497
1979	162	124	195	283	193	341	363	229	431	405	256	478
1980	174	109	187	296	181	337	376	224	415	415	254	459
1981	185	116	203	310	188	346	391	211	425	430	228	467
1982	192	133	217	327	201	358	411	245	435	449	269	472
1983	183	136	211	316	213	358	397	262	433	437	279	463
1984	182	151	206	309	231	349	388	261	432	427	286	480
1985	166	159	192	280	225	324	352	263	401	388	283	427
1986	162	130	192	273	197	328	344	230	403	378	254	433
1987	167	119	194	273	177	324	338	199	390	372	215	417
1988	175	113	191	285	162	324	351	187	384	382	202	415
1989	177	107	185	289	158	318	356	184	384	387	188	421
1990	179	97	194	291	149	325	359	175	390	391	195	422
1991	189	108	199	310	164	336	380	181	409	413	190	440
1992	185	125	195	308	179	332	377	200	399	411	226	424
1993	190	131	207	321	194	351	396	227	431	432	254	463
1994	189	143	208	319	209	354	394	237	428	429	246	458

Source: Carmichael and McDonald (1986); Webster (1995).

NM = Never married; W = Widowed; D = Divorced; figures to exact marriage duration 50 years only available from 1971 because data set commences with the 1921 real marriage cohort.

the latter have been much closer to the former than to rates for remarried widows and widowers. These nowadays are easily the lowest, with in the 1990s around a fifth of remarriages following widowhood likely to end in divorce within 30 years compared to around double that fraction of first marriages and remarriages following divorce.

What explains this change? The ages of persons remarried following widowhood again could be significant, having generated more resistance to new attitudes to divorce. Their marriages also may all along have been inherently more stable owing to both their maturity and a tendency to remarry cautiously. Comparing new and deceased spouses is a potential destabilizing force in remarriages following widowhood, but if a widely recognized danger may serve to promote extra care in choosing remarriage partners. The other interpretation to be placed on movement of the risk of divorce in first marriages away from that in remarriages following widow- hood toward that in remarriages following divorce is that it shows the extent to which first marriages previously were kept intact by social con- ventions that stigmatized divorce. Remarried divorcees never were as constrained by those conventions, but now that they are widely rejected, the two groups exhibit quite similar patterns of divorce behaviour.

Figure 5 shows female synthetic cohort percentages divorcing in partic- ular marriage duration intervals by prior marital status; equivalent graphs for males (not shown) exhibit similar patterns. The shift in the risk of dissolution of first marriages away from that of remarriages following widowhood towards that of remarriages following divorce either side of 1976 is clearly evident within most duration intervals. Differences by marital status in percentages divorcing at marriage durations 0-4 years have not been huge, although under the *Family Law Act* remarriages following widowhood have negotiated this period more successfully than other marriages. This greater stability is, however, more clearcut at longer marriage durations, over which the chief point of interest is the varying relative positions of the lines for women in first marriages and remarriages following divorce. Greater overall instability of remarriages following divorce has been due principally to greater instability at marriage dura- tions 5-14 years. Indeed, at durations 20-29 years, the differential since 1980 has been reversed. This evidence points to a more rapid tempo of dissolution among those remarried following divorce than among those in first marriages, even after allowing for the former's higher overall propen- sity to divorce.

Figure 6 shows cumulative rates of divorce at five-year intervals of exact marriage duration for real first marriage and remarriage cohorts. At durations 10 years and longer the ranking remarriages following divorce, first marriages, then remarriages following widowhood as the most through least divorce-prone is clearcut. As was observed for total real marriage cohorts, considerable stability, at levels similar to those recorded for recent synthetic cohorts (see Tables 1 and 2), is apparent in rates of depletion to given exact marriage durations of first marriage and remarriage cohorts formed during and after the late 1970s. This stability is less in evidence for cohorts remarrying following widowhood, but smallish numbers of cases are conducive to some volatility here. A distinctive feature of trend lines for cohorts of both sexes remarried after divorce is the series of V-shaped notches coinciding with the 1975-76 cohort. Technical uncertainties surround estimation of the size of this cohort and the allocation of divorces to it because of the huge increase (a doubling) in remarriages following divorce between 1975 and 1976.[4] However, the notches need not reflect these; they could mean that remarriages facilitated by the earliest *Family Law Act* divorces disproportionately involved very committed couples. To a greater extent than was usual they may have involved persons who had left previous spouses to live with new ones, and who hence under the *Matrimonial Causes Act* could petition for divorce only once separated for five years. With the new law overnight reducing this period to twelve months, a sudden, temporary, demand for divorce by persons long anxious, but hitherto legally unable, to formalize new relationships may have been released. Through tending to be associated with especially strong commitment to the new spouse and/or with the new relationship having already endured for several years, it could easily have been conducive to greater stability in remarriage.

Age at Marriage and Divorce

Extreme youth when marrying invariably has been found to elevate the risk of dissolution of first marriages (see, for example, the long list of studies cited by Carmichael, 1982, pp. 367-368). Data for Australia (Figure 7) reaffirm this finding. For both males and females cumulative divorce rates for 1977-94 synthetic first marriage cohorts have been far higher for those married as teenagers than for those married when older. First marriage at ages 20-24 also has more often been followed by divorce than first marriage at ages 25-29, 30-34 and 35-39, especially among males, but the immaturity and other destabilizing factors (lack of a sound economic base, frequency with which pregnancy is a precipitating factor, etc.) that regularly accompany teenage marriage cause it to stand apart. In the case of males Figure 7 shows divorce within 30 years to be well nigh universal among those married in their teens,[5] whereas for those married at ages 20-24 and at older ages the risks are respectively 40-45 percent and

FIGURE 5. Percentages Divorcing at Nominated Marriage Durations: Female Synthetic Marriage Cohorts 1961-1994 by Marital Status Prior to Marriage

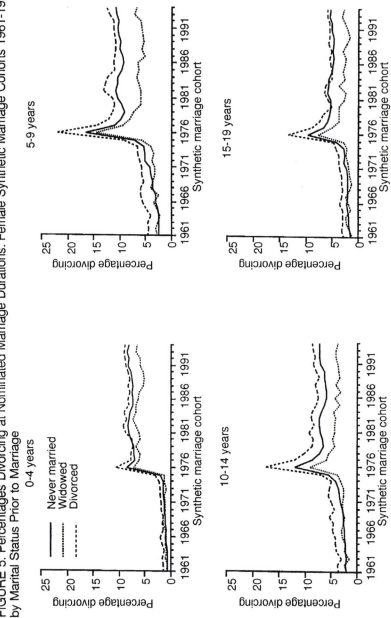

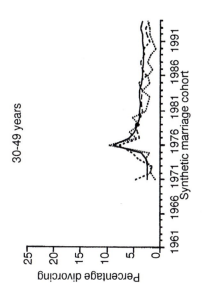

30-49 years

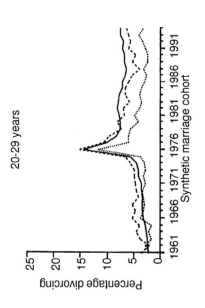

20-29 years

19

FIGURE 6. Cumulative Divorce Rates (per 1000 marriages) to Successive Exact Marriage Durations: Real Marriage Cohorts 1960-61 to 1989-90 by Sex and Marital Status Prior to Marriage

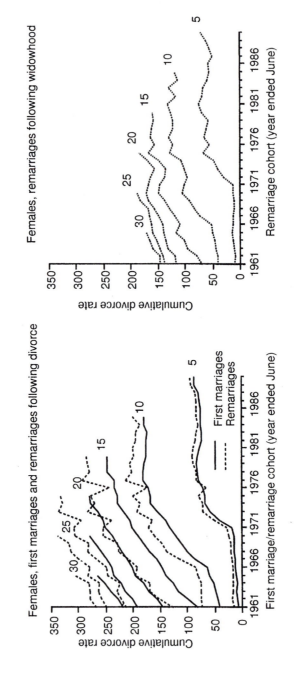

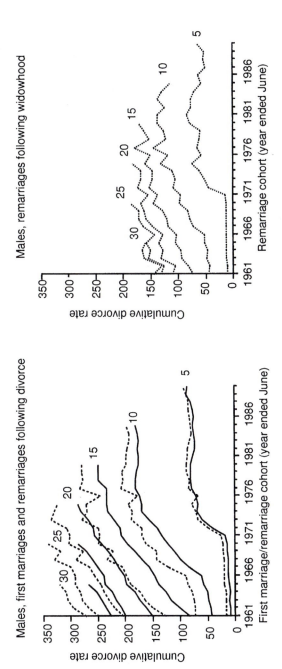

Males, first marriages and remarriages following divorce

Males, remarriages following widowhood

FIGURE 7. Cumulative Divorce Rates (per 1000 marriages) to Exact Marriage Durations 10, 20 and 30 Years: Synthetic First Marriage Cohorts 1977-1994 by Sex and Age at Marriage

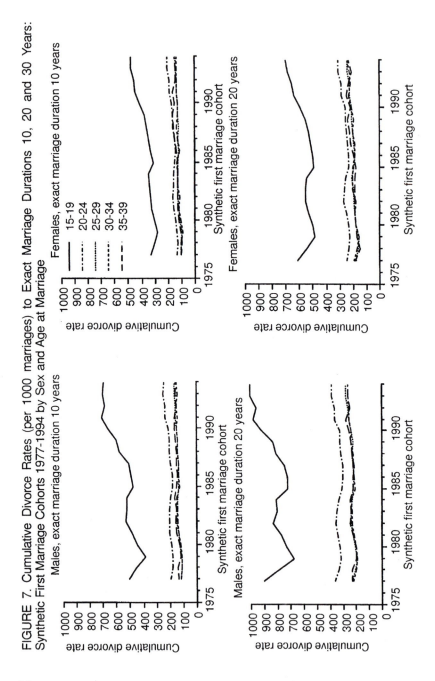

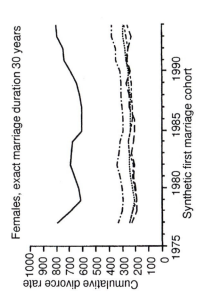

Males, exact marriage duration 30 years

Cumulative divorce rate

1000
900
800
700
600
500
400
300
200
100
0

1975   1980   1985   1990

Synthetic first marriage cohort

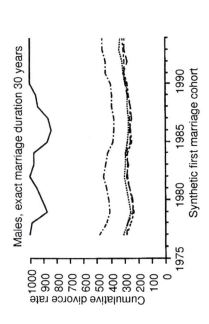

Females, exact marriage duration 30 years

Cumulative divorce rate

1000
900
800
700
600
500
400
300
200
100
0

1975   1980   1985   1990

Synthetic first marriage cohort

25-30 percent. Risks for females are lower. Teenage marriage is less aberrant, but still two-thirds or more of such marriages do not last 30 years, while the figures for those marrying at ages 20-24 and at older ages are of the order of 30-35 percent and 20-25 percent.

The period over which data on divorce by age and marital status at marriage are available is not sufficiently long for the experience of real first marriage cohorts by age at marriage to be tracked far. However, Webster (1995) shows levels of depletion to exact marriage duration 15 years for cohorts formed between 1975-76 and 1979-80 of around two-thirds and 40-45 percent for males and females married as teenagers, 25 and 20 percent for those married when aged 20-24, and 17-20 and 15-18 percent for those first married at ages 25-39. These figures are similar to synthetic cohort rates of divorce after 15 years recorded during the 1980s, but more recent synthetic cohort rates have been higher, possibly heralding higher real cohort rates by age at marriage in the near future. This pattern is especially noticeable for persons of both sexes married at ages 15-19 and 20-24, and may owe a good deal to the economic recession of the early 1990s, perhaps in interaction with later and less universal marriage having since the early 1970s made youthful marriers an increasingly select group.

Age at marriage also affects the likelihood of divorce among those remarrying following widowhood and divorce. Figure 8 shows cumulative rates of divorce after 10, 20 and 30 years for synthetic cohorts remarrying when aged 40-49 and 50 and over after being widowed, while Figure 9 shows comparable rates for synthetic cohorts remarrying at ages 30-39 and 40-49 after divorce. In both cases for both sexes the incidence of divorce to any exact duration of marriage is higher for the group remarrying younger. Differential competition from mortality as a force for marital dissolution is not a factor, divorce rates presupposing joint survival of husband and wife to each marriage duration. Those who remarry younger might tend to do so more rapidly and thus less carefully following termination of their previous marriages. They also subsequently reach any marriage duration with more of their lives still to live, whence if their remarriages are unfulfilling they may be more inclined (and in the case of women, economically better able) to seek renewed happiness, or at least to reject persisting in their current relationships, via divorce. With remarriages following divorce, moreover, 40-49 compared to 30-39 year-olds could be selected for greater commitment to marriage, having on average persevered longer in their first marriages. Any of these propositions might help explain the differentials observed.

Among remarrying divorcees it is notable that the divorce rate differen-

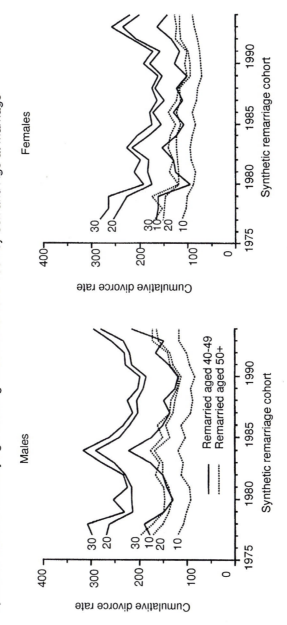

FIGURE 8. Cumulative Divorce Rates (per 1000 marriages) to Exact Marriage Durations 10, 20 and 30 Years: Synthetic Cohorts Remarrying Following Widowhood 1977-1994 by Sex and Age at Marriage

FIGURE 9. Cumulative Divorce Rates (per 1000 marriages) to Exact Marriage Durations 10, 20 and 30 Years: Synthetic Cohorts Remarrying Following Divorce 1977-1994 by Sex and Age at Marriage

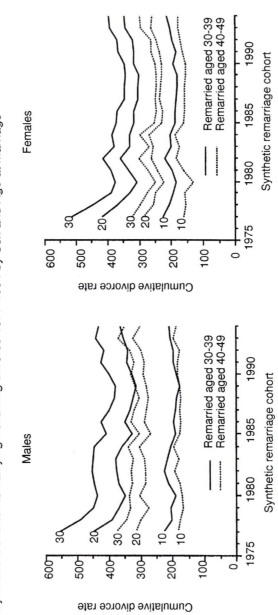

tial by age at marriage is small at exact marriage duration 10 years, particularly for males (Figure 9), but widens appreciably by duration 20 years. This could well constitute evidence supportive of the second proposition just advanced, for it suggests that retirement reduces the likelihood of divorce. Economic dependency could blunt the ability of women to end unfulfilling marriages in retirement; a sense that one's capacity to establish new relationships is waning may be common about this time; deteriorating health could increase spousal dependence and decrease attractiveness to alternative partners; and the opportunity to spend more time together might even reinvigorate some marital relationships. A point of interest in Figure 8 is how little divorce rates increase between exact marriage durations 20 and 30 years. These durations take even those remarried in their forties to retirement age and beyond, and the factors just listed, albeit speculatively, may again be implicated.

As with first marriages, divorce rates refined by age at marriage are available for only a few real cohorts of remarrying widowed and divorced persons, and only to shortish marriage durations (Webster, 1995). They largely confirm differentials just discussed. Cohorts of divorcees remarrying at ages 30-39 between 1976-77 and 1984-85 had been depleted by around 19-20 percent (males) and 18-19 percent (females) after 10 years, with figures for cohorts remarrying aged 40-49 lower on average only by about two percentage points. By exact marriage duration 15 years, however, these differentials by age at marriage had widened considerably for the five cohorts (1975-76 to 1979-80) able to be tracked that far. Real cohorts of remarried widows and widowers, on the other hand, though recording lower divorce rates than cohorts remarried following divorce, were distinctly more divorce-prone (about 40 and 50 percent more within the first 10 years for widows and widowers respectively) if remarried in their forties than if remarried at an older age.

DISCUSSION

The foregoing analysis has yielded a number of findings concerning Australia's participation in the upsurge of divorce in more developed countries over recent decades. In summary:

- The risk of a marriage ending in divorce has risen from about 10 percent in the 1950s and early 1960s to a new plateau at about 40 percent in the 1980s and 1990s.

- The increase in divorce was a period phenomenon, with marriages of all durations simultaneously affected.

- While real marriage cohorts have yet to be depleted by divorce to the extent indicated by cross-sectional cumulative divorce rates for synthetic marriage cohorts, the stability of these rates over an extended period gives them predictive credibility, as does the steepness of cumulative divorce trajectories for real marriage cohorts formed since 1980.

- Within the relative stability of cross-sectional divorce rates since the late 1970s, shifts in the balance between forces tending to raise and lower the level of divorce have produced distinct fluctuations.

- In shortening appreciably the interval between separation and becoming eligible to file for divorce, Australia's *Family Law Act,* aided by conducive socio-demographic trends, greatly increased the prominence of marriage durations 0-4 years in the distribution of divorces by duration of marriage.

- Reflecting the marked liberalization of attitudes to divorce in Australia, the risk of divorce in first marriages has assumed a level slightly below that in remarriages following divorce and well above that in remarriages following widowhood, where previously it lay distinctly below the former and only marginally above the latter.

- The tempo of marital dissolution by duration of marriage is more rapid in remarriages following divorce than in first marriages.

- Those marrying very young, especially as teenagers, have been especially susceptible to divorce.

- Differentials by age at marriage in divorce rates and in the tempo of divorce by duration of marriage for persons remarried following divorce and following widowhood suggest that post-retirement circumstances restrict divorce activity among these groups.

A natural inclination of lay observers of higher divorce rates in Australia has been to blame the *Family Law Act.* The divorce rate was, however, rising before the advent of 'no-fault' divorce; and the spate of divorces immediately after the Act came into effect points to substantial preexisting demand for it. Chester (1977) distinguishes between the *formal* availability of divorce (whether or not it is legally possible), its *effective* availability (taking in matters like cost, access to courts and the efficiency of the legal process) and its *normative* availability (determined by individual and societal attitudes to its legitimacy as a response to marital disharmony). The *Family Law Act* did not extend the possibility of divorce to anyone previously denied it. It did, though, enhance its 'effective' availability, by enabling it to occur more quickly, preventing aggrieved spouses from resisting it, making the process more efficient, cheaper and less intimidating, and ridding it of the need to air publicly details of marital conflict and misdeeds.

Undoubtedly the new law also promoted greater acceptance of divorce, but the size of its contribution defies measurement and it is impossible not to see the political process involved as a *product* of changing attitudes as well. The *Family Law Act*, in other words, accelerated a trend that it grew out of. Moreover, attitudes to divorce did not change in a vacuum, but as part of a major liberalist thrust that also embraced issues like premarital sexuality and nonmarital cohabitation, abortion, papal rejection of oral contraception, and the appropriateness of women having careers. Divorce laws do not undermine sound marriages. At most, by altering perceptions of the public acceptability of divorce and making the divorce process briefer and less intimidating, the *Family Law Act* helped reduce the *amount* of marital disharmony some would tolerate.

Several demographic and social trends laid the groundwork for higher divorce rates. By the 1960s marriages potentially lasted longer than in earlier generations (they occurred younger and expectations of life had increased), and prospects were that more of married life would be spent as a twosome (childbearing ended earlier and many children left home in late adolescence). The meaning of 'till death us do part' had changed, and partly in recognition of this the quality of marital relationships began to assume new importance. But the significance of the post-war marriage boom (McDonald, 1974; Carmichael, 1987, 1988) extends beyond its lengthening of the durations of 'lifelong' marriages. The post-war period brought appreciable decline in parental influence over mate selection and courtship in Australia (Carmichael, 1995b), and the more frequent assumption of family responsibilities by relatively immature couples, often in response to unintended pregnancy, was bound to increase the potential for marital disharmony. So, too, was near-universal marriage, for almost certainly some who were 'not the marrying type' were swept along by the tide.

Another important set of factors behind higher divorce rates has been women's growing economic independence and their demands for more egalitarian, role-sharing and emotionally fulfilling marriages. Evidence from an Australian study of property and income distribution in divorces granted in the early 1980s (Harrison, 1986) is that wives were the major decisionmakers in 60 percent of separations leading to divorce, with men taking this role around 25 percent of the time and the remainder being joint decisions. Arising out of the harshness and male dominance (including numerical dominance) of nineteenth century life, women's expectations of marriage in Australia historically were not lofty. Considerable potential for marital conflict long had laid dormant, and began to be realized as principles enunciated by the Women's Movement struck a responsive chord. Hitherto idealistic hopes of what marriage would offer became requirements. Men whose marriages had for years operated under one set of rules faced demands that the rules change; younger men found their wives unwilling to become clones of their mothers. Friction and casualties were inevitable as the sexes renegotiated marriage.

A major stimulus to this process was a newfound ability of women to live independently. It had two obvious dimensions: large post-war, and especially post-1960, increases in married female labour force activity (Young, 1990); and the introduction in 1973 of the Supporting Mother's Benefit (SMB). These developments greatly increased the feasibility of women opting out of unsatisfactory marriages, perhaps also signalling to men that one's wife could be deserted with a clearer conscience. The SMB extended reasonable welfare support to deserting wives, albeit (until 1979) after a six month qualifying period. Previously only deserted wives had been eligible for Federal assistance, again after waiting six months, while minimal State provision for deserting wives was characteristically 'austere, stigmatised and paternalistic' (Jones, 1980, p. 90). The economic disincentive to women ending unsatisfactory marriages also has been lessened by increased recognition of their non-financial contributions to their marriages in divisions of matrimonial property and, as previously noted, by initiatives to ensure the enforcement and adequacy of maintenance orders. The latter saw the establishment in 1988 of a Child Support Agency charged with collecting court-ordered maintenance (primarily through automatic withholding by employers of monies owed by liable parents), and the introduction in October 1989 of a formula for assessment of maintenance which takes account of fluctuations in taxable income and family composition via an annual review (Harrison et al., 1990).

Individualistic ideals now permeate marital relations in a way they formerly did not. Qualities like personal happiness, individual autonomy and self-realization feature prominently in Australia's value structure. The rise of individualism, observed in most developed countries (Lesthaeghe, 1992), is a major reason for the increased social acceptability of divorce; the reason, it has been argued, that attitudes to divorce changed was that society rejected the suppression of self entailed in keeping unhappy marriages intact (McDonald, 1984). Individualistic values stress idealism at the expense of the pragmatism that governs value systems based on conformity and obligation. Marriages in Australia thus have acquired an inherent instability formerly not present to the same degree. Tensions inevitably arise if a marriage is expected to serve both the collective interests of a family and the aspirations of individual partners.

Other arguments also can be advanced to help explain why divorce rates rose rapidly. Widening of the first birth interval consequent upon introduction of the pill in 1961 (Ruzicka and Choi, 1981) and a sharp fall in bridal pregnancy after 1971 (Carmichael, 1995b) had two implications for divorce rates. Because the early years of marriage more often were spent childless and with the wife still employed full-time, opting out became easier; and as a dual income start to married life became the norm a new point of potential marital conflict emerged—the decision to interrupt the wife's career to have children. Another adverse influence on divorce rates may have been unfavourable economic conditions after 1970. Rising unemployment and rapidly increasing housing costs (Burke et al., 1984) could have undermined some marriages. Married women's movement into the labour force also increased opportunities for both sexes to meet new partners. Finally, declining respect for religious morality very likely helped lift social sanctions against divorce.

These, then, have been the broad forces that generated the demand for more liberal divorce legislation and have underpinned the quadrupling of the likelihood of a marriage in Australia ending in divorce. That the more influential of them have been society-wide is apparent from the period nature of the increase in divorce rates. This characteristic, suggesting that backlogs of unfulfilling marriages were being terminated across all marriage durations, led briefly to optimism that clearing of those backlogs would leave more stable residues of intact marriages and result in a decline in cross-sectional divorce rates. The exercise of greater circumspection in the marriage market, manifested in marriage at older ages, also seemed conducive to such a development. Through the mid-1980s the optimism seemed well founded; the synthetic cohort cumulative rate of divorce to exact marriage duration 30 years fell from 406 per 1,000 marriages in 1982 to 342 per 1,000 in 1987, and that to exact duration 50 years fell from 444 to 376 per 1,000, all durations of marriage contributing to the trend. But these declines not only were not sustained, they were reversed.

The contemporary trend to later marriage dates from the early 1970s, and its strongest impact on the inherent stability of marriage cohorts was exerted during that decade at a time when that impact was swamped by opposing forces—a greatly liberalized legal environment for marriage dissolution, the demise of previously strong normative sanctions against divorce, and emergence of a much more individualistic value orientation. Analysis above has shown the major differential in divorce rates by age at marriage to be between those who marry in their teens and those who marry when older, with those (especially males) marrying in their early twenties also more divorce-prone than those first marrying in their mid-twenties and beyond. Most of the desertion of high-risk very young ages at marriage in Australia occurred during the 1970s, particularly in conjunction with the emergence of new options for dealing with unintended non-marital pregnancy–freer access to abortion after a late-1971 legal ruling in New South Wales; the 1973 introduction of the SMB; and a rise in community acceptance of consensual partnering (Carmichael, 1995b). Thus, while on the basis of 1971 first marriage ratios 33 percent of Australian females could expect to marry as teenagers and 29 percent of males before age 22, by 1982 both figures stood at 13 percent. They continued to fall, reaching 7 percent apiece in 1987 and 4 percent by 1993, so that the end of the trend may have been a factor in the divorce rate declining in the mid-1980s. But as ages at marriage continued to rise through the 1980s, increasingly they did so within an older range of ages over which little variation in the propensity to divorce occurs, the impetus for divorce rate decline consequently slackening. Lately counterforces to those for decline have dominated, an important one perhaps having been an ongoing trend to greater insistence on personal autonomy. Recent marriage cohorts may well have followed objectively sounder mate selection and marriage timing practices, including often prefacing marriage with periods of cohabitation, but they also have been formed over a period of significant lowering in levels of tolerance of marital disharmony. Whether difficult economic circumstances in the early 1990s and/or establishment of the Child Support Agency have been factors of moment in the divorce rate rising again is hard to assess, but they should not be discounted. With divorce rates seeming to have established something of a new equilibrium, such factors may well be the major determinants of future annual fluctuations.

The emergence of a new equilibrium in Australian divorce levels is, however, the key feature of the country's recent divorce experience. That the new regime has seen normative sanctions which once discouraged divorce greatly weakened is evident not only in the scale of the increase in divorce but in the convergence of the level of divorce in first marriages toward that in remarriages following divorce. With fear of social disapproval greatly diminished, determination to act in one's own best interests more widespread and the view now common that a clean break better serves children's interests than does prolonging a disharmonious marriage 'for their sake', first marriages have lost much of the ideological support for survival in the face of friction that formerly they enjoyed in greater measure than marriages in which previous divorce had substantially dissipated that support. The notions of a new equilibrium in divorce levels and of convergence of levels of divorce in first marriages and remarriages following divorce do, though, raise questions concerning consensual unions and the degree to which their proliferation may have influenced divorce trends. While not in the same league as Sweden and Denmark, Australia has participated decisively in the emergence of consensual partnering in the more developed countries since the mid-1960s (Carmichael, 1991, 1995a; Santow and Bracher, 1994; Australian Bureau of Statistics, 1995), and a substantial, if difficult to precisely quantify, minority of the nation's childbearing now takes place within consensual unions (Carmichael, 1995b).

To what extent has the divorce rate been kept in check by the increasingly informal nature of unions and hence union dissolution? Might closing of the differential in divorce levels between first marriages and remarriages following divorce be to some degree attributable to increased informal repartnering among divorcees? Australian evidence is lacking, but overseas studies (e.g., Trussell et al., 1992; Manting, 1994) suggest that consensual unions are less stable than marriages. Whether divorce rates would be higher in the absence of consensual partnering is, however, difficult to judge; consensual unions are not universally '*de facto* marriages', and hence dissolutions of such unions are not all informal divorces. Clearly more widespread consensual partnering has delayed marriages, but it has also eaten backward into the courtship process. Consensual unions often feature less than marriage-like commitment and are entered in circumstances in which marriage would not be contemplated; in many instances their dissolution is better likened to breaking off an engagement or ending a 'going steady' or even an experimental dating relationship than to a divorce. On the issue of repartnering following divorce, male and female rates of remarriage following divorce fell by almost two-thirds between 1976 and 1993 (Australian Bureau of Statistics, 1995), and there is little doubt that a major reason was the increased popularity of consensual repartnering, as both a prelude and an alternative to remarriage. Conceivably this repartnering has selected those who would have been higher-risk had they remarried and/or has performed a particularly strong 'winnowing' function in respect of relationships with the potential to result in remarriage following divorce. Consequently, although the divorce rate for remarriages following divorce rose sharply, its increase may have been restrained relative to that for first marriages.

CONCLUSION

This paper has sought to take stock of Australia's experience of divorce at a time when the main data source for doing so has recently been significantly impaired. It is to be hoped that the Family Court of Australia will soon see fit to reinstate the crucial data items, and thereby the capacity for ongoing monitoring of divorce trends at an appropriate level of detail. The other challenge for the future is to integrate into the picture an understanding of dissolutions of consensual unions and the extent to which they represent divorces that escape the official divorce statistics. As has been indicated, this is not a straightforward task. Consensual unions have a variety of meanings to those who live in them; meanings which range across levels of commitment typical of the varying stages of traditional dating and courtship as well as of marriage (Carmichael, 1995a). It follows that their dissolution can be the equivalent of anything from 'dropping' a casual boyfriend or girlfriend to divorce. Carefully designed, ideally longitudinal, survey research is needed to make these sorts of distinctions. Recent research into consensual partnering has relied heavily on retrospective event histories gathered in nationally representative surveys. It has made a valuable contribution, but has tended to invest the events of entry to and exit from consensual unions with statuses akin to marriage and separation prior to divorce respectively. There is a need to build into an understanding of consensual partnering and its relation to patterns of marriage and divorce an appreciation of the varied and changing perceptions partners may have of their relationships.

NOTES

1. A methodological appendix explaining the reduced events procedure used and the method by which denominators of divorce ratios were adjusted for 'disturbances' is available from the first author.

2. This series is based on data for real marriage cohorts commencing with that of 1921. Hence synthetic cohorts for the late 1940s are constructed to marriage duration 25 years, those for the 1950s and 1960s to durations 30 and 40 years respectively, and those for the 1970s, 1980s and 1990s to duration 50 years.

3. Adjustments for death and death of spouse built into these indices render them comparable across marital status categories. As noted in the 'Introduction', they assume joint survival of both parties to a marriage to any relevant exact marriage duration i.

4. This paper relies on Lexis diagram principles in estimating the size of financial year marriage cohorts and allocating divorces to them. Those principles, which assume even distributions of demographic events within calendar years and

within age or duration intervals, and which sometimes, for the sake of simplicity, trade off 'bits' of the experience of adjacent cohorts on the assumption that they are similar, can run into difficulty when a sudden change occurs in the intensity of a demographic process. In this instance, for example, estimating the 1975-76 remarriage cohort as half the number of persons remarrying after divorce in each of 1975 (pre-*Family Law Act*) and 1976 (post-*Family Law Act*) may produce an overestimate if, in 1976, remarriages actually were concentrated in the second half of the year. This in turn would tend to depress the cohort divorce rate, although the method used to estimate divorces occurring to that cohort might have had the opposite tendency, and the net effect is uncertain.

5. Indeed, for some synthetic cohorts cumulative divorce rates to exact marriage duration 30 years exceed 1000, although in Figure 7 they have been plotted with values of exactly 1000. This 'impossible' result sometimes occurs with synthetic cohort applications of reduced events methodology because of cross-sectional heaping of relevant demographic events. In general, this occurs either because circumstances temporarily are especially favourable to the demographic behaviour in question (i.e., divorce) or because, in successively more recent real cohorts, the behaviour is taking place earlier (i.e., at shorter marriage durations). The latter mechanism probably is at work in the present instance, although with numbers of male teenage marriages and divorces of males who married in their teens being small, deviation from an assumption built into present calculations that migration impacts equally on subgroups within marriage cohorts over time could also be a factor.

REFERENCES

Australian Bureau of Statistics. (1993). *Australia's families–Selected findings from the Survey of Families in Australia March 1992 to May 1992*. Canberra: Commonwealth Government Printer.

Australian Bureau of Statistics. (1995). *Australian social trends 1995*. Canberra: Australian Government Publishing Service.

Burke, T., Hancock, L. and Newton, P. (1984). *A roof over their heads: Housing issues and families in Australia*. Melbourne: Institute of Family Studies.

Carmichael, G.A. (1982). *Aspects of ex-nuptiality in New Zealand: Toward a social demography of marriage and the family since the second world war*. Unpublished doctoral thesis, Australian National University, Canberra.

Carmichael, G.A. (1987). Bust after boom: First marriage trends in Australia. *Demography, 24(2)*, 245-264.

Carmichael, G.A. (1988). *With this ring: First marriage patterns, trends and prospects in Australia*. Canberra: Department of Demography, Australian National University and Australian Institute of Family Studies.

Carmichael, G.A. (1991). A cohort analysis of marriage and informal cohabitation among Australian men. *Australian and New Zealand Journal of Sociology, 27(1)*, 53-72.

Carmichael, G.A. (1995a). Consensual partnering in the more developed countries. *Journal of the Australian Population Association, 12(1)*, 51-86.

Carmichael, G.A. (1995b). *From floating brothels to suburban semi-respectability: A history of non-marital pregnancy in Australia*. Working Papers in Demography No. 60, Research School of Social Sciences, Australian National University, Canberra.

Carmichael, G.A. and McDonald, P. (1986). *The rise and fall(?) of divorce in Australia*. Paper presented at the Annual Meetings of the Population Association of America, San Francisco.

Chester, R. (1977). England and Wales. Pp. 69-95 in R. Chester (Ed.), *Divorce in Europe*. Leiden: Martinus Nijhoff.

Harrison, M. (1986). Legal process. Pp. 40-56 in P. McDonald (Ed.), *Settling up: Property and income distribution on divorce in Australia*. Sydney: Prentice-Hall.

Harrison, M., Snider, G. and Merlo, R. (1990). *Who pays for the children? A first look at the operation of Australia's new child support scheme*. Melbourne: Australian Institute of Family Studies.

Jones, M.A. (1980). *The Australian welfare state*. Sydney: George Allen and Unwin.

Joske, P.E. (1952). *The laws of marriage and divorce in Australia and New Zealand*. Sydney: Butterworth.

Lesthaeghe, R. (1992). *The second demographic transition in Western countries: an interpretation*. IPD Working Paper No. 1991-2, Interuniversity Programme in Demography, Brussels.

Manting, D. (1994). *Dynamics in marriage and cohabitation: An inter-temporal, life course analysis of first union formation and dissolution*. Amsterdam: Thesis Publishers.

McDonald, P. F. (1974). *Marriage in Australia: Age at first marriage and proportions marrying, 1860-1971*. Canberra: Department of Demography, Australian National University.

McDonald, P. (1984). *Can the family survive?* Discussion Paper No. 11, Institute of Family Studies, Melbourne.

McDonald, P. (1988). Families in the future: The pursuit of personal autonomy. *Family Matters, No. 22*, 40-47.

McDonald, P. (1995). *Families in Australia: A socio-demographic perspective*. Melbourne: Australian Institute of Family Studies.

Moore, J.H. (1981). *Over-sexed, over-paid and over here: Americans in Australia 1941-1945*. St Lucia (Brisbane): University of Queensland Press.

Refshauge, W.F. (1982). *Non-marital pregnancy in Australia*. Unpublished masters thesis, Australian National University, Canberra.

Ruzicka, L.T. and Choi, C.Y. (1981). The recent decline in Australian fertility. *Year Book Australia, 65*, 114-127.

Santow, G. and Bracher, M. (1994). Change and continuity in the formation of first marital unions in Australia. *Population Studies, 48*, 475-496.

Stewart, D. and Harrison, M. (1982). *Divorce in Australia.* Working Paper No. 5, Institute of Family Studies, Melbourne.

Trussell, J., Rodriguez, G. and Vaughan, B. (1992). Union dissolution in Sweden. Pp. 38-60 in J. Trussell, R. Hankinson and J. Tilton (eds.), *Demographic Applications of Event History Analysis.* Oxford: Clarendon Press.

Webster, A. (1995). *Divorce rates by length of marriage: Australia, 1977-1994.* Demography Working Paper 95/1, Australian Bureau of Statistics, Canberra.

Wunsch, G.J. and Termote, M.G. (1978). *Introduction to Demographic analysis principles and methods.* New York: Plenum Press.

Young, C.M. (1990). *Balancing families and work: A demographic study of women's labour force participation.* Canberra: Australian Government Publishing Service.

Stress Following Marriage Breakdown: Does Social Support Play a Role?

Di Sansom
Douglas Farnill

SUMMARY. This study examined the relationship between social support and the everyday stress experienced by 139 individuals whose marriages had recently ended. Social support was measured by the Interview Schedule for Social Interactions (ISSI) which provides indices of community integration and attachment to close friends and family. Everyday stress was measured by a scale designed to be sensitive to the everyday stressors experienced by this category of people. Stress was inversely related to both indices of social support although more strongly to close attachment than community integration. The possible stress prevention role of social support in the post-separation period is discussed. *[Article copies available for a fee from The Haworth Document Delivery Service: 1-800-342-9678. E-mail address: getinfo@haworth.com]*

Marriage breakdown is now common in Australia with 40% of marriages ending in divorce (Australian Bureau of Statistics, 1995). Separation and divorce typically involve exposure to high levels of stress. The stress can be conceptualised as resulting from two sources; firstly, the cluster of discrete life events that people experience when a marriage ends (e.g., seeing a lawyer, selling the family home) and secondly, the ongoing

Di Sansom, PhD, and Douglas Farnill, PhD, are on the faculty, Department of Behavioural Sciences in Medicine, University of Sydney, Sydney, NSW, Australia 2006.

[Haworth co-indexing entry note]: "Stress Following Marriage Breakdown: Does Social Support Play a Role?" Sansom, Di and Douglas Farnill. Co-published simultaneously in *Journal of Divorce & Remarriage* (The Haworth Press, Inc.) Vol. 26, No. 3/4, 1997, pp. 39-49; and: *Divorce and Remarriage: International Studies* (ed: Craig A. Everett) The Haworth Press, Inc., 1997, pp. 39-49. Single or multiple copies of this article are available for a fee from The Haworth Document Delivery Service [1-800-342-9678, 9:00 a.m. - 5:00 p.m. (EST). E-mail address: getinfo@haworth.com].

or recurring everyday stressors that accompany life in the post-separation period (e.g., adjusting to new financial, living and social circumstances). These life events and everyday stressors are likely to be more intense than the life events and daily hassles which have been studied in the general population because marriage breakdown often entails major life changes and disruptions.

Recent research has demonstrated that both life events, and everyday stressors take their toll on the health of the separated/divorced and that everyday stress is particularly relevant to mental health (Garvin, Kalter & Hansell, 1993). While stress has been identified as adversely affecting the health of the recently separated/divorced little is yet known about factors that influence stress levels. A few researchers have investigated the role of social factors such as social support. Friedman, Chiriboga and Catron (1991) found that life events stress in the previous twelve months was not related to social support. They interpreted this finding as indicating that life events which occur within the separation and divorce timeframe are inevitably experienced as distressing and that social support can do little to alter this. However, another retrospective study, Kurdek (1988), found that social support was inversely related to the total stress (i.e., stress from life events and everyday stressors) experienced by a small group of mothers since separation. The question of whether social support is associated with the level of everyday stress in what McPhee (1984) terms the post-separation restructuring period remains largely unanswered. To explore this possibility the present study examined individual differences in both the everyday stress and social support experienced by the recently separated/divorced.

Social Support

While there are many definitions of social support in the literature most resemble one of the original descriptions offered by Caplan (1974). He described social support as a system consisting of enduring interpersonal ties to a group of people who can be relied upon to provide emotional sustenance, assistance and resources in times of need, and who provide feedback and share values. Payne and Jones (1987) contributed to the description of the concept by categorising possible sources of support: family, close friends, neighbours, co-workers, community members, professionals, and types of support: emotional, instrumental, informational, appraisal. The separated/divorced have often been found to need support in the areas of child care, finances, affect release, recreational and social activities, physical and sexual intimacy, divorce-related concerns, career and unemployment, housework and homemaking, and legal matters (Bloom, Hodges, & Caldwell, 1982; Henderson & Argyle, 1985; Hetherington, Cox & Cox, 1978). In respect of support source, they have been found to seek help from multiple sources including close friends and family, neighbours and acquaintances (Henderson & Argyle, 1985).

Social support has been extensively studied in stress research in the context of the stressor-illness model (Lin, Woelfel & Light, 1985). The idea that social support plays a role in the negative impact of stress on health is attractive because it opens possibilities for outside intervention. As Andrews, Tennant, Hewson and Vaillant (1978) point out, psychotherapeutic intervention can feasibly be directed towards bolstering support networks.

While it has been hypothesized that social support might affect the stress process at several points (Friedman, Chiriboga & Catron, 1991) most studies have examined the stress-buffering effects of support on illness (Kessler & McLeod, 1985). Little attention has been paid to the possibility that support can act at an earlier point in the stress-illness sequence, by preventing or limiting stress. This approach has been advocated by Pearlin (1989) who suggested that social support is most fruitfully evaluated in terms of limiting the number, severity, and diffusion of stressor constellations. In this capacity support may form a shield which insulates the individual from stress exposure, so that the supported individual experiences less stress than the unsupported individual. For example, the everyday stressors of the recently separated/divorced may be fewer in number and some may be less intense when supportive others provide help. Similarly adequate support may influence an individual's subjective appraisal of the stressors in his/her life so that they are regarded as less troublesome.

METHOD

Sample

Subjects of the study came from the Family Court of Australia and included individuals who had used the court in any capacity (i.e., counselling, register of separation, filing for divorce, litigation). This strategy of recruitment was more likely to produce a representative sample than the alternatives of advertising or selecting from a population who had sought counselling or some other kind of professional help. The study was focussed on the immediate post-separation period, and the sample was restricted to individuals who had been separated between one and twenty-four months (some had divorced during this period). Only subjects born in

Australia or another western culture were included as a means of controlling significant cultural variations in the variables under scrutiny.

By arrangement, and with appropriate ethical clearance, the Family Court sent letters to potential volunteers outlining the project. Confidentiality was guaranteed. Some potential volunteers were lost to the project as they had moved and could not be contacted and some were ineligible because they had remarried. Thirty-six percent were able to participate and completed the battery of scales and questionnaires. The final sample consisted of 77 women and 62 men most of whom were over 30 years of age (45% between 40 and 49, 38% between 30 and 39, 17% between 20 and 29). All levels of education and occupational status were covered although 49% of subjects were in white-collar employment. Fifty-nine percent of subjects were not living with another adult and 19% were living in a de-facto relationship. The majority (64%) had dependent children under eighteen years of age and the mean length of marriage until final separation was 11.8 years, while the mean length of separation was 14.7 months.

Measures

Everyday Stress

A number of authors suggest that in order to measure the everyday stress of a particular group in society it is necessary to construct tailored scales (Chamberlain & Zika, 1990; Kanner, Coyne & Schaefer, 1981). Accordingly, a scale was developed based on the Practical Living Problems Inventory developed by Jordan (1985) to explore the effects of marital separation. With advice from a reference group composed of professionals working in the field and recently separated individuals, an eighteen-item scale was developed. Items described recurring or persistent stressors which are likely to be part of everyday life following marital separation (e.g., doing domestic chores, maintenance and repair jobs at home, arranging child care, maintaining a good relationship with children, coping with access or custody arrangements, seeing or interacting with your (ex)spouse, adjusting to a different standard of living, making plans without a spouse). Subjects were asked to respond by stating whether the stressors were part of their lives at the moment. A four-point impact scale ranging from 0 to 3 (not difficult, slightly, very, extremely difficult) accompanied each item and subjects were asked to rate the impact of each stressor. Ratings were summed to produce a cumulative stress score.

Social Support

The Interview Schedule for Social Interaction (ISSI) is a psychometrically sound instrument developed by a group of Australian researchers to measure social support (Duncan-Jones, 1981; Henderson et al., 1980; Henderson, 1980; Henderson, Byrne & Duncan-Jones, 1981). The ISSI covers the broad range of support sources accessed by the separated/divorced and it is based on theoretically well-founded constructs (Thernlund & Samuelsson, 1993). It measures (i) social integration in the community defined as membership of a network of persons having shared interests and values (e.g., friends, neighbours and work associates), and (ii) attachment to others defined as affectional relationships with close friends and family which provide a sense of security and place. Social integration provides a base for social activities, outings and get-togethers preventing social isolation while attachment prevents the loneliness of emotional isolation (Thernlund & Samuelsson, 1993). Each facet is assessed on two dimensions, the extent to which it is available and the extent to which it is adequate, yielding four primary indices–availability of social integration (AVSI), adequacy of social integration (ADSI), availability of attachment (AVAT), adequacy of attachment (ADAT). The availability indices (AVSI, AVAT) reflect the amount of support available and the adequacy indices (ADSI, ADAT) reflect the adequacy of the available support. In its original form the ISSI is a structured interview, however, previous research has found comparable results with use of a questionnaire format (Thomas et al., 1985) and in this research a questionnaire format was used.

RESULTS

Table 1 lists the everyday stressors and shows the percentage of males and females who gave the stressor high ratings (i.e., very or extremely difficult). All stressors received a high rating from at least some respondents. The results for men and women tended to be similar. Three stressors were given high ratings by over 40% of men and women. Two related to dealing with the estranged spouse. Seeing or interacting with your wife/husband was rated as highly stressful by 45% of men and 43% of women; and negotiating with your wife/husband over money, children, etc., was rated highly by 44% of men and 46% of women. The third stressor referred to emotional problems. High stress ratings were given by fifty-eight percent of men, and 44% of women to coping with emotional turmoil. The fourth most prevalent stressor for both men and women referred to their financial situation. Thirty-four percent of men gave high ratings to the stressor of adjusting to a different standard of living and also making plans, and 36% of women gave high ratings to coping financially. In summary, the findings indicate that most respondents were troubled by the everyday stressors particularly associated with marriage breakdown concerning the estranged spouse, emotional turmoil and financial circumstances.

Descriptive statistics and Pearson product moment correlations between the variables appear in Table 2. Everyday stress was significantly and inversely correlated with all four indices of social support as expected with higher stress being associated with lower support. The correlations between stress and availability and adequacy of social integration were similar ($r = -.24$ AVSI, $r = -.25$ ADSI; $p < .01$); as were those between stress and the availability and adequacy of attachment ($r = -.38$ AVAT, $r = -.35$ ADAT; $p < .001$). Hotelling's t-test for differences between correlation co-efficients (Guilford & Fruchter, 1978) indicated that stress and availability of attachment were correlated significantly more strongly than stress and the availability of social integration ($t = 1.69$, $p < .05$, 1-tailed).

DISCUSSION

This is one of the first studies to report on the relationship between everyday stress and social support in a sample of recently separated/divorced people. While the findings are limited by the reliance on correlational data it would be unethical and impractical to conduct controlled manipulations of social support to study the effects on stress.

The findings of the study support the notion that the degree of everyday stress experienced by the recently separated/divorced is related to their level of social support. The stress experienced by people as they adjusted to their new separated/divorced state was lower amongst individuals who had more support. Furthermore, both aspects of social support were found to be significant, i.e., the extent to which people were socially integrated in a community, and involvement in close affectional relationships, although the latter appeared to be more important. However, the finding that social integration was related to everyday stress is particularly noteworthy, as most of the social support literature has focussed on the relevance of close relationships and largely neglected social network interactions (Bolger & Eckenrode, 1991; House & Kahn, 1985; Tardy, 1985; Vaux, 1988).

While causal inferences cannot be drawn from the data, it is likely that social support played a preventive role in everyday stress. As Thernlund and Samuelsson (1993) point out, social integration provides people with

TABLE 1. Percentage of Respondents Rating Everyday Stressors as Very or Extremely Difficult

Everyday Stressors	Male (N = 62)	Female (N = 77)
1. Doing domestic chores, e.g., cleaning and tidying the house, cooking meals, shopping.	16	13
2. Maintenance and repair jobs at home, e.g., household repairs, taking care of the car.	10	23
3. Coping with transport arrangements, e.g., between home, work, school.	0	12
4. Arranging child care, domestic help, etc.	3	8
5. Meeting your schedule of activities.	11	21
6. Doing your job at work.	15	13
7. Maintaining a good relationship with your children.	18	12
8. Dealing with your child's or children's behaviour.	8	17
9. Coping with access or custody arrangements.	23	14
10. Seeing or interacting with your husband/wife.	45	43
11. Negotiating with your husband/wife over money, children, etc.	44	46
12. Adjusting to a different standard of living.	34	29
13. Coping financially.	26	36
14. Participating in social activities, e.g., talking to people, making new friends, and attending social functions.	29	20
15. Coping with boredom.	23	14
16. Making plans.	34	22
17. Coping with your emotional turmoil.	58	44
18. Making decisions.	27	22

TABLE 2. Pearson Product Moment Correlations Between Variables and Descriptive Statistics

Variables	1	2	3	4	Mean	SD	Range
1. Stress					13.9	8.9	0-36
2. AVSI	-.24*				8.68	4.1	0-16
3. ADSI	-.25*	.51**			9.06	4.58	0-17
4. AVAT	-.38**	.45**	.47**		5.14	2.06	0-8
5. ADAT	-.35**	.28*	.54**	.53**	56.67	26.32	1-100

* $p < .01$; ** $p < .001$

information, advice, evaluation of behaviours, and help through the device of favour exchange. Attachment provides the emotional support which comes from confiding in, and generally talking to, close friends and relatives. Clearly, help from both sources may reduce stress associated with carrying out a range of domestic chores, maintaining a household and a car, making transport arrangements, managing finances, and the emotional demands of interacting with one's ex-spouse and children, being alone, and making decisions without a partner.

A stronger association between stress and support from close relationships is consistent with research on divorced and non-divorced subjects which has revealed a tendency for close friends and family to be the primary sources of support, providing not only emotional help but also instrumental, informational and appraisal support (Cohen & Syme, 1985; Henderson & Argyle, 1985).

Finally, the results have practical implications for, although the stress following marriage breakdown results from an interplay between many different factors, services designed to boost the social support of the recently separated/divorced are likely to reduce their stress. Moreover, the strong association found in this study between the availability and adequacy indices of each support dimension ($r = .51$ social integration; $r = .53$ attachment) suggests that if amount of support was increased, so might satisfaction with support. The need for help is underlined by recent empirical research which has shown that poor health and adjustment outcomes among the separated/divorced can be largely attributed to economic hardship, quality of social support, and increased stress emanating particularly from work and parenting responsibilities (Garvin, Kalter & Hansell, 1993; Nelson, 1994; Wyke & Ford, 1992).

REFERENCES

Andrews, G., Tennant, C., Hewson, D.M., and Vaillant, G.E. (1978). Life events stress, social support, coping style and risk of psychological impairment. *Journal of Nervous and Mental Disorders, 166*, 307-316.

Bloom, B.L., Hodges, W.F., and Caldwell, R.A. (1982). A preventive program for the newly separated: Initial evaluation. *American Journal of Community Psychology, 10*, 251-254.

Bolger, N., and Eckenrode, J. (1991). Social relationships, personality, and anxiety during a major stressful event. *Journal of Personality and Social Psychology, 61*, 440-449.

Caplan, J. (1974). Support systems and community mental health. New York: Behaviour Publications.

Chamberlain, K., & Zika, S. (1990). The minor events approach to stress: Support for the use of daily hassles. *British Journal of Psychology, 81(4)*, 469-481.

Cohen, S., and Syme, S. L. (Eds.). (1985). Social support and health. San Diego, CA: Academic Press.

Duncan-Jones, P. (1981). The structure of social relationships: analysis of a survey instrument, Parts 1 and 2. *Social Psychiatry, 16,* (1) 55-61, (2) 143-149.

Friedman, L., Chiriboga, D. A., and Catron, L. S. (1991). Social Supports in the Context of Divorce. In D. A. Chiriboga & L.S. Catron & Associates (Eds.), *Divorce: Crisis, Challenge or Relief?* (pp. 195-223). New York: New York University Press.

Garvin, V., Kalter, N., and Hansell, J. (1993). Divorced women: individual differences in stressors, mediating factors, and adjustment outcome. *American Journal of Orthopsychiatry, 63,* 232-240.

Guildford, J. P. and Fruchter, B. (1978). *Fundamental Statistics in Psychology and Education* (pp. 163-164). New York: McGraw-Hill.

Henderson, M. and Argyle, M. (1985). Source and Nature of Social Support Given to Women at Divorce/Separation. *Br. J. Social Wk., 15,* 57-65.

Henderson, S. (1980). A development in social psychiatry: the systematic study of social bonds. *Journal of Nervous and Mental Disorders, 168(2),* 63-69.

Henderson, S., Byrne, D., and Duncan-Jones, P. (1981). *Neurosis and the social environment.* Sydney: Academic Press.

Henderson, S., Byrne, D.G., Duncan-Jones, P., Scott, R. and Adcock, S. (1980). Social Relationships, Adversity and Neurosis: A Study of Associations in a General Population Sample. *Brit. J. Psychiat., 136,* 574-583.

Hetherington, E.M., Cox, M. and Cox, R. (1978). The aftermath of divorce. In J.H. Stevens, Jr. & M. Matthews (Eds.), *Mother-child, father-child relations* (pp. 149-176). Washington, DC: National Association for the Education of Young Children.

House, J.S., and Kahn, R.L. (1985). Measures and concepts of social support. In S. Cohen and S.L. Syme (Eds.), *Social support and health* (pp. 83-108). San Diego, CA: Academic Press.

Jordan, P. (1985). *The effects of marital separation on men.* Family Court of Australia Research Report No. 6.

Kanner, A.D., Coyne, J.C., and Schaefer, C. (1981). Comparison of two modes of stress management: daily hassles and uplifts versus major life events. *Journal of Behavioural Medicine, 4,* 1-39.

Kessler, R.C. and McLeod, J.D. (1985). Social support and mental health in community samples. In S. Cohen and S.L. Syme (Eds.), *Social Support and Health.* San Diego, CA: Academic Press.

Kurdek, L.A. (1988). Social support of divorced single mothers and their children. *Journal of Divorce, 11,* (3-4), 167-188.

Lin, N., Woelfel, M.W. and Light, S.C. (1985). The Buffering Effect of Social Support Subsequent to an Important Life Event. *Journal of Health and Social Behaviour, Vol. 26* (September): 247-263.

McPhee, J.T. (1984). Ambiguity and change in the post-divorce family: towards a model of divorce adjustment. *Journal of Divorce, 8(2),* 1-16.

Nelson, G. (1994). Emotional well-being of separated and married women: long term follow-up study. *American Journal of Orthopsychiatry, 64(1)*, 150-160.

Payne, R.L., and Jones, J.G. (1987). Measurement and methodological issues in social support. In S.V. Kasl and C.L. Cooper (Eds), Stress and Health: Issues in Research Methodology. Chichester: John Wiley and Sons Ltd.

Pearlin, L.I. (1989). The sociological study of stress. *Journal of Health & Social Behavior, Vol 30(3)*, 251-256.

Tardy, C.H. (1985). Social support measurement. *American Journal of Community Psychology, 13*, 187-202.

Thernlund, G.M. and Samuelsson, A.K. (1993). Parental Social Support and Child Behaviour Problems in Different Populations and Socioeconomic Groups: A Methodological Study. *Soc. Sci. Med., Vol 36*, No. 3, pp. 353-360.

Thomas, P.D., Garry, P.J., Goodwin, J.M., and Goodwin, J.S. (1985). Social bonds in a healthy elderly sample. *Social Science and Medicine, 20*, 365-369.

Vaux, A. (1988). Social support. New York: Praeger.

Wyke, S., and Ford G. (1992). Competing explanations for associations between marital status and health. *Social Science & Medicine, 34(5)*, 523-32.

CHILE

Children of Divorce: Academic Outcome

Arturo Roizblatt
Sheril Rivera
Tzandra Fuchs
Paulina Toso
Enrique Ossandón
Miguel Guelfand

SUMMARY. A case-control study was done to observe the association between the parents' divorce and their children's results in school.

The information was obtained from a questionnaire which was answered by the counselors of 8 public schools in Santiago, Chile.

The authors are on the faculty, Universidad de Chile, Facultad de Medicina, Campus Oriente, Departamento Psiquiatria y Salud Mental, Departamento de Salud Publica.

Address correspondence to: Arturo Roizblatt, MD, Málaga 950, Apt. 52, Las Condes, Santiago, Chile.

[Haworth co-indexing entry note]: "Children of Divorce: Academic Outcome." Roizblatt, Arturo et al. Co-published simultaneously in *Journal of Divorce & Remarriage* (The Haworth Press, Inc.) Vol. 26, No. 3/4, 1997, pp. 51-56; and: *Divorce and Remarriage: International Studies* (ed: Craig A. Everett) The Haworth Press, Inc., 1997, pp. 51-56. Single or multiple copies of this article are available for a fee from The Haworth Document Delivery Service [1-800-342-9678, 9:00 a.m. - 5:00 p.m. (EST). E-mail address: getinfo@haworth.com].

From one class of each school, 52 pupils of divorced marriages were searched. The control group of 52 pupils of non-divorced parents was chosen by selecting the name following the case on the class list.

The children of divorced parents were: 37 (71%) girls, 15 (29%) boys, the average age was 11. 8 ± 0. 8 years; 12 (29%) had failed the year; the average marks were 5.2 ± 0.7 (range 1-7) and the average attendance was 92 ± 8 %.

The controls were: 33 (63%) girls, 19 (37%) boys, the average age was 11.4 ± 0.6 years; 3 (5.7%) had failed the year; the average marks were 5.9 ± 0.5 (range 1-7); the average attendance was 94.5 ± 4.5%.

The conclusion is that children of divorced marriages have 4.9 more estimated relative risk (RR) of failing year and 7.1 times more estimated relative risk of having an average mark of 5.5 or lower than children of non-divorced parents.

These numbers must be observed with caution because of the small size sample and show an association but are not cause-effect. *[Article copies available for a fee from The Haworth Document Delivery Service: 1-800-342-9678. E-mail address: getinfo@haworth.com]*

INTRODUCTION

The parents' divorce can be seen as a stressful event for children, becoming sometimes a critical situation for their academic development, which may be reflected by a low academic outcome,[1] associated with different levels of hostility, aggression, anxiety and depression that can last until adulthood.[2-17]

Studies demonstrate that students coming from families in which both parents live at home have less absence and delays to class, have better average marks and more positive behaviour towards teachers, in comparison to those coming from reconstructed families or living with one parent.[1,12,13] On the other hand, it is known that children of split marriages that maintained their academic level were those who spent more time with both parents.[14,15]

From the clinical experience and international research on this matter, the authors became interested in knowing if there was an association between separation of the parents and some effects on academic outcome of these children in Santiago, Chile. For this purpose they were compared with children of non-divorced parents.

The following hypotheses are expected to be demonstrated in this study; these are, that children of divorced parents in comparison with children of non-divorced parents:

a. - Have higher risk to fail the year.
b. - Have higher risk of getting lower marks.
c. - The percentage of absence is higher.

METHOD

A case-control study was done in the last trimester of 1994, in Santiago, Chile. Eight public schools were chosen randomly. The universe was constituted by students in 6th grade in these primary schools, a total of 446 children. The sample of children was selected from one class of each of these schools and made up of 289 children. The information was obtained by a questionnaire created for this research, which was sent to the schools.

Fifty-two pupils were found being children of divorced parents; they corresponded to 100% of the cases.

The control group were pupils in 6th grade whose parents lived together. They were selected by choosing the name following the case on the class list, that fulfilled the requirement.

The variables in the study were: Age, sex, incidence of repeating, and average marks of both control groups and children of separated parents.

The average marks were considered from the trimester previous to the study, on a scale from 1-7.

The attendance to class was considered from the trimester previous to the study. The information was obtained from the class book.

The information was analyzed in averages, percentages, estimated odds ratio and chi square test (X^2) with confidence level of 95%.

RESULTS

The children of divorced parents were: 37 (71%) girls and 15 (29%) boys; the average age was 11.8 ± 0.8 years; 12 (23%) had failed; the average marks were 5.2 ± 0.7; the average attendance was $92 \pm 8\%$ during the third trimester of 1994.

The controls were: 33 (63%) girls and 19 (37%) boys; the average age was 11.4 ± 0.6 years; 3 (5.7%) had failed; the average marks were 5.9 ± 0.5 %; the average attendance was $94.5 \pm 4.5\%$ during the third trimester of 1994.

In average marks, the difference observed between both groups is statistically significant ($p \leq 0.05$) and children of divorced parents have 7.1 times higher estimated relative risk of having average marks (≤ 5.5) than a pupil of non-divorced parents (Table 1).

In failing year, the difference observed between both groups is statistically significant (p $\leq$ 0.05) and children of divorced parents have 4.9 times higher estimated relative risk of failing at least one year than a pupil of non-divorced parents (Table 2).

In percentage of attendance, the difference observed between the groups is not statistically significant (p > 0.05), so the pupil of divorced parents does not have more risk of absence than a pupil of non-divorced parents (Table 3).

DISCUSSION

It can be concluded that there is an association between repeating grade, a worse academic outcome and being a child of divorced parents; similar

TABLE 1. Average marks $\leq$ 5.5 or $\geq$ 5.6 of 6th grade pupils who are children of divorced parents (Case) or non-divorced parents (Control). October-December, 1994. Santiago, Chile.

Average marks	Case	Control	Total
< 5.5	34 (65.6%)* **	12 (23.1%)**	46 (44.2%)
> 5.6	16 (30.6%)	40 (76.9%)*	56 (53.8%)
Sub-total	50 (96.2%)	52 (100%)	102 (98%)
Unknown	2 (3.8%)	0 (0%)	2 (2%)
Total	52 (100%)	52 (100%)	104 (100%)

*significant ODDS RATIO (RR > 1)
**significant by chi square test (p < 0.05)

TABLE 2. 6th grade pupils who are children of divorced parents (Case) or non-divorced parents (Control) who failed a year. October-December, 1994. Santiago, Chile.

Failed Year	Case	Control	Total
Yes	12 (23%)* **	3 (5.8%)**	15 (14.4%)
No	40 (77%)	49 (94.2%)*	89 (85.6%)
Total	52 (100%)	52 (100%)	104 (100%)

*significant ODDS RATIO (RR > 1)
**significant by chi square test (p < 0.05)

TABLE 3. Percentage of attendance more or less than 90% of 6th grade pupils who are children of divorced parents (Case) or non-divorced parents (Control). July-September, 1994. Santiago, Chile.

% Attendance	Case	Control	Total
< 89%	10 (20%)* **	8 (15.4%)**	18 (17.3%)
> 90%	40 (76.2%)	44 (84.6%)*	88 (80.7%)
Sub-total	50 (96.2%)	52 (100%)	102 (98%)
Unknown	2 (3.8%)	0 (0%)	2 (2%)
Total	52 (100%)	52 (100%)	104 (100%)

*significant ODDS RATIO (RR > 1)
**significant by chi square test (p < 0.05)

results were described in the literature in relation to effects that parents' divorce has on children.[1,8]

There was no association found between more absence and being a child of divorced parents. The literature describes that these children have higher absence.[6,9]

It is known that divorce per se is not the one event that produces the change in the members of the family, but the dysfunctional conducts usually are generated before, during and after the separation, when an aggressive and unstable atmosphere is usual and contributes to anxiety, depression[2,5,15] and a lower academic outcome in the children.[1,6]

We think it is essential to continue a line of research that would allow us to know more about children who have divorced parents, to understand the effects in their life and personality[3,4,9-13]; and then introduce new efficient approaches and supports for them[7,16,17] in more areas of which the school system can be one.

BIBLIOGRAPHY

1. Mulholland DJ, Watt NF, Philpott A et al. Academic Performance in Children of Divorce: Psychological Resilience and Vulnerability. Psychiatry, Aug. 1991, 54 (3).
2. Beck D, Lemmp R. The Meaning of Abnormal Family Behavior Situations for the Origin and Type of Psychoreactive Disturbances. Zeitshrift für Psychotherapie und Medizinische Psychologie, 1969, 19(1).
3. Aro H. Parental Discord, Divorce and Adolescent Development. Eur Arch Psychiatry Neurol Sci, 1988, 237(2).

4. Molanen I, Rantakallio P. The Single Parent Family and the Child's Mental Health. Soc Sci Med, 1988, 27(2).
5. Spigelman G, Spigelman A, Englesson I. Hostility, Aggression and Anxiety Levels of Divorce and Nondivorce Children as Manifested in Their Responses to Projective Tests. J Pers Assess, Jun 1991, 56(3).
6. Karr SK, Johnson PL. School Stress Reported by Children in Grades 4, 5 and 6. Psychol Rep, Apr 1991, 68(2).
7. Wolchik SA, Ruehlman LS, Braver SL et al. Social Support of Children of Divorce: Direct and Stress Buffering Effects. Am J Community Psychol, Aug 1989, 17(4).
8. Featherstone DR, Cundick BP, Jensen LC. Differences in School Behavior and Achievement Between Children From Intact, Reconstituted and Single Parent Families. Adolescence, Spring 1992, 27(105).
9. Felner RD, Ginter MA, Boike MF et al. Parental Death or Divorce and School Adjustment of Young Children. Am Jour Comm Psycho, Apr 1981, Vol 9(2).
10. Bisnaire LM, Firestone P, Rynard D. Factors Associated With Academic Achievement in Children Following Parental Separation. Am J Orthopsychiatry, Jan 1990, 60(1).
11. Ziemska M. Educational and Psycho-Hygienic Functions in Divorced Families With Well and Maladjusted Children. International Sociological Association, 1978.
12. McDermont JF Jr. Parental Divorce in Early Childhood. Am J Psychia, 1968, 124(10).
13. Portes PR, Howell SC, Brown JH et al. Family Functions and Children's Postdivorce Adjustment. Am J Orthopsychiatry, Oct 1992, 62(4).
14. Romelsjo A, Kaplan GA, Cohen RD et al. Protective Factors and Social Risk Factors for Hospitalization and Mortality Among Young Men. Am J Epidemiol, Mar 1992, 135(6).
15. Spigelman H, Spigelman G. Indications of Depression and Distress in Divorce and Nondivorce Children Reflected by Rorschach Test. J Pers Assess, Aug 1991, 57(1).
16. Roizblatt A, García P, Maida M. Is Valentine Still Doubtful? A Workshop Model for Children of Divorce. Contemporary Family Therapy, Vol 12, N°4, August 1990.
17. Roizblatt A, Riquelme F. Effects of Divorce on Adult Children of Divorced Families in Chile. Family Conciliations Courts Review, Vol 29, N° 4, October 1991.

Interaction Behaviour of Preschool Children from Single and Two Parent Families

Elisabeth Sander
Claudia Ermert

SUMMARY. Subjects of this study were 30 children, 19 boys and 11 girls, three to six years of age and their mothers. Fourteen children came from mother-child and 16 from two parent families. The children and their mothers were videotaped while doing a puzzle. An observation system for measuring parent-child interaction was developed and the perceived stress of the mothers was rated. There were no significant differences between the interaction behaviour of children from two and single parent families, but there were significant differences depending on the degree of maternal stress. *[Article copies available for a fee from The Haworth Document Delivery Service: 1-800-342-9678. E-mail address: getinfo@haworth.com]*

Dr. Elisabeth Sander and Dr. Claudia Ermert are on the faculty, Institute for Psychology, University of Koblenz, Rheinau 1, 56075 Koblenz, Germany.

[Haworth co-indexing entry note]: "Interaction Behaviour of Preschool Children from Single and Two Parent Families." Sander, Elisabeth and Claudia Ermert. Co-published simultaneously in *Journal of Divorce & Remarriage* (The Haworth Press, Inc.) Vol. 26, No. 3/4, 1997, pp. 57-63; and: *Divorce and Remarriage: International Studies* (ed: Craig A. Everett) The Haworth Press, Inc., 1997, pp. 57-63. Single or multiple copies of this article are available for a fee from The Haworth Document Delivery Service [1-800-342-9678, 9:00 a.m. - 5:00 p.m. (EST). E-mail address: getinfo@haworth.com].

INTRODUCTION

In the literature, behaviour disorders of children from single parent families are often reported, as well as interaction problems in the relationship between single parent and child.

Stress connected with single parentship is considered to be the reason for these findings. First of all, stress caused by a life crisis is mentioned, as for instance, feelings of loss after divorce or death of a parent or partner, or the stress connected with the related coping processes or the processes of adaptation to the new life situation or the new role. In addition, there are stressors as a consequence of the socio-economic situation of the single parent family which is usually a poor one (Cierpka et al., 1992; Sander, 1989; Noack, 1992).

In the last few years, a lot of empirical studies have been carried out, which demonstrate that children in single parent families as well as single parents cope very differently with the situation and that coping depends on personality as well as on environmental factors (Beelmann & Schmidt-Denter, 1991; Fthenakis et al., 1982; Hetherington, 1989; Niepel, 1992; Sander, 1993; Simons et al., 1993).

These findings suggest that there is a chance of trying to change the given conditions in the sense of an optimization, instead of interpreting the single parent family as an unchangeable disadvantageous condition for children's development, as is often done in psychological textbooks (e.g., Toman, 1988, p. 21).

In taking such an optimistic view, one certainly has to consider that the obstacles opposing changes of several conditions are varied, and that the level of intervention has to be varied too, depending on the desired changes, and that sometimes psychological intervention will have no influence at all. Thus, for instance, it is possible to improve childrearing practices by counselling single parents, while an improvement of the socio-economic situation can only be reached by political measures.

On the other hand, the view mentioned nevertheless opens up possibilities of effective counselling. It therefore is necessary to know the conditions inhibiting or promoting the development of the members of the single parent family. Actually, in the literature of the last ten years, several conditions could be identified, which promote the development of children in single parent families (Gately & Schwebel, 1992; Sander, 1988).

There are only a few studies concerning the influence of attitudes, values, perceived stress and similar cognitions of the single parent on the development of children. Some studies concentrating on these questions hint at an existing relation (Beatti & Viney, 1980; Klein-Allermann & Schaller, 1992; Noack, 1992).

From literature about parent-child relations in general, family climate or patterns of parental leadership, it can be hypothesized that maternal states of emotions, attitudes and related cognitions will influence the development of the child to a high degree.

In the present study we were interested in these questions, as we believe that maternal states of emotions and attitudes may be influenced by counselling to a certain degree. We think that this may be the starting point, from which the developmental conditions for children in single parent families may be improved by counselling offers for single parents. We were also interested in the question of a possible difference in the importance of the maternal cognitions mentioned above, especially of the perceived stress of mothers from single and two parent families.

As an indicator of behaviour disorders of the child, we concentrated in the present study on children's interaction behaviour. As we assumed that the influence of maternal cognitions will be stronger the younger the children are, we only examined preschool children.

Because of the age of the sample children, we chose the method of observation for measuring interaction behaviour. The behaviour setting was interactive play between mother and child with a puzzle, a well-known everyday situation in our culture.

We wanted to answer the following questions:

- Are there differences in the interaction behaviour of children from single parent and two parent families?

- Are there differences in the interaction behaviour of preschool children in relation to the estimated amount of perceived maternal stress?

On the basis of the results of empirical studies mentioned above, we expected significant differences between children from single parent and two parent families, as well as between children from high versus low stressed mothers.

METHOD

Sample

Subjects were 30 children, 19 boys and 11 girls, three to six years of age and their mothers. Fourteen children came from mother-child and 16 from two parent families. The single parent mothers were divorced or had been separated for two to four years. It was a random non-clinical sample of children from the region of Koblenz whose mothers took part in a one-time counselling offer of the Psychological Institute of the University.

Procedure

The basis of the observation of interaction behaviour was the standard-ized puzzle play setting. The children and their mothers were videotaped while doing a puzzle. The video camera was situated behind one-way glass. The observation was carried out in the observation room of the Psychological Institute of the University and was embedded in a play hour. Video recording and discussing the videotape with the mothers several days later was an element of the above-mentioned counselling offer.

Observation Categories

There are several sufficiently evaluated observation systems for mea-suring parent-child interaction (see for instance the survey of Mann et al., 1988). Since observation systems have to be constructed for very specific situations, the existing observation systems may give useful hints or may serve as patterns of construction. Nevertheless, it is necessary to develop new or adapted systems if the evaluated observation setting cannot be taken over in quite the same form. We decided therefore to develop a category system for our observation situation, relying on Lütkenhaus (1981). The observation system was developed for the mothers' as well as for the children's behaviour. For answering the questions of the present study, only the observation system for the children's behaviour is relevant. Therefore the observation system for the mothers' behaviour is not de-scribed here.

For developing the category system, some tapes were first evaluated unsystematically, and, by including the relevant literature, a first category system was developed. After an observation training (the course of the training was based on Eller & Winkelmann, 1983), the trained observers then categorized 12 videotapes by means of the observation system. The space of time to be observed was the first 12 minutes of each puzzle sequence. These 12 minutes were divided into 48 intervals of 15 seconds each. At the end of each interval, the most frequently observed category was coded. The category system was improved several times. Finally, the 30 videotapes were categorized by two observers by means of the final version of the improved system. The category system is presented in Table 1.

By means of the category system, the entire behaviour, without any category left over, could be categorized. The interrater agreement was measured by Kappa, K = .88.

TABLE 1. Categories of Children's Interaction Behaviour

Orientation	Explanation
Searching	Explaining by color or form
Searching/Sorting	Explaining by "there"
Observing	Answer to mother's question
Searching for help	
Making use of help	
Ignoring help	
Refusing help	
Play	Classifications (assignments)
Play activity	Classification of a puzzle piece
Symbolic play	Trying out
Commenting to mother	Contradicting
Talking to oneself (monologue)	
Avoidance tactics	
Gestures of the child	Evaluation of self
Showing embarrassment	Negative evaluation of self
Putting a finger in mouth	Positive evaluation of self
Vocalizing	Positive evaluation of self
Embarrassed smile	and smiling
Positive smiling of joy	
Common smiling of embarrassment	
Common smiling of joy	

From these data we conclude that the internal validity (content validity, objectivity, reliability) of the category system is satisfactory.

Rating Maternal Stress

On the basis of detailed anamnesis, behaviour observations and an intensive counselling interview, the counsellor rated the subjectively perceived stress of the mothers (high stressed versus low stressed).

Statistical Procedures

In order to answer the questions of this paper, contingency tables were formed and relations between the categories of the observation system and the categories "single parent/two parent family" and "rather stressed/ rather not stressed" were examined by means of a Chi^2-Test.

RESULTS

There were no significant differences between the interaction behaviour (categories) of children from two and single parent families. On the other hand, we could find significant differences depending on the degree of maternal stress:

Children of rather stressed mothers compared to rather non-stressed mothers ignored mother's help more often (Chi^2 = 5.32, df = 1, p < .05), more explained the selection of a puzzle piece by colour and form (Chi^2 = 5.13, df = 1, p < .05) and smiled more often out of embarrassment (Chi^2 = 10.54, df = 1, p < .01).

CONCLUSIONS

Contrary to our hypothesis, there was no significant difference between the behaviour of children from single and two parent families, while there were, in accordance with our expectations, significant differences between the interaction behaviour of children whose mothers had varied perceptions of stress.

These results support the interpretation that the fact of living in a single parent or two parent family has less influence on the observed behaviour of children than the way their mothers perceive and evaluate their concrete life situations.

The quality of the observed behaviour differences points to the fact that there are behaviour disorders of children of high versus low stressed mothers: ignoring maternal help, rare verbal explanations for decisions and rare smiling may be indices of a rather problematic mother-child relation, resulting in rather inhibited interaction behaviour of the child.

The results fit well into a theoretical framework which postulates a connection between maternal cognitions and attitudes and the development of children. This fact supports the plausibility of our findings, although they should not be generalized because of the small sample.

Also, the results of our study support the demand for counselling opportunities for mothers, independent of family type (single parent/two parent family).

REFERENCES

Beatti, S. & Viney, L.L. (1980). Becoming a lone parent: a cognitive interactionist approach to appraising and coping during a crisis. *British Journal of Social and Clinical Psychology, 19*, 343-351.

Beelmann, W. & Schmidt-Denter, U. (1991). Kindliches Erleben sozial-emotionaler Beziehungen und Unterstützungssysteme in Ein-Elternteil-Familien. *Psychologie in Erziehung und Unterricht, 38*, 180-189.

Cierpka, A., Frevert, G. & Cierpka, M. (1992). "Männer schmutzen nur!"-Eine Untersuchung über alleinerziehende Mütter in einem Mutter-Kind-Programm. *Praxis der Kinderpsychologie und Kinderpsychiatrie, 41*, 168-175.

Fthenakis, W.E., Niesel, R. & Kunze, H.-R. (1982). *Ehescheidung. Konsequenzen für Eltern und Kinder*. München: Urban & Schwarzenberg.

Gately, D. & Schwebel, A. I. (1992). Favorable outcomes in children after parental divorce. *Journal of Divorce & Remarriage, 18*, 57-78.

Hetherington, E.M. (1989). Coping with family transitions: Winners, losers, and survivors. *Child Development, 60*, 1-14.

Klein-Allermann, E. & Schaller, S. (1992). Scheidung-Ende oder Veränderung familialer Beziehungen? In M. Hofer (Hrsg.), *Familienbeziehungen* (S. 266-288). Göttingen: Hogrefe.

Niepel, G. (1992). Die Bedeutung sozialer Netzwerke und sozialer Unterstützung für Alleinerziehende-ein Trendbericht über ein in der deutschen Forschung vernachlässigtes Gebiet. *Frauenforschung, 4*, 60-76.

Noack, P. (1992). Allein zu Zweit: Ein-Elternteil-Familien. In M. Hofer (Hrsg.), *Familienbeziehungen* (S. 289-310). Göttingen: Hogrefe.

Sander, E. (1989). Alleinerziehende Eltern. In. B. Paetzold und L. Fried (Hrsg.), *Einführung in die Familienpädagogik* (S. 69-86). Weinheim: Beltz.

Sander, E. (1988). Überlegungen zur Analyse fördernder und belastender Bedingungen in der Entwicklung von Scheidungskindern. *Zeitschrift für Entwicklungspsychologie und Pädagogische Psychologie, 20 (1)*, 77-95.

Sander, E. (1993). Die Situation des Alleinerziehens aus der Sicht betroffener Mütter. *Psychologie in Erziehung und Unterricht, 40*, 241-248.

Simons, R.L., Beaman, J., Conger, R.D. & Chao, W. (1993). Stress, support, and antisocial behavior trait as determinants of emotional well-being and parenting practices among single mothers. *Journal of Marriage and the Family, 55*, 385-398.

Toman, W. & Egg, R. (1985). *Psychotherapie. Ein Handbuch*. Stuttgart: Kohlhammer.

CHINA

Impacts of Social Pressure and Social Support on Distress Among Single Parents in China

Chau-kiu Cheung
Elaine Suk-ching Liu

SUMMARY. A sample of 301 single parents in Guangzhou, China enabled a study of relationships between distress on one hand and social pressure and social support on the other. Confirmatory factor analysis showed that social pressure and social support, including emotional support and instrumental support, were only weakly correlated. They were shown to have equal contribution to distress, which included depression and anxiety. Distress was positively related to social pressure and negatively related to social support. No sex differential was detected for these relationships. Results indicate the importance of the so-

Chau-kiu Cheung, PhD, and Elaine Suk-ching Liu, MSW, are on the Faculty of Medicine, Department of Applied Social Studies, Centre for Clinical Trials and Epidemiological Research, City University of Hong Kong, Prince of Wales Hospital, Shatin, N.T., Hong Kong.

[Haworth co-indexing entry note]: "Impacts of Social Pressure and Social Support on Distress Among Single Parents in China." Cheung, Chau-kiu and Elaine Suk-ching Liu. Co-published simultaneously in *Journal of Divorce & Remarriage* (The Haworth Press, Inc.) Vol. 26, No. 3/4, 1997, pp. 65-82; and: *Divorce and Remarriage: International Studies* (ed: Craig A. Everett) The Haworth Press, Inc., 1997, pp. 65-82. Single or multiple copies of this article are available for a fee from The Haworth Document Delivery Service [1-800-342-9678, 9:00 a.m. - 5:00 p.m. (EST). E-mail address: getinfo@haworth.com].

cial context for the Chinese single parent's distress. *[Article copies available for a fee from The Haworth Document Delivery Service: 1-800-342-9678. E-mail address: getinfo@haworth.com]*

The literature has consistently suggested that single parents suffer from higher distress than married parents (Amato & Patridge, 1987; Nelson, 1985; Simons et al., 1993). In China, rigorous research on the distress of single parents is missing. Yet, anecdotal evidence concurs with the view that single parents are in higher distress than married parents (Sun, 1991). An important factor contributing to higher distress among single parents appears to be the social factor, including social pressure and social support which single parents receive in their daily lives. The present study aims at verifying the contribution of the social factor to single parents' distress in China.

Single Parents in China

A single parent is a parent who takes care of a child aged below 18 years, in the absence of a spouse in the household. The single parent is particularly susceptible to social influence in China because of its structural and cultural characteristics. As regards structural characteristics, single parents are a minority group in China. Although direct statistics of this proportion are unavailable, an indirect statistic in terms of the divorce rate shows that divorce in China (0.15% in 1993 [State Statistical Bureau, 1994]) is far less prevalent than in the United States (0.48% [U.S. Bureau of the Census, 1994]). It seems that only 2.5% of all households in China consist of single parents, as compared with 8% in the United States (U.S. Bureau of the Census, 1994). This structural difference would create variation in stigmatization by two cognitive processes. First, according to the thesis of illusory correlation, people are likely to have prejudiced attitudes toward the minority group because they tend to ascribe undesirable attributes to members of atypical groups (Hamilton & Sherman, 1989). Second, according to the thesis of the spiral of silence, members of the minority are less likely to speak up for themselves, thus strengthening the negative perception of the majority group (Granovetter & Soong, 1988). As a result of stigmatization, which is a negative societal reaction toward a person because of the person's particular status, people likely treat single parents unfavorably (Sibicky & Dovidio, 1986).

Cultural dimensions of familism and social orientation in China also enhance social influence on single parents. Familism emphasizes maintenance of an intact family and roles and responsibilities of all family members (Yang, 1988). China is a family-centered society in which family members and relatives shoulder most of the caring task (Pearson & Phillips 1994). At the same time, Chinese are curious about others' affairs (Pearson & Phillips 1994). They like to comment on deeds of single parents (Sun, 1991, p. 118). Moreover, Chinese single parents are particularly susceptible to social influence, because of their adherence to the norm of social conformity (Sun, 1991, p. 60; Yang, 1986). Familism and social orientation are probably the heritage of the agricultural, feudal society in China which emphasized labor-intensive production and cooperation (Sun, 1991, p. 60; White, 1979). These ideologies, nevertheless, highlight the importance of social influence in terms of social pressure and social support in China.

Impact of Social Pressure and Social Support

Social pressure and social support derive from notions of negative social interaction and positive social interaction respectively. Negative social interaction occurs when some people make a person feel very bad, unhappy, upset, or angry (Okun et al. 1990). Finch et al. (1989) operationalized negative social ties in terms of criticism, being taken advantage of, broken promise, being let down, being neglected, and provoking feelings of conflict or anger. They showed that the factor deriving from these negative interaction items was independent of the factor comprising positive interaction items, including help, companionship, confiding, consultation, and sharing things. These items tap the central concept of social support, specifically, functional social support which involves support in various daily life aspects (Wohlgemuth & Betz, 1991). Emotional social support and instrumental social support are two typical examples which involve verbal support for one's emotion and tangible assistance to one respectively (Wortman & Dunkel-Schetter, 1987). In sum, social support is defined as interpersonal transactions that involve the expression of positive affect, the affirmation or endorsement of the person's beliefs or values, and the provision of aid or assistance. By contrast, social pressure is defined specifically by criticism and pressure on a single parent concerning his or her custodial role. It is hypothesized, like the finding by Finch et al. (1989), that social pressure and social support, when applied to a sample of single parents in China, are independent.

Social pressure is hypothesized to lead to or maintain a single parent's distress. This hypothesis derives from findings that negative social interaction brings along one's depression and anxiety as found in the study of college students (Lakey et al. 1994), patients (Helgeson, 1993), and older adults (Finch & Zautra, 1992; Okun et al. 1990). Notably, Finch and Zautra (1992) employed distribution-free structural equation analysis to show that negative social interaction increased an older adult's depression both contemporaneously and over time. Their findings were replicated by Helgeson (1993). Lakey et al. (1994) showed that Time 1 negative social interaction, which was measured by a list of 40 items, increased a student's Time 2 dysphoria and anxiety. Okun et al. (1990) showed that negative social ties were related to an older adult's distress with cross-sectional data. With divorced persons, studies also found that negative social interaction, which included the quality of social relation (Katz, 1991), pressure to remain married (Green, 1987), and challenge to the parent's authority (Nelson, 1985) increased one's distress. However, the effect of social pressure on a single parent's distress has not been directly tested, although it has been suggested that children's expectation for tolerant parenting may become pressure particularly on a single mother (Ambert, 1985, p. 24).

Social support is hypothesized to reduce a single parent's distress. This hypothesis derives from significant findings concerning the effect of social support on the psychological adjustment of single parents (D'Ercole, 1988; Gladow & Ray, 1986; Kurdek, 1988; Leslie & Grady, 1988; Shinn et al., 1989; Simons et al., 1993). Whereas it is suggested that social support would only reduce distress when the person is under stress (Cohen & Wills, 1985), these studies demonstrated the direct effect of social support. It may be because being a single parent is already a source of chronic stress and events of divorce and widowhood are highly stressful (Compas & Williams, 1990; Forgatch et al., 1988, p. 135; Nelson, 1985, p. 98; Straus, 1988, p. 229). Therefore, the thesis of stress-buffering holds when social support reduces a single parent's affective distress.

In the study of students (Lakey et al., 1994) and old adults (Okun et al., 1990), it was found that negative social interaction significantly related to distress. However, effects of social support on distress were not significant in some cases. Lakey et al. (1994, p. 42) suggested that negative social interaction is a better predictor of affective distress than social support. This is a hypothesis to be tested in this study.

There may be a sex differential in the effect of social support on a single parent's distress. Clarke-Stewart (1990) found that social support was significantly positively related to a divorced woman's psychological adjustment but was not so to a divorced man's. In a broader context, social support has been found more effective in reducing a person's distress (Gore & Cotten, 1991, p. 151; Wohlgemuth & Betz, 1991). This sex differential may be explained by a female's higher interpersonal sensitivity (Eagly, 1987, p. 16) and dependency on social relation (Gore & Cotten, 1991, p. 151).

Hypotheses

From the preceding discussion, the following hypotheses arise.

Hypothesis 1: A single parent's received social pressure and social support are independent.

Hypothesis 2: A single parent's received social pressure is positively related to his or her distress.

Hypothesis 3: A single parent's received social support is negatively related to his or her distress.

Hypothesis 4: For a single parent, the relationship between distress and social pressure is stronger in magnitude than the relationship between distress and received social support.

Hypothesis 5: Relationships between distress and received social pressure and social support are stronger in a single mother than in a single father.

Besides these 5 major hypotheses, relationships between distress and years of custody, widowhood, spouse's imprisonment, spouse's desertion, education, family income, age, sex, and the age of the elder child were examined. It was hypothesized that years of custody was associated with lower distress. Prior research has indicated that the recency of single parenthood was associated with high depression (Goldberg et al., 1992) and months since separation was associated with low anxiety (Propst et al., 1986). A widowed parent is hypothesized to suffer higher distress than a divorced parent. Amato and Patridge (1987) found that a widowed person was less psychologically adjusted than a divorcee. They explained this by the higher uncontrollability and irreparability of the death of a spouse (Amato & Patridge, 1987, p. 316). The spouse's imprisonment and desertion are two other conditions leading to single parenthood. They are examined for control purpose. It is hypothesized that a more highly educated single parent shows lower distress. Propst et al. (1986) showed that education was related to lower anxiety. A higher family income is hypothesized to lead to lower distress in the single parent. Katz (1991) found that earning was negatively related to the depression of divocees and widows. Green (1987) found that the more spending money a divorcee had, the more the adjustment to divorce. An older single parent is hypothesized to have lower distress. Cook (1988) found that older single mothers were more satisfied with the neighborhood. It was hypothesized that a single mother was more depressed and anxious than a single father. Prior research tends to report higher distress in a single mother than in a single father (Clarke-Stewart, 1990; Green, 1987; Nelson, 1985, Straus, 1988). Clarke-Stewart (1990, p. 89) speculated that single mothers would find their situations more trapped, their goals as wives frustrated, and having lower social and occupational status than single fathers even when the financial condition was controlled. It is hypothesized that the elder child's age is negatively related to the single parent's distress. Umberson (1989) documented that an average parent whose offspring is under 18 years old was more depressed. Because all the aforementioned hypotheses derive from Western studies, their applicability should be tested among single parents in China.

METHODS

Data were obtained from personal interviews with 301 single parents in Guangzhou, during the last 2 months in 1993. With the assistance of the Women's Federation of China, these parents were recruited from 52 secondary schools, 31 primary schools, and 50 kindergartens and nurseries. In this sample, 199 (66.8%) were single mothers and 99 (33.2%) were single fathers (and the data concerning the sex of 3 parents were carelessly omitted in the questionnaire). Their average age was 38.5 years, among a range from 28 to 59 years. They had an average length of custody experience of 3.63 years. Most of them (191, 63.7%) attained the primary level of education. Virtually all of them were employed, as only 5 single mothers were not. Most of them were ordinary workers (112, 37.5%). There were 79 (26.4%) parents working in technical or minor professional or administrative posts. Their average family income was 687 yuans, with a range from 150 to 6,000 yuans. They had on average 1.15 children, and among them 0.63 boys and 0.51 girls. The average age of their elder children was 10.2 years, with a range between 3 and 21 years.

Measurement

The parents were interviewed face-to-face by trained interviewers from the Women's Federation. With a structured questionnaire, the single parents' depression, anxiety, social support, and social pressure received were measured by questions adapted from corresponding measurement instruments. These measures were based on composite scores of the parents' responses to a number of questions which were scored on a 5-point Likert-type scale. The wording of each question was made relevant to Chinese culture. These questions were interspersed in the questionnaire to avoid grouping them according to the concepts to be measured. This was to eliminate the order bias (Tourangeau & Rasinski, 1988). The internal consistency of each measure, as expressed by reliability alpha, was found acceptable for each measure.

Depression. Depression was measured by 14 questions adapted from the Center for Epidemiologic Studies Scale of Depression (CES-D) (Radloff, 1977). This scale of depression could be used for all general populations and was the most popular scale ever used (Radloff, 1991). The marker item, with the highest corrected item-total correlation was: "Did you have crying spells?" The reliability alpha of the composite score was .826.

Anxiety. Anxiety was measured by 4 questions adapted from Sherbourne et al. (1991). The marker item was: "Did you have difficulty trying to calm down?" The other items were: "Were you bothered by nervousness?" "Did you feel rattled?" "Were you restless?" The reliability alpha of the composite score was .788.

Social Support. Social support received by the single parent was measured by 8 questions adapted from Sherbourne et al. (1991). The strength of this conceptualization of social support was on treating social support as actually received, rather than wishfully perceived (Wethington & Kessler, 1986). This avoided the problem of confounding social support by a subjective projection or rationalization of one's psychosocial adjustment (Slavin and Compas 1989). Hence, this concept of social support as received was more objective than the one that was purely subjectively perceived. Two dimensions of social support were discerned, that is, emotional social support and instrumental social support. A marker question of emotional social support, having the highest corrected item-total correlation, was: "Is there anyone showing you love and affection?" The reliability alpha of the composite measure of emotional social support, consisting of 5 items, was .848. A marker question of instrumental social support was: "Is there anyone who takes care of the housework for you when you are sick?" The composite score, consisting of 3 items, yielded a reliability alpha of .668. Instrumental social support correlated .532 with emotional social support.

Social Pressure. Social pressure on the single parent was measured by two questions. These two questions were: "Did the people around you put pressure on you regarding matters of custody?" and "Did the people around you criticize your performance in custody?" The reliability alpha of the composite measure was .587.

For the convenience of interpretation, these composite measures were scored from 0 to 100. The end of 100 indicated the highest level of depression, anxiety, emotional social support, instrumental social support, and social pressure.

Analytic Strategy

Much of the analysis relied on the use of LISREL (Jöreskog & Sörbom, 1993). LISREL is a versatile statistical program that can perform complicated factor analysis and path analysis (Bollen, 1989). Its strength lies in the flexibility to test particular sets of parameters, including factor loadings and regression coefficients. To test Hypothesis 1, LISREL involved confirmatory factor analysis of items measuring social pressure, emotional and instrumental social support. This analysis restricted and estimated factor loadings of corresponding factors of social pressure, emotional social support, and instrumental social support. The goodness of fit of the confirmatory factor model would be indicated by a low likelihood chi-square (L^2), and root-mean-square residual (RMSR), and a high Goodness-of-Fit Index (GFI), and a high Comparative Goodness-of-Fit Index (CFI) (Bentler, 1990). A Comparative Goodness-of-Fit Index above .90 would show the good fit of the model (Feldman, 1993).

Regression analysis tested Hypotheses 2, 3, 4, and 5 were tested. The regression analysis first entered social pressure, emotional social support, instrumental social support, together with years of custody, widowhood, spouse's imprisonment, spouse's desertion, education, family income, age, sex, the age of the elder child, numbers of sons and daughters into the model. Examination of regression coefficients of social pressure and emotional support and instrumental support gave a test of Hypotheses 2 and 3. Hypothesis 4 was tested by using LISREL (Jöreskog & Sörbom, 1993) to constrain the regression coefficient of social pressure equal to the negative of the sum of regression coefficients of emotional support and instrumental support. The difference in the likelihood ratio chi-square of this constrained model from the unconstrained model yielded a test of Hypothesis 4. This procedure was performed for depression and anxiety alternately. To test Hypothesis 5, the interaction terms between sex and emotional support and instrumental support were added to the regression model. It was the technique of moderator regression analysis (Wohlgemuth & Betz, 1991).

RESULTS

The proportions of single parents whose spouses were dead, imprisoned, having deserted the families, or divorced were 33.1%, 1.7%, 7.7%, and 57.5%. Thus, divorce and widowhood accounted for most cases of single parenthood. On a scale running from 0 to 100, the means of depression, anxiety, social pressure, emotional social support, and instrumental social support were 37.1 (SD = 13.4), 33.0 (SD = 19.0), 35.7 (SD = 23.3), 67.1

($SD = 18.8$), and 59.6 ($SD = 22.3$) respectively. The depressive items, when transformed to approximate the CES-D, yielded a mean score of 16.2, on a scale from 0 to 60. This was substantially higher than the mean (10.3) obtained from a survey of the population in Beijing (Lin, 1989), and the mean (11.3) from a survey of white American women (Case et al., 1989). Furthermore, 48.2% of the single parents were depressives classified according to the cutoff point at 15/16. This was higher than the percentage (26.5%) in white American women (Case et al., 1989). These comparisons verified the view that single parents are in higher distress than others.

Hypothesis 1 was supported by the nonsignificant correlation between the social pressure factor and instrumental social support factor. These factors and the emotional social support factors were identified by their respective items in the expected way (see Table I). That is, estimated loadings on these factors were significant and high and the model fitted the data quite well ($L^2(33) = 163$, *RMSR* = .064, *GFI* = .907, *CFI* = .882). The correlation between social pressure and emotional social support was weak ($r = -.175$). Furthermore, the correlation between social pressure and a total social support score which included both emotional and instrumental social support was nonsignificant ($r = -.106, p = .060$). This showed that social pressure and social support were relatively independent.

Hypothesis 2 was supported by the significant regression coefficients of social pressure in predicting depression and anxiety (.308 & .269) (see Table II). Hypothesis 3 was supported by the significant negative relations of emotional support and instrumental support to depression. It was partly supported in predicting anxiety when only instrumental support was significantly negatively related to anxiety.

Hypothesis 4 which stated that distress was more related to social pressure than social support had to be rejected. This was indicated by the nonsignificant chi-squares in constraining the coefficients of social pressure equal to the negative sum of those of emotional support and instrumental support in predicting depression ($L^2(1) = 1.00, p = .316$) and anxiety ($L^2(1) = 1.35, p = .245$). These results suggested that the relations between distress and social pressure and those between distress and social support, which was the sum of emotional support and instrumental support, were equally strong.

Hypothesis 5, which stated that relations between distress and social pressure and social support differ between sex, was rejected. None of the 6 interactive terms between sex and social pressure and social support added significant contribution to explaining distress.

Years of custody was significantly negatively related to depression anxiety as hypothesized. Widowhood led to higher depression, but not higher

TABLE I. Confirmatory Factor Analysis: 3-Factor Model

	Social pressure	Emotional social support	Instrumental social support
Social pressure:			
Being criticized about custody	0.646*		
Pressure on custody	0.646*		
Social support:			
Have someone giving good advice		0.545*	
Have someone to confide in		0.547*	
Have someone understanding own problems		0.810*	
Have someone expressing care		0.884*	
Have someone sharing worry with		0.827*	
Have someone taking care of housework			0.781*
Have someone caring for children			0.522*
Have someone accompanying to the doctor			0.607*

	Interfactor correlations		
Social pressure	1.000		
Emotional social support	−0.175*	1.000	
Instrumental social support	−0.094	0.715*	1.000

$L^2(33) = 163$, RMSR = .064, GFI = .907, CFI = .882
*: significant at the 2-tailed .05 level.

anxiety, than divorce. Education and family income exerted no significant effect on distress. Sex was only significantly related to depression but not anxiety. The effect of sex on anxiety might have been mediated by other variables included in the regression equation. Effects of age, the elder child's age, and number of sons and daughters were not significant.

DISCUSSION

Although not supporting Hypothesis 1 in full, confirmatory factor analysis of items of social pressure and social support of Chinese single parents reveals that the two concepts are relatively independent. The social pressure factor did not significantly correlate with the instrumental social

TABLE II. Regression Analysis of Depression and Anxiety

	Depression			Anxiety		
	r	Beta	b	r	Beta	b
Before the entry of interaction terms						
Social pressure	.317*	.302*	0.173	.271*	.275*	0.225
Emotional support	−.343*	−.201*	−0.143	−.140*	−.026	−0.026
Instrumental support	−.342*	−.186*	−0.111	−.174*	−.136*	−0.116
Custody years	−.164*	−.143*	−0.763	−.210*	−.217*	−1.657
Widowhood	.033	.175*	4.946	−.077	.042	1.683
Spouse's imprisonment	.066	.031	5.580	.100	.076	11.345
Spouse's desertion	−.037	.037	2.704	.020	.050	3.611
Education	−.109	−.001	−0.161	.005	.052	1.389
Family income ('000)	−.065	.017	0.440	.035	.082	2.991
Age	−.144*	−.058	−0.163	−.167*	−.082	−0.326
Female	.134*	.130*	3.651	.126*	.086	3.488
Number of sons	−.021	−.029	−0.725	−.008	−.004	−0.143
Number of daughters	−.012	−.006	−0.153	−.006	.002	0.067
Age of the elder child	−.066	−.028	−0.108	−.088	.054	0.296
R^2		.328*			.190*	
After the entry of interaction terms						
Female social pressure	.336*	−.279	−0.083	.279*	−.363	−0.514
Female emotional support	−.171*	−.358	−0.103	−.042	−.451	−0.185
Female instrumental support	−.217*	−.158	−0.045	−.091	−.233	−0.096
R^2		.339*			.210*	

*: significant at the 2-tailed .05 level.
The regression analyses also controlled for occupation.

support factor and was only weakly correlated with the emotional social support factor. When emotional support and instrumental support were combined, this total social support score showed no significant correlation with social pressure. Thus, the result tends to support Finch et al.'s (1989) proposition that negative social interaction is unrelated to social support.

Hypothesis 2 and most of Hypothesis 3 are supported by results of regression analysis. Accordingly, social pressure and instrumental social support were related to both depression and anxiety. Emotional social support was significantly negatively related to depression but not to anxiety. This latter finding is consistent with the stress-buffering interpretation. Accordingly, emotional social support buffers the stress of being a single parent by reducing depression, that is, senses of frustration and guilt. However, emotional social support does not affect anxiety which is more the result of the anticipated failure to carry out the role of a single parent than the result of frustration and guilt resulting from divorce, widowhood, spouse's imprisonment or desertion. Hereby, depression and anxiety can be distinguished by being underrewarded in the past as in depression and feeling underprepared for the future as in anxiety (Garber et al., 1980). The former is stress to be buffered and the latter is not stress experienced at all and not to be buffered. Thus, reduction of future anxiety is not necessarily involved in the stress-buffering function of emotional social support.

Hypothesis 4, which states that social pressure is more related to distress than social support is, finds no support from LISREL analysis. The finding is that social pressure and social support, comprising emotional and instrumental social support, are equally important to the single parent's distress. If negative social interaction is more important than social support in predicting college students' and old adults' distress as found in Lakey et al.'s (1994) and Okun et al.'s (1990) studies, then social support will be especially important in buffering stress in single parents. That is, the effect of social support is relatively stronger on single parents' distress than on students' and older adults'.

Hypothesis 5 which states that there is a sex differential in the relationship between distress and social pressure and social support is not supported by moderator regression analysis. It may cast doubt on Clarke-Stewart's (1990) study that detected the sex difference. Problems with this study are the smallness of the sample ($N = 45$) and the absence of a statistical test of the sex difference. The present finding is consistent with Loscocco and Spitze's (1990) proposition that processes of social support are the same for men and women.

There are significant effects due to years of custody and widowhood on distress. With the passage of time, single parents tend to be more psychologically adjusted. They will eventually acquire necessary coping and supportive resources with sufficient time. Gradually, they may become accustomed to the status change. Widowed parents, when compared with divorced parents, suffered more distress. This finding echoes Amato and Patridge's (1987, p. 316) explanation that because the death of a spouse is uncontrollable and irreparable, it is especially stressful. This stress increases one's depression but not anxiety. Because depression is a result of past dissatisfaction, it is particularly affected by the past stress of being widowed. On the other hand, because anxiety results from anticipated danger (Garber et al., 1980), it results more from divorce than being widowed. Single parents whose spouses deserted the families or were imprisoned had distress at a similar level with divorced parents.

Effects of material resources seem to be minimal on the psychological adjustment of Chinese single parents. Both family income and education were not associated with lower distress. It seems that financial strain does not contribute to distress directly. This finding, however, may be specific to the urban sample in that all single parents except five single mothers were employed. Thus, they might not suffer much from economic pressure which would contribute to their distress (Elder et al., 1995).

Age and sex were weakly related to single parents' affective distress. Only sex showed a significant relationship with depression. Single mothers were more depressed than single fathers. As Clarke-Stewart (1990, p. 89) speculated, single parenthood may be more frustrating and nonrewarding to a mother than to a father. Family structure, in terms of the number of sons and daughters and the elder child's age, exhibited no significant relationship to distress.

In all, this study illustrates the importance of the social context in maintaining single parents' psychological adjustment in China. The social context affects their psychological adjustment through two relatively independent ways, that is, social pressure and social support. Both these social impacts are roughly equal. They also affect both single fathers and mothers.

Implications

In view of substantial impacts of social pressure and social support, efforts to alleviate Chinese single parents' distress should consider social factors as well as person-centered factors. Focusing on the single parent, empowerment work can enhance the single parent's social networking and stigma management (Kissman, 1991). Social networking involves the effective use of social support from the family and friends. To facilitate the single parent's social networking, social skills training is a necessary tool. Through this training, the single parent would learn how to plan for seeking help, including the identification of the nature, time, and providers of help. As regards stigma management, work to enhance the single parent's confrontation and dissonance reduction is useful (Levy, 1993). Because the severity of stigmatization and social pressure depends on the single parent's perception, the single parent can alleviate the negative impact by proper adjustment. Confrontation is an act to challenge the nature and consequences of a behavior and dissonance reduction is an act to evoke others' sense of justice and compassion. By confrontation, the single parent challenges the rationale of social pressure and by dissonance reduction, the single parent negotiates with the person who exerts social pressure. Rather than being a passive recipient of social pressure, the single parent can employ confrontation and dissonance reduction to redefine social pressure. Furthermore, the single parent should discern and adjust to the part of social pressure that is helpful, while resisting the rest of it. In this way, social pressure can become good advice.

This study highlights that distress is not merely personal, but also the result of one's social context. People's beliefs that single parenthood is bad and single parents are problematic in behavior and personality are responsible for creating social pressure on single parents. These beliefs are wrong in that a single parent is not fully responsible for single parenthood and having high social pressure and low social support together (as shown in Hypothesis 1). To prevent social pressure, mass programs that disclose facts to the public regarding the normal functioning of single parents and their families are necessary. Drama may be an effective programming means for such educational and normalizing purposes (Fink & Tasman, 1992, p. 217).

Further Study

The present study can be improved by a longitudinal design and enhanced measurement of key variables. The measure of social pressure can be improved by adapting Lakey et al.'s (1994) Inventory of Negative Social Interaction, which includes 40 items. Similarly, the measure of social support can be strengthened by adapting a comparable 40-item inventory (Barrera et al., 1981). The present cross-sectional design makes conclusive causal inferences difficult. Thus, whereas it is hypothesized that social pressure and social support influence distress, it is likely that distress determines one's social pressure and social support received. It is the thesis of self-selection (Nelson, 1985, p. 117; Simons et al., 1993). Accordingly, a depressed or anxious person would attract more criticism and discourage support from others (Wortman & Dunkel-Schetter, 1987). Conversely, one would feel more pleased to lend support to psychologically adjusted people. These plausible reverse cause-effect relationships prevent making conclusive causal inferences in one direction. This inconclusion may be relieved by employing a longitudinal panel design.

REFERENCES

Amato, P.R., & Patridge, S. (1987). Widows and divorcees with dependent children: Material, personal, family and social well-being. Family Relation, 36, 316-320.

Ambert, A.M. (1985). Custodial parents: Review and a longitudinal study. In B. Schlesinger (Ed.), The one-parent family in the 1980s: Perspectives and annotated bibliography 1978-1984 (pp. 13-34). Toronto, Canada: University of Toronto Press.

Barrera, M., Jr., Sandler, I.N., & Ramsay, T.B. (1981). Preliminary development of a scale of social support: Studies on college students. American Journal of Community Psychology, 9, 4, 435-447.

Bentler, P.M. (1990). Comparative fit indexes in structural models. Psychological Bulletin, 107, 238-246.

Bollen, K.A. (1989). *Structural equations with latent variables.* New York: John Wiley & Sons.

Callahan, C.M., & Wolinsky, F.D. (1994). The effect of gender and race on the measurement properties of the CES-D in older adults. *Medical Care, 32,* 341-356.

Clarke-Stewart, K.A. (1990). Adjusting to Divorce: Why do men have it easier? Journal of Divorce, 13(2), 75-94.

Cohen, S., & Wills, T.A. (1985). Stress, social support, and the buffering hypotheses. Psychological Bulletin, 98, 310-357.

Compas, B.E., & Williams, R.A. (1990). Stress, coping, and adjustment in mothers and young adolescents in single- and two-parent families. American Journal of Community Psychology, 18, 525-545.

D'Ercole, A. (1988). Single-mothers: Stress, coping, and social support. Journal of Community Psychology, 16, 41-54.

Eagly, A.H. (1987). Sex differences in social behavior: A social-role interpretation. Hillsdale, NJ: Lawrence Erlbaum.

Elder, G.H., Jr., Eccles, J.S., Ardelt, M., & Lord, S. (1995). Inner-city parents under economic pressure: Perspectives on the strategies of parenting. Journal of Marriage and the Family, 57, 771-784.

Feldman, L.A. (1993). Distinguishing depression and anxiety in self-report: Evidence from confirmatory factor analysis on nonclinical and clinical samples. Journal of Consulting and Clinical Psychology, 61, 631-638.

Finch, J.F., Okun, M.A., Barrera, M., Jr., Zautra, A.J., & Reich, J.W. (1989). Positive and negative social ties among older adults: Measurement models and the prediction of psychological distress and well-being. American Journal of Community Psychology, 17, 585-605.

Finch, J.F., & Zautra, A.J. (1992). Testing latent longitudinal models of social ties and depression among the elderly: A comparison of distribution-free and maximum likelihood estimates with nonnormal data. Psychology of Aging, 7, 107-118.

Fink, P.J., & Tasman, A. (1992). Stigma and mental illness. Washington, DC: American Psychiatric Press.

Forgatch, M.S., Patterson, G.R., & Skinner, M.L. (1988). A mediational model for the effect of divorce on antisocial behavior in boys. In E.M. Hetherington & J.D. Arasteh (Eds.), Impact of divorce, single parenting, and stepparenting on children (pp. 135-154). NJ: Lawrence Erlbaum.

Garber, J., Miller, S.M., & Abramson, L.Y. (1980). On the distinctions between anxiety and depression: Perceived control, certainty, and probability of goal attainment. In J. Garber & M.E.P. Seligman (Eds.), Human helplessness: Theory and applications (pp. 131-169). New York: Academic Press, 131-169.

Gladow, N.W., & Ray, M.P. (1986). The impact of informal support systems on the well being of low income single parents. Family Relations, 35, 113-123.

Gore, S., & Cotten, M.E. (1991). Gender, stress, and distress: social-relational influences. In J. Eckenrode (Ed.), The social context of coping (pp. 139-163). New York: Plenum Press.

Granovetter, M., & Soong, R. (1988). Threshold models of diversity: Chinese restaurants, residential segregation and the spiral of silence. Sociological Methodology, 18, 69-104.

Green, R.G. (1987). The influence of divorce predictive variables on divorce adjustment: An expansion and test of Lewis and Spanier's theory of marital quality and marital stability. Journal of Divorce, 7(1), 67-81.

Hamilton, D.L., & Sherman, S.J. (1989). Illusory correlations: Implications for stereotype theory and research. In Daniel Bar-Tal, Carl F. Graumann, Arie W. Kruglanski, and Wolfgang Stroebe (Eds.), Stereotyping and prejudice: Changing conceptions (pp. 59-82). New York: Springer-Verlag.

Helgeson, V.S. (1993). Two important distinctions in social support: Kind of support and perceived versus received. Journal of Applied Social Psychology, 23, 825-845.

Jöreskog, K.G., & Sörbom, D. (1993). LISREL 8 user's reference guide. Chicago, IL: Scientific Software.

Katz, R. (1991). Marital status and well-being: A comparison of widowed, divorced, and married mothers in Israel. Journal of Divorce & Remarriage, 14(3/4), 203-218.

Kissman, K. (1991). Feminist-based work with single-parent families. Families in Society, 72, 23-28.

Kurdek, L.A. (1988). Social support of divorced single mothers and their children. Journal of Divorce, 11(3/4), 167-188.

Lakey, B., Tardiff, T.A., & Doea, J.B. (1994). Negative social interactions: Assessment and relations to social support, cognition, and psychological distress. Journal of Social and Clinical Psychology, 13(1), 42-62.

Leslie, L.A., & Grady, K. (1988). Social support for divorcing mothers: What seems to help? Journal of Divorce, 11(3/4), 147-165.

Levy, A.J. (1993). Stigma management: A new clinical practice. Families in Societies, 34, 226-231.

Lin, N. (1989). Measuring depressive symptomatology in China. Journal of Nervous and Mental Disease, 177, 121-131.

Loscocco, K.A., & Spitze, G. (1990). Working conditions, social support, and the well-being of female and male factory workers. Journal of Health and Social Behavior, 31, 313-327.

Nelson, G. (1985). Family adaptation following marital separation/divorce: A literature review. In B. Schlesinger (Ed.), The one-parent family in the 1980s: Perspectives and annotated bibliography 1978-1984 (pp. 97-151). Toronto, Canada: University of Toronto Press.

Okun, M.A., Melichar, J.F., & Hill, M.D. (1990). Negative daily events, positive and negative social ties, and psychological distress among older adults. Gerontologist, 30, 193-199.

Pearson, V., & Phillips, M. 1994. "Psychiatric Social Work and Socialism: Problems and Potential in China." Social Work 39: 280-287. 162-182.

Propst, L.R., Pardington, A., Ostrom, R., & Watkins, P. (1986). Predictors of coping in divorced single mothers. Journal of Divorce, 9, 33-53.

Radloff, L.S. (1977). The CES-D scale: A self-report depression scale for research in the general population. Applied Psychological Measurement, 1, 385-401.

Radloff, L.S. (1991). The use of the Center for Epidemiologic Studies Depression Scale in adolescents and young adults. Journal of Youth and Adolescence, 20, 149-166.

Sanders, C.M. (1988). Risk factors in bereavement outcome. Journal of Social Issues, 44(3), 97-111.

Sherbourne, C.D., & Stewart, A.L. (1991). The MOS social support survey. Social Science and Medicine, 32, 705-714.

Shinn, M., Wong, N.W., Simko, P.A., & Oritiz-Torres, B. (1989). Promoting the well-being of working parents' coping, social support, and flexible job schedules. American Journal of Community Psychology, 17, 31-55.

Sibicky, M., & Dovidio, J.F. (1986). Stigma of psychological theory: Stereotype, interpersonal reactions, and the self-fulfilling prophecy. Journal of Consulting and Clinical Psychology, 33, 148-154.

Simons, R.L., Beaman, J., Conger, R.D., & Chao, W. (1993). Stress, support, and antisocial behavior trait as determinants of emotional well-being and parenting practices among single mothers. Journal of Marriage and the Family, 55, 385-398.

Slavin, L.A., & Compas, B.E. (1989). The problem of confounding social support and depressive symptoms: A brief report on a college sample. American Journal of Community Psychology, 17, 57-66.

State Statistical Bureau (1994). Statistical Yearbook of China 1994. Beijing, China: China Statistical Publishing House.

Straus, M. (1988). Divorced mothers. In B. Birns & D.F. Hay (Eds.), The different faces of motherhood (pp. 215-238). New York: Plenum.

Sun, W.L. (1991). Divorce in China. Beijing, China: Chinese Women.

Tourangeau, R., & Rasinski, K.A. (1988). Cognitive processes underlying context effect in attitude measurement. Psychological Bulletin, 103, 299-314.

Umberson, D. (1989). Relationships with children: Explaining parents' psychological well-being. Journal of Marriage and the Family 51, 999-1012.

Umberson, D., and Williams, C.L. (1993). Divorced fathers: Parental role strain and psychological distress. Journal of Family Issues, 14, 378-400.

U.S. Bureau of the Census (1994). Statistical abstract of the United States 1994. Washington, DC.

Wethington, E., & Kessler, R. (1986). Perceived support, received support, and adjustment to stressful life events. Journal of Health and Social Behavior, 27, 78-89.

White, L.T., III. (1979). Agricultural and industrial values in China. In R.W. Wilson, A.A. Wilson & S.L. Greenblatt (Eds.), Value change in Chinese society (pp. 141-154). New York: Praeger.

Wohlgemuth, E., & Betz, N.E. (1991). Gender as a moderator of the relationships of stress and social support to physical health in college students. Journal of Counseling Psychology 38, 367-374.

Wortman, C.B., & Dunkel-Schetter, C. (1987). Conceptual and methodological issues in the study of social support. In A. Baum & J.E. Singer (Eds.), Handbook of psychology and health, Vol. 5: Stress (pp. 63-108). Hillsdale, NJ: Lawrence Erlbaum Associates.

Yang, C.F. (1988). Familism and development: An examination of the role of family in contemporary China Mainland, Hong Kong, and Taiwan. In D. Sinha & H.S.R. Kao (Eds.), Social values and development: Asian perspectives (pp. 93-123). New Delhi, India: Sage.

Yang, K.S. (1986). Chinese personality and its change. In M.H. Bond (Ed.), The psychology of the Chinese people (pp. 106-170). Hong Kong: Oxford University Press.

HUNGARY

The Regional Variation of Divorce in Hungary

David Lester
Zoltan Rihmer

SUMMARY. In both Hungary and the United States, marriage and suicide rates predicted regional divorce rates. In Hungary, but not the United States, higher birth rates were associated with lower divorce rates. *[Article copies available for a fee from The Haworth Document Delivery Service: 1-800-342-9678. E-mail address: getinfo@haworth.com]*

Yang and Lester (1991) studied the regional variation of divorce rates over the states of America and found that the divorce rate was higher in states where indices of social instability (such as suicide, interstate migration and alcohol consumption) were higher. It is of interest to explore

---

David Lester, PhD, is Executive Director for the Center for the Study of Suicide, RR41, 5 Stonegate Court, Blackwood, NJ, USA. Zoltan Rihmer, PhD, is on the faculty at the National Institute for Nervous & Mental Disease, Budapest, Hungary.

[Haworth co-indexing entry note]: "The Regional Variation of Divorce in Hungary." Lester, David and Zoltan Rihmer. Co-published simultaneously in *Journal of Divorce & Remarriage* (The Haworth Press, Inc.) Vol. 26, No. 3/4, 1997, pp. 83-85; and: *Divorce and Remarriage: International Studies* (ed: Craig A. Everett) The Haworth Press, Inc., 1997, pp. 83-85. Single or multiple copies of this article are available for a fee from The Haworth Document Delivery Service [1-800-342-9678, 9:00 a.m. - 5:00 p.m. (EST). E-mail address: getinfo@haworth.com].

83

whether such single-nation studies have results which are applicable to other nations. Accordingly, a data set for the 20 regions of Hungary (Lester and Rihmer, 1992) was examined to explore the social correlates of regional divorce rates in Hungary.

METHOD

The data for Hungary were from 1985 and included marriage, divorce, birth, suicide and death rates per 100,000, the perinatal mortality rate for infants aged zero to six days per 1,000 live births, and the percentage of residents in each county who migrated internally from 1984 to 1985. The data were obtained from the Central Statistical Bureau (1985).

A comparable data set for the 48 contiguous states of the United States for 1980 was available from Lester (1994). The data were the same except that perinatal mortality rates were for the first 28 days of life and interstate migration was from 1975 to 1980.

RESULTS AND DISCUSSION

The results are shown in Table 1. In both nations, marriage and suicide rates contributed significantly to the multiple regression prediction of regional divorce rates. Divorce rates were higher in regions where marriage and suicide rates were higher. In addition, birth rates were negatively associated with divorce rates in the multiple regression for Hungary, while interregional migration was positively associated with divorce rates in the United States.

The results confirm that indices of social instability, such as suicide rates and interregional migration are associated with divorce rates in the United States. These same associations are found for Hungary, except that the contribution of interregional migration to the multiple regression was not statistically significant.

Interestingly, in both nations, marriage rates predicted divorce rates, suggesting that higher divorce rates may result in high remarriage rates, thereby increasing the overall marriage rate. Finally, in Hungary alone, the presence of children appears to be associated with lower divorce rates, suggesting that it might be useful to study the impact of children upon divorce in both nations in studies of individuals to see whether this difference appears at the individual as well as at the aggregate level.

TABLE 1. Regional Correlates of Divorce Rates in Hungary and the United States

	Hungary		United States	
	correlation r	regression beta	correlation r	regression beta
marriage rate	0.04	0.54*	0.80***	0.51***
birth rate	− 0.53*	− 1.38***	0.24	0.08
death rate	0.31	− 0.40	− 0.34*	0.08
infant mort.	0.13	0.09	− 0.24	0.04
migration	− 0.22	0.10	0.74***	0.26*
suicide rate	0.28	0.62**	0.78***	0.29*
R^2		0.78		0.81
adjusted R^2		0.68		0.78
F		7.65**		29.27
df		6/13		6/41

*   two-tailed p < .05
**   two-tailed p < .01
*** two-tailed p < .001

REFERENCES

Central Statistical Bureau. *Demographic yearbook.* Budapest: Central Statistical Bureau.

Lester, D. *Patterns of suicide and homicide in America.* Commack, NY: Nova Science.

Lester, D., & Rihmer, Z. Sociodemographic correlates of suicide rates in Hungary and the United States. *Psychiatrica Hungarica*, 1992, 7, 435-437.

Yang, B., & Lester, D. Correlates of statewide divorce rates. *Journal of Divorce & Remarriage*, 1991, 15, 219-223.

ICELAND

An Icelandic Study of Five Parental Life Styles: Conditions of Fathers Without Custody and Mothers with Custody

Sigrún Júlíusdóttir

SUMMARY. An Icelandic family study[1] of a nationwide random sample of 846 responding parents is presented. It consists of (a) a comparative group of married/cohabiting parents and four groups of single parent families, i.e., (b) widowed parents, (c) parents never in cohabitation, (d) divorced parents with custody (mainly women) and finally (e) divorced parents without custody (mainly men). Fathers without custody is a special group of single parent families in Iceland (that relates to the social family profile, legislation, divorce rate and proportion of children born out of marriage). The main results of the fathers' situations, their complaints and wishes are presented. The fathers express more discontent with the custody arrangements

Dr. Sigrún Júlíusdóttir is Associate Professor at the Department of Social Work, University of Iceland, IS-101, Reykjavík, Iceland.

[Haworth co-indexing entry note]: "An Icelandic Study of Five Parental Life Styles: Conditions of Fathers Without Custody and Mothers with Custody." Júlíusdóttir, Sigrún. Co-published simultaneously in *Journal of Divorce & Remarriage* (The Haworth Press, Inc.) Vol. 26, No. 3/4, 1997, pp. 87-103; and: *Divorce and Remarriage: International Studies* (ed: Craig A. Everett) The Haworth Press, Inc., 1997, pp. 87-103. Single or multiple copies of this article are available for a fee from The Haworth Document Delivery Service [1-800-342-9678, 9:00 a.m. - 5:00 p.m. (EST). E-mail address: getinfo@haworth.com].

than their visiting rights. For the other (single parent) groups family interaction is frequent and makes up a strong network of (social and emotional) support. The divorced fathers' marginal position in the family is reflected, i.e., in their restricted pattern of family interaction. The children of divorced parents lose more contact with their grandparents and other relatives in their fathers' family than with their mothers' family. The divorced fathers without custody have longer working hours and less good housing than the other groups. They express their unhappiness over loss of responsibility of their children. They suffer more than the other groups from sleep disturbances and sad thoughts. *[Article copies available for a fee from The Haworth Document Delivery Service: 1-800-342-9678. E-mail address: getinfo@haworth.com]*

INTRODUCTION

The social changes of the last decades are not the least reflected in changes in close relationships and within the family. Prerequisites to fulfil parental roles and emotional needs within the family are constantly varying in correlation with a changing society and consumption habits, revised gender roles, new family forms and different life styles. Family policy discussions and statistical information about family matters and children's living conditions in Iceland[2] have revealed lacking family support and poor attention to children's affairs, their welfare and human rights, compared with the other Nordic countries. This is striking because the Icelandic society has a relatively high material living standard and educational level. Furthermore, the nation is characterized by a proportionally young population, children under 15 being around 25% of the population. At the same time only 13% of what is allocated to health and social matters goes to family issues (SBI 1994: 232-233). This is much lower than in the other Nordic countries (NOSOSCO 1992:46).

In a recent study where parents were interviewed and both fathers and mothers expressed their discontent and frustration over lacking support, an interesting gender difference appeared. The mothers complained about not being able to use their education and professional training due to lacking day-care services and low salaries. Icelandic women have good education and their participation in the labour market is approximately 80%, 47% of them work part-time and only 53% full-time (Vinnumarkaðurinn 1994). The fathers complained about long working hours, 56 hours per week on the average, not having the opportunity to spend time together with the family and their children (Júlíusdóttir 1993:104-129, 144, 265-273). Women in families with young children are not only taking care of their children. As service for the elderly is limited, middle-aged women more-over take care of their ageing parents (Júlíusdóttir 1993; Sigurgeirsdóttir 1994; Sigurðardóttir 1993; Broddadóttir et al. 1996). In the families this results in strain and conflicts which are a common theme in family work and marital counselling.

It represents a striking change in the Icelandic family structure that the number of children per woman has decreased from 4+ in the period 1940-1960 to 2.2 in 1993 (SBI: 1994, 62, 58). The strain also appears in that the divorce rate in Iceland has been increasing markedly during the last decades. In the fifties divorces were 9% of the weddings, but since the eighties they are 40% plus (SBI: 1994, 62, 58). Women take more initia-tive to divorce than men. Women more often than men ask for the custody of the children and get it in 90% plus of the cases (SBI 1994).

In the study presented below the overall conditions of the different family types are described. The emphasis is on portraying the difference between fathers without custody and the mothers with custody,[3] in some cases also compared with the other parental groups.

THE STUDY: METHOD AND SAMPLE

To convey information to politicians and initiate attitude change in family matters, the Icelandic Committee for the Year of the Family de-cided to sponsor a study in the domain of child issues and family life. This should simultaneously serve the practical purpose of revealing which in-terventions were most urgent.

To prepare the selection of the sample and to have up to date informa-tion on Icelandic family structure, we started with a representative tele-phone survey on family forms, size of households, number of children in the family, etc., see Table 1. (You may note that three generation families in total amount to 5.2% of the households).

The definition of the family concept was discussed. The team agreed to use a broad and flexible understanding of what a family is and hence decided to study *five* types of parental groups which all were defined as *family*. Referring to clinical experience and that fathers having their chil-dren staying in their homes on a regular basis in fact constitutes a special family form, we decided to include fathers without custody as a special group (Table 2).

The final sample of 1150 parents is a nation-wide representative group selected from the Icelandic National Register of 1994. Those selected were parents having at least one child below the age of sixteen in 1991. A

TABLE 1. Icelandic Family Structure. Division of Households

Total N = 1042	%	N
Married with own children[4]	50.2	523
Married with (own and) step-children	7.4	77
Married with children and parents	3.0	31
Single parents with children and parents	2.2	23
Single parents with children	6.4	67
Only adults (singles, cohabiting without children, elderly)	30.8	321
Total	100.0	1042

TABLE 2. Five Types of Parental Groups

(1) married (or cohabiting) parents
(2) parents never married nor in cohabitation
(3) widowed parents
(4) divorced parents with custody of their child(ren)
(5) divorced parents without custody of their child(ren)

further limitation of the group was that they should not have lost the other parent through death or divorce or had a child outside cohabitation, during the period of one year before the survey. Thus we avoided getting parents who quite recently had been through the key event and probably were still in crisis. One more limitation was that they should not be in (registered) cohabitation again.

The questionnaire consisted of 115 questions whereof 58 questions applied to all parental groups but 57 extra questions were only intended for the single parents. These four groups thus answered questions about the birth of a child outside cohabitation, about their divorce and about the death of the other parent.

Answers were obtained from 846 respondents so that the response rate was 74%. The single parent families with custody of their children are headed by women in 96% of the cases. Thus in the following text we may refer to these parents alternatively as "divorced mothers" or "parents with custody." In the same way, "divorced fathers" is almost the same group as "parents without custody."[5]

The difference in answering behavior between the groups is rather striking and constitutes a part of the results.

It is well known in social research that people who are satisfied with their conditions, well adjusted and better off socially seem to be more willing to participate and tell about their lives. The other groups are often not so easy to reach, nor are they willing or motivated to co-operate. In the same way we have reason to think that the responding fathers without custody in the study–being proportionally the smallest group–make up a rather well adjusted and conscious subgroup of divorced fathers. Married and widowed parents share not only similar interest in answering but they have also several important features in common (see Table 3).

The average age of the respondents was 36. Even here there were differences of interest, the never married parents being youngest (34) and the widowed parents being oldest (42; see Table 4). Age of the children is, accordingly, somewhat different in the different groups. The children (oldest child) of the widowed parents are the oldest, 12.7 years on average; children of the divorced are 10.7 years and children of the never married parents are 8.6 years old. Another finding, although not surprising, is the uneven participation of the sexes, the women being in majority in all groups except for the divorced parents without custody.

TABLE 3. Number of Respondents and Response Rate in Each Parental Group

Number of recipients N = 1150	Number of respondents	Response rate, %
Married (or cohabiting) parents	238	82
Parents never married nor in cohabitation	186	69
Divorced parents with custody of child(ren)	309	74
Divorced parents without custody of child(ren)	71	55
Widowed parents	42	84
Total/Average	846	74

TABLE 4. Average Age and Sex Composition of Parental Respondent Groups

	Average age, years	F, %	M, %
Married (or cohabiting) parents	37	58	42
Parents never married nor in cohabitation	34	98	2
Widowed parents	42	78	22
Divorced parents with custody of child(ren)	34	95	5
Divorced parents without custody of child(ren)	38	10	90

FINDINGS

Social Characteristics of the Parental Groups

Occupational Status. There was a significant difference between the social group or class affiliation of the various parental groups. From Table 5 we can see how fathers without custody share similar status with the married parents as these two most often belong to social group 1. Most of the fathers without custody are skilled industrial workers or seamen while the single mothers with custody are most often in skilled service jobs.

The same profile appears in education. Thus we find that married parents and parents without custody in our study have to a greater extent some kind of a higher (university or special) education. Proportionally a great number of the widowed parents (78% women) had only general public education (up to 10th grade) while the single (never married and divorced) parents (over 95% women) more often (30%) are getting further education now or have done so during the last four years.

Working Hours. As Table 6 shows, the fathers without custody work most of all, 51 hours, whereas the average for all groups is 44 hours a week. More women (58%) than men (42%) answered in the group of married parents. Icelandic women work less (more part time) than single mothers in general. This might explain the relatively low number of working hours in the married group.

Income. The difference between the income of the parental groups is significant (Table 7). As the number of persons is different in the households the distribution per person in the home was also calculated. Divorced parents without custody (90% men) have the highest income. Divorced parents with custody (95% women) have the lowest income of all groups.

TABLE 5. The Social Group Affiliation of the Different Parental Groups

N = 846	Of the married, %	Of the never married, %	Of the widowed, %	Of the divorced w.custody, %	Of the divorced without custody, %	Of the total respondent group, %
1. Specialists, private enterprise	19	15	10	15	19	16
2. Higher service jobs	30	44	35	42	14	36
3. Seamen, farmers, industry	27	9	23	10	45	19
4. Workers, service jobs	24	32	32	33	22	29
	100	100	100	100	100	100

Housing. Single parents with custody (except widows) most often live in apartment buildings (Table 8). Unexpectedly, the parents without custody come next after the married and the widows in living in villas.

While single parents with custody have the lowest number (2.5) of bedrooms, parents without custody have 2.6 bedrooms on average. As in many other matters the widowed and married parents have similar standards, i.e., 3.6 and 3.3 bedrooms, respectively. Their housing in square meters is also larger (99m^2) than that of the single parents with custody (91m^2). While widowed parents almost always (98%) own their housing and 80% of married parents do so, it is interesting that only 60% of the other groups of single parents own their housing and only 40% of the parents without custody.

TABLE 6. Number of Working Hours per Week for the Various Parental Groups

	Married	Never married	Widowed	Divorced with custody	Divorced without custody	Total
Working hours	43.8	42.8	34.9	43.5	51.0	43.6

TABLE 7. Income in the Different Parent Groups

(Thousands of kronur before tax)	Married	Never married	Widowed	Divorced with custody	Divorced without custody	Total
Income per home	208	106	138	106	154	144
Income per person	51	45	41	38	94	47

TABLE 8. Housing Conditions of the Different Parent Groups

N = 846	Married %	Never married %	Widowed %	Divorced with custody, %	Divorced without custody, %	Total group, %
Villas	39	18	32	13	27	25
Houses for 2-4 families	33	33	41	32	32	33
Larger apartment buildings	26	48	22	53	34	40
Other	2	1	5	2	7	2
Total	100	100	100	100	100	100

Leisure and Family Network Relations

Parents without custody (90% men) report the lowest level of variety and frequency of leisure activity. Only the group of married parents report so little leisure activity. Parents without custody go most often alone to the cinema or they go to a coffee-house and sometimes they visit friends. On the other hand they have only seldom friends coming to their house and they visit other family members far less than the parents in the other groups.

The family network is strong in Iceland. Approximately 44% on the average of all parental groups are likely to visit parents (their children's grandparents) *three times a week or more,* 16% are likely to get visits from parents and 66% are likely to call parents on the telephone. Single parents visit their own parents more than married parents do. Parents without custody are least likely (37%) out of the single parents to visit their own parents but they visit their siblings on the average as much as the other single parents. Parents without custody are also least likely (10%) to get visits from their own parents and to call them. In the same way they seem to almost cut off the contact with their ex-in-laws as they rarely visit or call them or receive calls from them.

Regarding participation in family parties or special family occasions the parents (fathers) without custody are obviously neither involved in their own family nor in the family-in-law. The divorced parents with custody do participate in family occasions quite as often as the married parents. Among the single parents it is however only the widowed parents who participate to some extent in family occasions with their ex-in-laws.

Thus parents without custody (90% men) seem to be on their own without company from the family. It seems that the single parents with custody seek company or support for children from the grandparents while married parents seem to be more on their own. They visit parents more seldom and they visit their siblings even more seldom. Regarding contact with the family-in-law the pattern is similar but more striking. Here we find that even the divorced parents with custody reduce their contact with the children's grandparents on the fathers' side markedly after the divorce and only quite seldom have them visiting their (and the children's) own house. Fathers without custody have in general relatively poor relation-ships with their family members, i.e., in all regards except contacts with siblings and, to some extent, to brothers or sisters-in-law. See Table 9.

Also in the divorce process the parents with custody discuss their expe-rience and feelings more often with family members than the other parents do and they do so far more often with friends. Twice as many of the parents without custody as of parents with custody do not talk at all with anyone about the divorce. Divorced parents seek much less support from

TABLE 9. Family Network Relations: Percentage Reporting Contact More than Three Times per Week

N = 846	Married	Never married	Widowed	Divorced with custody	Divorced without custody	Total group
I visit parents	36	57	53	46	37	44
Parents visit me	18	15	34	14	10	16
I call them	61	71	72	73	42	66
I visit parents-in-law	15		13	3	5	8
Parents-in-law visit me	12		8	0	0	5
I call parents-in-law	34		50	7	5	20
I call brother or sister-in-law	18		17	8	9	13
I visit siblings	14	32	21	23	21	21
Siblings visit me	13	20	18	19	11	16
I call siblings	36	56	50	56	41	48
I visit grandparents	9	18	0	6	5	9
Grandparents visit me	1	5	0	1	0	2
I call grandparents	13	22	13	15	5	15
I spend leisure time with family members	15	33	18	19	8	20
We meet on family occasions	70	82	59	70	41	70
I spend leisure time with in-laws	7		11	1	0	5
We meet on family occasions	42		28	8	6	28

the other parent than married parents do when there are problems with the children.

The changed pattern of family interaction after divorce is noteworthy and it seems to affect both the children and the parents, especially the parents without custody. The pattern that appears in their case is probably harder for them to deal with as it so markedly deviates from what is the culturally acknowledged and expected.

The respondents were also asked to what extent they got some kind of *direct assistance from their families,* advice, practical or economic help or support with the children. In general people seem to seek more help from their own families of origin than from the families-in-law. After the divorce there is a decrease in this kind of supportive contact from the in-laws. The help parents seek from their families is mainly emotional support in the form of advice. Also here the parents (fathers) without custody ask least for support, assistance and advice from their families. Unexpectedly, they get as little help with the children as the married parents who would have each other to ask and to rely on. Simultaneously the parents without custody report that they are *worried about the children while at work* and that they have *difficulties with the children when they are sick* in the same proportions as the other parental groups. They are also less than others asked to help or give advice in the family. Those who get most assistance from their families, especially with the children, are the never married parents but they have almost no contact with the family of the other parent. Compared with this it is interesting that the divorced parents with custody (and the children) report that they get direct assistance from both their families of origin and from the in-laws.

Evaluation of the Marriage and the Process of Divorce

A factor analysis revealed that the most outstanding source of conflict among the divorced parents is *communication*. The second most outstanding source of conflict is that of *boundaries and behavioral pattern* (fidelity, sexuality, drinking, philosophy of life). Here the divorced mothers express somewhat more conflicts than the divorced fathers. In the third conflicting issue, *the division of housework and time,* the difference between the sexes is clearly significant and it explains more of the distribution than the difference between parental groups.

A majority of the divorced mothers says that the marriage was rather or very difficult but less than half of fathers say so. Thus also the parents with custody (95% mothers) say in 56% of the cases that they themselves took the initiative in the decision of divorce but only 26% of the parents without custody (90% fathers; this accords with general statistics). There is also a clear difference in the view of the decision of divorce. Both mothers and fathers say they themselves had thought about divorce for more than a year before the separation. On the other hand it turns out that when they were asked, twice as many of the non-custodial parents as of the custodial parents think that the ex-partner had thought about this decision for a longer time than themselves, i.e., more than a year before separation.

The families were rarely involved in the decision process, and in different ways for the mothers and fathers. Thus some of the fathers say that parents-in-law recommended the divorce but only a very small part of the mothers say so about their parents-in-law. Some fathers say that their siblings advised them against divorce but the mothers say to the same extent the opposite, i.e., that their siblings recommended them to divorce.

From this it seems that the families, in some cases, support their own family member, such that the mothers get support in their decision to divorce and keep the children and the fathers get support against divorce and losing the children.

The majority of divorced parents say that they reached the divorce decision rather or very easily. Approximately 20% could negotiate on their own after some conflicts and a small group had a dispute that was solved with help from divorce counsellors or attorneys. In this group no couple needed to go to court.

Regarding the emotional part of the divorce there is a clear difference between the sexes in that the fathers are discontent twice as often as the mothers. Also regarding the economic outcome of the divorce the fathers are significantly more often discontent than the mothers. When there was a conflict on economic issues there was also conflict regarding the children, i.e., custody arrangements and visiting habits. Even regarding the attitudes and reactions of other people the fathers without custody are still more often discontent than the mothers who report only in few cases that they are discontent with the reactions they get in their social surroundings.

From this it is clear that the fathers without custody are more discontent than the mothers with almost all parts of the divorce process, from the very beginning and to the end.

Custody Arrangements and Visiting Rights

When asked how content parents are with custody arrangements, 92% of parents with custody (95% mothers) are content while only 59% of the parents without custody (90% fathers) say so and 28% of them even report they are very discontent. Joint custody had been in the debate for many years at the time of the survey but had not yet been legislated. When asked, 76% of parents without custody wished they could get joint custody but only 20% of the parents with custody say so. The difference between the sexes is strongly significant here.

Regarding the visiting form it is striking that a third of the never married mothers report no visiting at all between child and father and more than half of them say the visiting habits are varying. A somewhat more stable visiting form seems to be used among the divorced parents although more than a third of both mothers and fathers say it is varying and not following a special agreement about frequency and form. Mothers with custody say more often than the fathers without custody that the children see their father on an irregular basis or don't see him at all.

When asked about attitudes and wishes in this connection there is again a significant difference between the custody groups and the sexes, but in the opposite direction. Now the majority of parents without custody say they are content with the visiting form, a fourth says they do not wish more frequent visiting and only a small part of them is discontent with the visiting form. Almost two thirds of the parents with custody say they are content but a third of them say they are discontent with the father's visiting habits. In this connection it is interesting that again two thirds of the parents with custody (mothers) further say they wish that the parents without custody (fathers) would share more of the economic responsibility for the children. For a comparison the parents with custody don't complain more than the never married mothers about being alone with the responsibility for the children but they complain more than them about the financial burden. The divorced mothers express more negative attitudes toward the fathers than the never married mothers. Single mothers with custody (both divorced and never married) also report more negative attitudes towards the fathers than fathers do towards the mothers. The parents without custody say twice as often as the others that they think the children were against the divorce while the parents with custody report the opposite, saying the children expressed their content.

From this it is obvious that the sexes have clearly divided views of rights and duties regarding their children. The parents with custody seem to be eager to keep for themselves the responsibility and care for the children but they could allow the fathers to share more of the financial burden. The parents without custody, on the opposite, wish they could have more formal responsibility through joint custody but they are not interested in more visiting. Another interesting finding is the difference in attitude among single mothers, the divorced mothers reporting more negative attitudes toward the father than the never married mothers.

Parents' Health the Last Six Months

Most parents say they are healthy. The total group reports good health in 69% of the cases. Most healthy are the widowed parents, 78%, and the married parents, 73%. The groups of single parents complain more of health problems than the married ones. Difference between the parental groups is not found in the physical health factors but in the emotional and psycho-somatic factors. Factor analysis reveals that the frequency of the emotional and psycho-somatic factors is lowest for the married parents, with a mean score of 0.36. The mean score for the single parents increases from the never married (0.50) through divorced parents with custody (0.65) and the widowed (0.70) to the highest for the divorced parents without custody (0.89).

All groups of single parents living together with their children express more often insecurity and *attacks of anxiety*. They also get more often headache and sense of fatigue. Both divorced mothers and fathers feel *constantly anxious* more than others. Parents without custody seem to have similar grief feelings as the widows and they feel significantly more than other parents often worried and lonely and complain of *sleeplessness or sleeping disturbances.* The average frequency for all groups is 16% but 26% for parents without custody. They are also more likely to feel more often *depressed and pessimistic,* the average frequency for all groups being 16% but for parents without custody and for the widows 36%.

Parents who had lost their partner through death or divorce were asked how they dealt with feelings of loneliness. Parents without custody react most seldom with inviting people to their house. They say they avoid seeing people. Their leisure activity is poor, and they are more alone than other single parents, going to the cinema or taking a glass of alcohol as a remedy against their feeling of loneliness.

DISCUSSION

The conditions of the parents without custody are different from other parental groups. Their daily lives are characterized by long working hours in skilled work and a relatively high income. Different from what is most common in Iceland they are not owning their relatively large housing. However, they offer their children a bedroom of their own, even more often than other single parents. They avoid social contacts.

The fathers without custody suffer from emotional stress more than other parents, feeling constantly anxious, having depressive feelings and sleeping problems. They have less contact (visits, calls, help, advice) with the family network than other parents. They also talk less about personal matters with family and friends than the divorced mothers. This applies to the divorce experience and their worries about the children no less than other issues. They do not see the marriage having been so unsuccessful as the mothers and are more discontent than the mothers about the decision of divorce. Although they are more accepting of the divorce process itself, they are more discontent than the mothers with both the emotional and the financial outcome for themselves. They are more discontent with the custody arrangement than the visiting form and express clearly their wish to have joint custody.

The overall results on the non-custodial fathers' situation indicate frustration and even resignation. Their helplessness in dealing with their feelings related to loss, sadness and isolation manifest themselves as withdrawal and complaint.

It seems that the fathers without custody feel they are the losers in the divorce case. This might be related to or even cause lowered self-esteem. Their withdrawal from family, friends and social activity seems to push them to escape into work which is economically rewarding and culturally and socially acknowledged. This, in turn, could indicate increased insecurity in their–restrictedly granted–role as fathers in which they, however, say they would like to take more responsibility.

In group work with divorced mothers and fathers where family life education is given and a possibility to share experiences and get support is offered, there are often cases where fathers without custody describe their unhappiness and frustration over not knowing how to handle the painful feelings of loss and rejection, mainly related to the contact with their children.[6] There are several examples where these fathers have described their shame and anger and how it caused them not to see their children at all, as "no contact is better than being reminded of the pain of personal failure" or "feeling like a stranger together with my own child is unbearable." Thus a possible explanation of the fathers in this study not wishing to have more visiting rights but simultaneously wishing so strongly for joint custody, might be that they feel weak and powerless when seeing their children under the conditions of time limits and restricted possibilities of participation and influence in their daily lives (Júlíusdóttir et al. 1995: 104-115). Also the mothers' negative attitude towards the fathers without custody is likely to complicate the visiting habits and weaken their motivation to take initiative as a responsible parent.

It even seems that the fathers without custody feel cheated in that the mothers had a kind of a head-start in planning the divorce in their mind long before it was a joint or verbalised issue. In the negotiation process it seems that they feel vanquished as they see themselves as losers (more discontent) on all counts.

In clinical work with divorced fathers who don't have the custody of their children it is common that they express their frustration and helplessness. They seem to feel ashamed of not being accepted in the family. As found in this study they do not talk to family and friends nor seek support with the children, so it is not surprising that they feel helpless and don't know how to behave or act when they are together with their children. Instead of taking the initiative and asking for support they feel hampered in sharing their inadequacies. A common solution is to start a new relationship and even prematurely try to build a new family. In the case when this happens rather soon after the divorce it often seems to influence negatively the contact with the ex-wife and subsequently their contact with the children.

In the study presented we get the parents' report about children's conditions. It shows that both in divorce cases and in loss of a parent through death, the children seem to be the forgotten part. Attention is not given to their crisis, their grief and their need of knowing what is going on and getting adequate support. Instead, these children are more responsible, take more care of siblings and even help and support their parents more than children who are brought up by both parents. Through the divorce the children not only lose the daily contact with their father but they also lose contact with their grandparents on the father's side. It is a remarkable pattern that the mothers in most cases ask for and get the custody of the children. At the same time as their economic and social conditions become worse after the divorce and they complain about strain and worries, they do not wish more co-operation from the father on the raising of the children, except financially. Regarding the visiting form it is noticeable that more than a third of the never married mothers report no visiting at all between child and father and more than a half say the visiting habits are varying. This indicates that the father-child relationship in these families is very weak and the needs and rights of the children are ignored, even more than in the divorced families.

This leads to thinking about both fathers' and children's ethical and legal rights, not to mention the importance of their emotional and social relationships. The different dilemmas of the sexes, i.e., the female caring responsibility, or ethics of emotional care, and the male working responsibility, or ethics of financial and practical support, seem to become still stronger after divorce than before. The gender effect seems to become still more unfair and the lacking equality in the parental roles increases.

Some of the conditions that play a part in the decision of divorce seem to deteriorate after divorce. Married men who complain over much work and too little contact with their children while staying in marriage are likely to increase their working hours and their income and the contact with their children seems to diminish both in quantity and in quality after divorce. Married women who complain over low salaries and lacking day-care–choosing to work part-time to be able to take the responsibility for the children in the home while in marriage–are likely to have worse living conditions after the divorce as they get lower income and work more and take still more responsibility for the children.

NOTES

1. The study was carried out by a research team at the Faculty of Social Sciences, University of Iceland, consisting of Sigurðardóttir, N.K., Jónsson, F.H., Grétarsson, S.J. and the author, who was project leader. It was financed by The Icelandic Committee for The International Year of the Family 1994.

2. Iceland is a small society of 260,000 inhabitants. It is historically and culturally a part of the Nordic countries although geographically located in the middle of the North Atlantic Ocean. Its language is Icelandic and it has been an independent state since 1944.

3. Custody here refers to legal responsibility and physical care. The study was done one year before Icelandic legislation allowed joint custody. Only legal joint custody is possible according to this law.

4. If we on the other hand look at the division of only families with children (0-17 years) then the married and cohabiting parents are 80% but single parents 20% (NOSOSCO 1995).

5. Since respondents among fathers with custody and mothers without were so few we have nothing significant to say about these groups as such nor any subdivisions.

6. For further description of this project see Sigurðardóttir N., 1981, and Júlíusdóttir S., 1984.

BIBLIOGRAPHY

Broddadóttir, I., Eydal, G., Hrafnsdóttir, S., Sigurðardóttir, S., 1996. "The Development of Local Authority Social Services in Iceland." *In* Sipilä, J. (ed.), *The Rise and Reconstruction of Personal Social Services. A Comparative Nordic Study.* London: Avebury.

Giddens, A. 1993. *Modernity and Self-Identity. Self and Society in Late Modern Age.* Oxford: Polity Press. (1st edn 1991).

Jónsdóttir, S., 1993. "Gamlar norrænar konur og velferðarkerfið." *Morgunblaðið 28. December.*

Júlíusdóttir, S., 1984. "Experience with Post Divorce Education: Seminar report." *Parent-Child Relationship Post-Divorce.* Copenhagen: Dansk Socialforskningsinstitut. pp. 184-197.

Júlíusdóttir S., 1993. *Den Kapabla Familjen i det isländska samhället: En studie om lojalitet, äktenskapsdynamik och psykosocial anpassning.* Félagsvísindastofnun HÍ/Goteborgs Universitet.

Júlíusdóttir, S., 1994. "Enforälderfamiljer: Deras Struktur och villkor i det isländska samhället." *Fokus på Familjen* Vol. 22 (1), 11-23.

Júlíusdóttir, S., Sigurðardóttir, N.K., Jónsson, F.H., Grétarsson, S.J., 1995. *Barnafjölskyldur. Samfélaglifsgildi-mótun.* Reykjavík: Félagsmálaráðuneytið.

NOSOSCO, 1992. *Social Tryghet i de nordiske land. Omfang, utgifter og finansiering 1990.* Nordisk statistisk skriftserie nr 58. Copenhagen.

NOSOSCO 1995. *Social Security in the Nordic Countries. Scope 1993. Expenditure and financing 1993. Copenhagen.*

Ólafsson, S., 1990. *Lifskjör og lífshættir á Íslandi.* Reykjavík: Félagsvísindastofnun HÍ/Hagstofa Íslands.

Sigurðardóttir, N., 1981. "Kurser for nyfraskilte." *Nordisk Socialt Arbejd,* 1 (4), 18-25.

Sigurðardóttir, S., 1993. "Isländska livsloppsformer," in Wærness, K. et al. (eds.) *Livslöp blant gamle i Norden.* Norsk Gerontologisk Institutt, Rapport 2, 51-97.

Sigurgeirsdóttir, S., 1994. "Aldraðir innan fjölskyldunnar," in *Fjölskyldan-uppspretta lífsgilda.* Reykjavík: Félagsmálaráðuneytið. pp. 215-218.

The Statistical Bureau of Iceland (SBI), 1994. *Landshagir.* Reykjavík.

The Statistical Bureau of Iceland (SBI), 1994. *Vinnumarkaðurinn (1991-1994).* Reykjavík. pp. 50-52.

The "Invisible" Figure
of the Deceased Spouse in a Remarriage

Shoshana Grinwald
Tsvia Shabat

SUMMARY. When people remarry after a spouse has died, there is a continuing relationship with the dead spouse. This article deals with theoretical types of this continuing relationship as described by a couple, each of whom has been widowed. *[Article copies available for a fee from The Haworth Document Delivery Service: 1-800-342-9678. E-mail address: getinfo@haworth.com]*

INTRODUCTION

Remarriage is a choice. The basic purpose is the desire to satisfy important basic needs. Remarriage for widows and widowers is an indication of

---

Shoshana Grinwald, PhD, is a lecturer at the School of Social Work at Bar-Ilan University, Ramat-Gan, Israel. Her address is PO Box 358, Kochav Yain, 44864, Israel. Tsvia Shabat, MA, is a Social Worker practicing in Israel.

[Haworth co-indexing entry note]: "The 'Invisible' Figure of the Deceased Spouse in a Remarriage." Grinwald, Shoshana and Tsvia Shabat. Co-published simultaneously in *Journal of Divorce & Remarriage* (The Haworth Press, Inc.) Vol. 26, No. 3/4, 1997, pp. 105-113; and: *Divorce and Remarriage: International Studies* (ed: Craig A. Everett) The Haworth Press, Inc., 1997, pp. 105-113. Single or multiple copies of this article are available for a fee from The Haworth Document Delivery Service [1-800-342-9678, 9:00 a.m. - 5:00 p.m. (EST). E-mail address: getinfo@haworth.com].

emerging from crisis and adaptation to a new situation (Parkes and Weles, 1983). The way to success includes a transition period as a couple enters the new relationship.

This article focuses on the complexity of the relationship with the spouse who has died, within the situation of a new marriage.

THE RELATIONSHIP WITH THE DEAD SPOUSE

The fact of death physically separates the couple. When a spouse dies, the source of love, liking, friendship, and concern is lost. It is a breaking of continuity from time-past to time-future, and the loss of what might have been. The invisible figure of the dead spouse indicates all those ways in which a relationship with him/her is maintained (Schuchter and Zisook, 1988). Among these are memories, dreams, sharing important information, a feeling of concern or agreement that can supply comfort, relief, and support.

Society respects the marriage relationship and tries to preserve it. When a spouse dies, the one remaining is known as "her" widower or "his" widow. A phrase that implies an ongoing belonging. Interpersonal relationships formed within the framework of marriage reflect the bio-social needs for a relationship. Although the spouse is not a blood relation, the ongoing closeness of the marriage relationship is equal in worth to a biological relationship (Moss and Moss, 1980). There is, therefore, a social expectation of strong loyalty to the dead spouse, accompanied by idealization of the latter and the marriage (Lopata, 1979 in Moss & Moss, 1980).

Loyalty to the original family and its tradition with regard to grief, can influence the process of grief and harm the psychological willingness of widow or widower to accept the loss and come to peace with it, in order to adapt in a healthy manner and continue living.

In the sphere of the intrapsychic, during the early mourning process, widow or widower often experiences hallucinations and physically sense the presence of the dead spouse. These experiences are usually understood to be messages from the dead and do not necessarily mean a distortion of reality. This connection is almost always seen as a conscious effort to keep the dead spouse alive in his/her heart which allows him/her confidence and support (Schuchter & Zisook, 1990).

Working through grief helps to accept loss, the fact that the spouse will not return, and to separate from him/her. However, even after a process of mourning, when widow or widower is going through new experiences, new attitudes to him/herself, the intrapsychic connection with the dead spouse prevails.

The notion of an ongoing relationship with the dead spouse destroys the myth regarding the finality of such a relationship. Farber (1990) presents historical attitudes to the mourning process: Freud's attitude in 1917 regarding the finality of a relationship with a beloved spouse who has died, when the victory of the ego is an ability to disconnect from the object no longer alive. He is followed by Lindeman who, in his classical teachings, not only emphasised disconnection with the dead, but also determined the period normal for this process.

These points of view were popular for a long time and were questioned in an article by Burgoyne and Goim (Burgoyne & Goim, 1979 in Farber, 1990), "The Timeless Connection with Someone who has Died." This article described two analyses of women widowed for about six years, among them one who remarried, who discussed the ongoing "relationship" with their dead spouses. Other researchers followed: Vaillant, 1985 in Farber, 1990; Moss and Moss, 1980; Schuchter and Zisook, 1990; all of whom reinforced the change of attitude regarding the relationship with the dead.

The basic relationship was defined as a threesome: A widow/widower, spouse, and the dead spouse (Moss & Moss, 1980). Widow or widower must live with the fact that their memories are associative and that the years spent in the first marriage are an integral part of their personal development and maturity: In time these fade, but the dead spouse is not silent in the new marriage.

Husband or wife seem to enter a vacant role, but the physical, psychological and socio-cultural patterns woven with the dead spouse exist, and they prevail, together with the intruding relationship from the first marriage. This is the meaning of a threesome in a replaced relationship and how it works in a remarriage (Moss & Moss, 1980).

Plans not carried out, or completed, with the first spouse can flow into the new marriage and be realized. Usually, family relations with the original family (extended) still exist as well as friends from the first marriage, and, at the same time, they are expected to be involved with the social structure of the new husband or wife.

Unrelated to the quality of the first marriage or the period of mourning, widow or widower sees the new partner through the prism of the first marriage, although the level of intensity has changed. Widow or widower notices similarities or differences on all levels of the relationship. Even small daily things such as a favorite expression or preferred food can rouse memories of the first husband or wife.

THE NEW FAMILY IN THE REMARRIAGE

Each member of the nuclear family reaches "togetherness" quickly and must deal with the fact that each person has a family, interpersonal communicational history from the past, before the formation of the new family. At the same time, each new step represents new challenges and roles for each family member, that is, a new personal adaptation to the framework is required.

A family formed from a new marriage must let go of the patterns and norms that they have known from the nuclear family and which are inappropriate for the complex reality and different norms of the new family (Visher & Visher, 1990).

Awareness and knowledge of what can be expected in a new marriage lessens the pressure and allows an easier transition.

THE LAVI/REGEV FAMILY

There are many, varied types of connection with the dead spouse (Schuchter and Zisook, 1990). Some of these will be described through the experience of the Lavi/Regev family, the second marriage of a widow and a widower.

The family graph (Figure 1) includes both nuclear families. Ayalla's (46) nuclear family includes her dead spouse, Elly, who had died aged 32, fourteen years previously, and her two children, Dana (20), and Noam (14.5). The couple were married for 10 years. Her extended family includes her sister Raya (51), her husband and their three children, and her dead husband's parents, Tsipora (72) and Chanan (73).

Danny's nuclear family includes his wife Dalia, who had died aged 52, two years previously, and his two daughters, Adi (31), and Noah (28), both married with children. The couple had been married for 31 years. The extended family includes his mother Sarah (76) and his brother Ezra (59) and his family.

The couple, Ayalla and Danny, have been married for one year. Ayalla's nuclear family moved into Danny's house.

TYPES OF CONTINUING RELATIONSHIP

The continuing relationship exists in many shapes. Among these: living legacies, symbolic representation, the original family of the dead husband, ceremonies and events, and memories.

FIGURE 1.

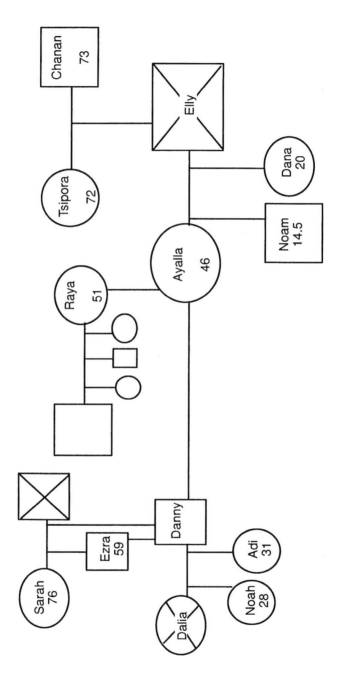

Following are types of this relationship and examples.

Living Legacies

Legacies are real representations of personality, ideas, appearance, the various ways of the dead person. The widow or widower may identify with the dead spouse by being in close touch with these representations or by fusing with them. For the widow/widower, identification with the dead spouse can create significant changes in his/her personality, habits and tastes (Schuchter & Zisook, 1990). After Dalia's death, Danny began to tidy the house as she had done. Things he hadn't done before her death.

In comparison with identification with the dead person, an unconscious process, his/her desires, interests, or purposes are conscious, and chosen action significantly guards the relationship with the dead spouse. A remarriage can entail continuing "education" taken on by the widow or widower with regard to the everyday, by completing or preserving projects. Danny helped his daughters pay their mortgage according to his first wife's request. Likewise he contributed a stereo set in her memory to the baby ward at the hospital where she had worked. Ayalla and her parents created a fund for an outstanding student at the high school which Elly, her first husband, had attended.

The dead also "live" on through family friends by means of such qualities as appearance, personality, mannerisms, habits, and abilities, the contributions of genetic relationship.

Noam, aged 14, an adolescent, only recently began to resemble his father in build, voice, and facial features, and this could not be ignored. Friends and family react to the resemblance to his father. He has lately done his psychometric exams and his talents are also similar to those of his father.

Danny, Ayalla's new husband, became a grandfather and went to the States to visit his daughter Noah. He was there for the birth and stayed to help her. He felt he had to fill her mother's role (had she been alive, she would undoubtedly have gone for the birth). Danny is enthusiastic about the resemblance between his granddaughter and his first wife, Dalia.

Symbolic Representation

This is a process whereby belonging, or experiences, or memories shared with the dead partner have become fused with his/her spirit. This process develops slowly before the death, and continues to develop until fusion after the death of the partner (Schuchter & Zisook, 1990). The objects of symbolic representation are experienced in a wide sphere of ambivalent feeling–both as painful memories and as an opportunity for ongoing connection. Danny works in the garden where Dalia, his first wife, had spent many hours working, this enabling him to feel close to her.

Symbolic representation of the relationship allows widow or widower to keep alive not only their beloved, but also their relationship. Elly's many love letters to Ayalla are experienced with ambivalence. Ayalla cannot read the letters from her first husband, but neither can she get rid of them, and she keeps them in a cupboard.

THE RELATIONSHIP WITH THE DEAD SPOUSE THROUGH THE ORIGINAL FAMILY– HIS/HER PARENTS/INLAWS/GRANDPARENTS

Fusing of families by remarriage creates an extended family. Unlike the extended family created by the first marriage, some of the roles belong to the step parent, brother or sister. The remarriage suprasystem describes the relationship between the families of the remarried couple (Sager et al., 1983).

Many decisions must be made by the couple regarding the fusion of the families. Some of them are connected to normal organisation of the supra-system. Ayalla and Danny's marriage confronted two strange families with a fairly obvious daily life and traditional family customs. Ayalla's relation-ship with her in-laws had always been close. After her husband's death, they had continued to help physically with the upbringing of the children and were a pillar of strength for Ayalla and her children. When Ayalla met Danny, they accepted him and encouraged her to build another family with him. It was therefore natural that she should want to continue the warm relationship. The positive attitude of the suprasystem to the remarriage undoubtedly aided family feeling and effort to build another family. The patterns formed during the year between the remarried family and the parents of the first husband, were not formed in a day, but as they were being tested. Tsipora and Chanan, the grandparents, continue to visit their grandchildren regularly, at the new family home, and they continue their close relationship with the new couple. Likewise, the family visits Tsipora and Chanan, the parents of Ayalla's dead husband, in the home where she had met Elly in her youth, before they were married. In this home, Elly, "Daddy's room," is there for the children and they use it on their visits there. Elly's image accompanies Ayalla in the home of her in-laws by virtue of the experiences there and his belonging to the place, and by virtue of the close relationship with the parents of the dead spouse.

Ceremonies and Events

Memorial days, birthdays, holidays, and other significant dates are often experienced with great emotion in connection with the dead spouse. The symbolism of these events is likely to arouse long-buried emotions. The partner who experiences a stronger emotion than usual, and who is a part of a new relationship, needs understanding and empathy from his/her new partner. Lately, towards the second anniversary of Dalia's death, Danny went through a period of memories and great pain that increased as the day approached. Ayalla's sensitivity to his situation, her standing by him while respecting his relationship with his first wife, constituted both support and reinforcement for Danny.

Memories

People use memories to preserve what has been lost. Preserved images arouse past feelings. These living relationships allow relations with the dead spouse and they are an inseparable part of regular life in the new marriage framework. The couple, Ayalla and Danny, tell each other about their previous marriages and experiences in the context of relevant subjects that arise.

Many contexts arouse the presence of the first spouse in the home of the remarriage. The question is how much these contexts affect each partner. The new partner is accepted as the second husband or second wife. He or she is placed second and defined as second in relation to the first. The new husband or wife sees him/herself as second in the triad.

Although the partner has died, the newly married person still has to cope with him/her. He/she knows the dead spouse through the rose-colored glasses of the widow/widower, original families, and their friends. Despite the tendency to turn the dead partner into something "hallowed," and very difficult to live up to, the new husband or wife needs to be patient with regard to the "invisible" figure, and respect the ability of the partner to choose a new appropriate partner. The husband or wife who has died will always be a presence in the new family home, either physically or spiritually, although this will lessen as time goes by.

In Ayalla and Danny's family, both have been widowed, and there are two triad frameworks. In such a situation, each one is usually able to be sensitive to the needs of the other. To be a partner to each other, in a new marriage, each in his/her own right and not as a replacement, or someone who has to resemble the partner who has died.

CONCLUSION

This article focuses on the importance of awareness of the widow/widower and their partners in a remarriage, on normalised relations between widow/widower and spouses who have died. Recognition of types of possible relationships with spouses who have died, and understanding their presence in the new marriage framework, constitutes key help for the couple in the transition to a new beginning.

BIBLIOGRAPHY

Farber, S.R. (1990). Widowhood: Integrating loss and love in E.M. Stren (ed). *The Psychotherapy and the Widowed Patient*. pp. 39-48. New Rochelle, NY: Iona College.

Moss, S.M., and Moss, Z.N. (1980). The image of the deceased spouse in remarriage of elderly widow(er)s. *Journal of Gerontological Social Work*. (3)2, pp. 59-70.

Parkes, C.M., and Weles, R.S. (1983). *Recovery from bereavement*. New York: Basic Books.

Sager, C.J., Brown, H.S. Crohn, T.T., Engel, T., Rodstein, E. and Walker, L. (1983). *Treating the remarried family*. New York: Brunner Mazel.

Seaburn, B.D. (1990). The ties that bind: Loyalty and Widowhood in E.M. Stren (ed.) *The Psychotherapy and the Widowed Patient* pp. 139-146. New Rochelle, NY: Iona College.

Shuchter, S.R., and Zisook, S. (1988). Widowhood: The continuing relationship with the dead spouse. Bulletin of the Menninger Clinic. 52 (3) pp. 269-279.

Visher, E.B., and Visher, J.S. (1988). *Old Loyalties New Ties: Therapeutic Strategies with Stepfamilies*. New York: Brunner/Mazel.

A Model for the Evaluation
of Readiness for Divorce

Yedidya Tova
Yerushalmi Hassia

SUMMARY. The purpose of the model presented here is to examine the readiness of a couple for separation, for divorce, and their ability to negotiate and go through a mediation process. The model is based on tools from the area of Art Therapy and relates to the dimension of the personality of each of the couple, to the inter-personal dimension and the connection between the two dimensions. The model was developed by the two writers and was applied to many couples. The article will present the model and a description of a case study in order to demonstrate its use. The article will not relate to such additional aspects in the process of mediation as the functioning of parents or an evaluation of the children's situation. *[Article copies available for a fee from The Haworth Document Delivery Service: 1-800-342-9678. E-mail address: getinfo@haworth.com]*

THE RATIONALE FOR THE DEVELOPMENT OF THE MODEL

There has lately been increased awareness among couples who apply for divorce mediation as a way to reach a divorce agreement. Even when couples apply for mediation the process often breaks down. The reason for

---

Yedidya Tova, PhD, is a clinical social worker, The School of Social Work, Bar-Ilan University, Israel. Yerushalmi Hassia, PhD in Psychology, is affiliated with "Maavarim" Clinic for Psychotherapy, Herzlia-Pituach, Israel.

[Haworth co-indexing entry note]: "A Model for the Evaluation of Readiness for Divorce." Tova, Yedidya and Yerushalmi Hassia. Co-published simultaneously in *Journal of Divorce & Remarriage* (The Haworth Press, Inc.) Vol. 26, No. 3/4, 1997, pp. 115-123; and: *Divorce and Remarriage: International Studies* (ed: Craig A. Everett) The Haworth Press, Inc., 1997, pp. 115-123. Single or multiple copies of this article are available for a fee from The Haworth Document Delivery Service [1-800-342-9678, 9:00 a.m. - 5:00 p.m. (EST). E-mail address: getinfo@haworth.com].

this can usually be found in the fact that the therapist has not located the underlying conflicts or the position of the couple with regard to their readiness for the process of divorce (Kressel, 1983). The central questions facing the therapist are how ready the couple is emotionally to end the marriage, and how able the couple is to negotiate a divorce agreement appropriate for their needs and those of the children.

The model is based on an evaluation process that is intended to answer these questions. It is intended to design the divorce mediation process according to the unique pattern of each couple who applies or who is referred. The model also examines the possibility of reconciliation with an appropriate therapy program.

The phase before divorce is characterised by a sense of emotional upheaval mixed with such feelings as alienation, distance, fear, distress, ambivalence. The behavioral implications of these are confrontations and quarrels on the one hand and, on the other, denial, a pretence of things being alright, and, generally speaking, an inability to function (Kaslow, 1981). In this situation of stress, expressed by physical and emotional retreat, the couple is required to make significant decisions and to negotiate sensibly in order to reach an agreement.

But the nature of stress situations is the loss of the tools to cope effectively, characterised by a feeling of helplessness (Haynes, 1981).

The effective activating of a couple during the process of evaluation increases clients' sense of self-efficacy, their ability to cope and to cooperate. Clients are able to discard the role of helplessness in the face of the crisis that has brought them to therapy and to connect with their strength and ability (Talmon, 1990, Yerushalmi, 1993).

Divorce is a process of many stages and dimensions, including a disconnection and renewal in many areas of life: legal, economic, physical, emotional, functional, sexual, social and parental (Wallerstein & Kelly, 1980). The process of evaluation must therefore be multi-dimensional and relate to interaction on various levels (hidden and explicit) and to various aspects (personal and interpersonal) and their compatibility. The ability of the couple to cope with the process of mediation and separation must be examined from 3 viewpoints:

1. The interpersonal aspect (the couple).
2. The personality aspect.
3. The degree of the spouses' mutual readiness for divorce.

Relying on research and therapeutic work done with divorcing couples (Kressel, 1983), we have discovered that the following criteria create a unique map of coping for each couple:

A. The interpersonal-couple aspect:

1. The degree and openness of the conflict.
2. The degree of mutuality in the decision to divorce, the degree of ambivalence.
3. The ability to negotiate, communicate, degree of openness in communication.

B. The personality aspect, each spouse's dealing with the crisis:

1. The degree of personal flexibility.
2. The ability to accept decisions.
3. Dependence as opposed to independence.
4. The ability to withstand pressure.
5. Self-esteem and self-image.
6. The ability to accept support.

C. The degree of mutual readiness:

1. Adaptation to the idea of divorce.
2. Personal ability to cope with the crisis.
3. The ability to create a support system.

THE CHOICE OF EVALUATION TOOLS FOR COUPLE AND FAMILY INTERACTION

The evaluation of a couple's relationship is multi-dimensional. It must relate to spousal's interaction on the level of content (verbal and non-verbal behavior), and on the level of process (closeness, distance, space, cooperation). When evaluating a relationship, observation ensures reliable information, allowing more clinical application than would a questionnaire.

The most significant aspect of evaluating spousal interaction in the process of divorce is verbal and non-verbal communication. Evaluation of the communication between spouses can be achieved by means of observing their interaction during a session, or the interaction created as a result of simulated enactment when relating to verbal tasks (such as planning an event together) or joint creativity. When a couple works together to resolve abstract problems, their behavioral patterns, attitude to challenges, ability to negotiate and to resolve problems, as well as coping with new social/environmental challenges, all emerge.

The process of evaluation of marital interactions by means of tasks given to the spouses, allows enactment of the problems and strengths of the couple, and thus enables the therapist to design a therapeutic program appropriate for each couple (Yerushalmi, 1993).

THE USE OF ART THERAPY FOR EVALUATION

By means of fulfilling talks, creativity and art therapy, people express the ways in which they perceive the world around them, relate to it, and to their place in the world. The way in which one paints, sculpts or makes a collage reflects the way in which one sees the reality of one's life (Rapaport, Gill & Schafer, 1968).

By means of tools from the area of Art Therapy, one can reach unconscious content, hidden desires, impulses, feelings of pain and fear, that are expressed symbolically on paper (Kramar, 1971).

The way in which someone approaches art work indicates the way in which he/she copes with life's tasks–confidently or hesitantly, with trust or suspicion, etc. (Hammer, 1957).

The basis of evaluation through art is the uncovering of the symbols in the content of the product, and by observing a patient's method of work as reflecting, on a personality level, his/her self-image, sexual identity, quality of interpersonal relationships, together with specific functional evaluations such as flexibility of thought, coping with stress, and motivation (Yedidya, 1993).

By means of tools from the sphere of Art Therapy, a therapist can help his/her patient to build a bridge from the abstract and the hidden to the structured and the open, from diffused feelings to defined feelings that can be experienced and labelled. This process, experienced through art, can help a patient to better organise and control his/her emotional world, to differentiate between fantasy and reality and between him/herself and others, and thus to be able to communicate actively and effectively with the environment (Hedges, 1983).

THE TOOLS OF THE MODEL

A Socio-Metric Mapping of "Myself and My Close Environment"

The couple are instructed to make a map of the meaningful people in their lives. The tool examines the situation of each one in relation to support systems, and the attitude to the other partner and his/her importance as illustrated by his/her place on the map (Yedidya, 1993). Our work with a couple who came to therapy, the wife considering a divorce, is an illustration of the clinical use of the tool. The husband drew his mother as the biggest figure and closest to himself. On his other side he drew his two children and further on his "little wife." The painting illustrated very clearly to both the husband and the wife the focus of their marital problems, namely, the husband's lack of individuation from his mother, which would not allow him to be a real partner in their marriage.

Building a Tower Together

The couple are instructed to build a tower with straws and adhesive paper. This tool examines the behavior of the couple in a situation that requires cooperation while coping with a task. The task examines personality scales, coping with a crisis, the ability to accept a decision, the ability to withstand pressure, and behavioral flexibility, interpersonal scales–the level and openness of conflict, and the ability to negotiate (open communication) (Yerushalmi, 1993).

The following example illustrates the use of this tool:

The husband dominated the process of building the tower, while the wife cooperated with his disorganized work, saying: "It would not stand on its own." The product of this work was a flat tall tower, with no basis to stand upon, which, of course could not stand on its own. It illustrated very clearly the role of the codependent wife cooperating with the husband who was a gambler, in the misery of their marital life.

Family Task–Family Album

The family album is a collage, created by the couple, by cutting and gluing figures and images from magazines offered to them.

Each spouse is instructed to introduce on a separate paper, their family, as he/she sees it. The family album serves as a symbol of how the family is perceived and the separation from it. The task examines denial as opposed to working through the separation, idealization, feelings towards the family. Analysis of the work is done together with the couple.

An illustration of this tool is the collage of a woman, who chose a picture of a man leaning on a stick. She explained that she chose the picture because the man resembled her husband, but viewing the collage more carefully, made it clear that she perceives her husband as weak and dependent.

CASE STUDY

Background Details

The couple, Amnon and Tamar (fictitious names), about 40 years old, married for almost 20 years, parents of 3 children, have reached the point of divorce proceedings. Both are independent professionals. Both describe the marriage as unsatisfactory from the beginning, one of convenience, not based on warmth or love. The wife has initiated divorce proceedings, although in the past the husband also raised the subject several times.

ANALYSIS OF FINDINGS

Coping with Tasks

The two spouses related differently to the tasks. The wife approached the work with confidence; she was preoccupied with her own product and did not relate to her husband. She showed no curiosity with regard to his work. The husband, on the other hand, procrastinated, hesitated, tried to see what his wife was doing, and even after choosing a method of work, still hesitated, stopped and started, examining her product again before finishing.

Description of the Products

In all of the products made by the couple, what stood out was the husband's dependency on the wife, and his emotional difficulty in considering separation. We will illustrate this by means of the products.

MAPPING THE FAMILY

The husband placed his wife, children, and his wife's family (parents and brother) close to him, closer than friends. Whereas the wife, only after she'd completed the map, noticed that she had not included her husband. She then added him alongside friends. The wife's map was full of friends, whereas the husband's map reflected loneliness and the lack of a support system. The husband had no family.

THE TOWER

The wife separated the materials and built a structured and stable tower for herself. The husband reacted with a feeling of paralysis and difficulty at the separation initiated by his wife. Once he'd pulled himself together, he built a separate tower with a shaky foundation. When the couple were asked to create a connection between the two towers, the husband put his tower on top of his wife's. She removed it, placing it at a distance from her own.

THE FAMILY ALBUM

The wife placed the picture of a man and a woman on the paper, at some distance from each other. The only picture of a couple showed them ignoring one another. (It is interesting to note that when she described her choice of certain pictures, she was particular about matching colors and features, and she wasn't aware of any of the other things she'd created). She placed the children close to the figure of the woman, at a distance from that of the man. Her husband's paper was very empty and, in the top corner, he chose to stick two pictures of a couple and two children. The female figure in the husband's picture appeared to be a powerful career woman, whereas he cut out the figure of the man he'd chosen and stuck it next to that of the woman, slightly leaning against her.

Analysis of Findings

The analysis is based on their method of working, the products, and the attitudes of the patients to the products. From these it is possible to learn about the couple in three ways:

1. *Personality Differences*–The wife initiated, she had confidence and belief in herself, (seen by the husband as being powerful), independent. The husband was passive, dependent, threatened, lacked confidence, hesitated. The husband expressed a sense of detachment and loneliness both in the family album and in the mapping.
2. *The Level of the Couple*–The husband perceived himself as being outside of the family. He expressed alarm at the separation. The wife seemed to have begun a process of separation and detachment. It should be noted that according to the figures in the family collage, the couple had a normal sexual and functional identity.

3. *Differences with Regard to the Readiness of the Two*–In a discussion about the products with each of the two, they could connect emotionally with inner content, and became aware of their own process as well as each other's. The wife understood that she was communicating a subtle, powerful message to her husband: "Get out of my life and the lives of the children." This as opposed to the verbal, open message of invitation to a process of mutual examination regarding separation. The strong sense of abandonment the husband experienced caused him to feel threatened and to continue to hang on to a framework lacking emotional content.

THE INTERVENTION PROGRAM

The special program of intervention was determined for the couple according to the process of evaluation. It enabled the husband to go through a process of preparation for separation and the wife to discover empathy and tolerance for the feelings of her husband and his process. Preparation of the separation agreement took place only after the husband was emotionally ready for this.

CONCLUSION

The evaluation process illustrated by this case study allows therapist and moreover the spouses to understand their two levels of functioning– the practical/open level and the hidden/emotional level, and the interaction between these two levels. When the hidden is revealed, one can work through it. Creative tools that allow the avoidance of defenses let one become aware of unconscious content. The couple's active cooperation in the process helps them become a part of the evaluation, understand the problematic aspects as well as the strength of their relationship, and cooperate in structuring a program of intervention.

REFERENCES

Hammer, E.F. (1958). *The Clinical Application of Projective Drawing.* Springfield, Illinois: Charles C. Thomas.
Haynes, J.M. (1981). *Divorce Mediation.* Springer Publishing Company N.T.
Hedges, L. E. (1983). *Listening Perspectives in Psychotherapy.* New York: Yasam Aronson Inc.

Kaslow, F.W. (1981). Divorce & Divorce Therapy. In A.S. Gurman & D.P. Kniskern (Eds). *Handbook of family therapy* (pp. 662-696). New York: Brunner/ Mazel.

Kramar, E. (1971). *Art as Therapy with Children*. New York: School Books Inc.

Kressel, K.E. (1983). Typology of Divorcing Couples Implications, Mediation and the Divorce Process. *Family Process* Vol. 19.

Rapaport, D., Gill, M.M. & Schafer, R. (1968). *Diagnostic Psychological Testing.* New York: International University Press, Inc.

Talmon, M. (1990). *Single-Session Therapy.* San Francisco: Jossey-Bass Publishers.

Wallerstein, J.S. & Kelly, K. (1980). *Surviving the breakup: How children and parents cope with divorce.* New York: Basic Books.

Yedidya, T. (1993). *Developing diagnostic tools taken from the expressive therapy for diagnosing youth in distress.* Unpublished Dissertation, The Union Institute, Cincinnati, Ohio.

Yerushalmi, H. (1993). *Integrative tool for evaluation of marital interaction activating the clients with the use of videotape.* Unpublished Dissertation, The Union Institute, Cincinnati, Ohio.

JAPAN

Marriage and Divorce in Japan

Masahito Sasaki
Terry L. Wilson

SUMMARY. This paper investigates the current nature of the institution of marriage and the practice of divorce in Japan with reference to historical trends and shows a special concern for legal and ethical issues affecting the status of the custodial parent and the serious matter of support. Attention is drawn to the generalized outcome of the divorce process in Japan and the need for reform. *[Article copies available for a fee from The Haworth Document Delivery Service: 1-800-342-9678. E-mail address: getinfo@haworth.com]*

Japan witnessed its highest recorded divorce rate before the turn of the century. After 1900 a steadily declining rate of divorce was reported

Masahito Sasaki, DSW, is Assistant Professor and Terry L. Wilson, LSTh, is a Research Advisor, Nihon Shakaijigyo Daigaku (The Japan College of Social Work), 3-1-30 Takeoka, Kiyose-shi, Tokyo-toh 264, Japan.

The authors wish to express their appreciation to Professors Sheila B. Kamerman and Steven Paul Schinke, Columbia University School of Social Work, for their encouragement and helpful advice in pursuing this research.

[Haworth co-indexing entry note]: "Marriage and Divorce in Japan." Sasaki, Masahito and Terry L. Wilson. Co-published simultaneously in *Journal of Divorce & Remarriage* (The Haworth Press, Inc.) Vol. 26, No. 3/4, 1997, pp. 125-135; and: *Divorce and Remarriage: International Studies* (ed: Craig A. Everett) The Haworth Press, Inc., 1997, pp. 125-135. Single or multiple copies of this article are available for a fee from The Haworth Document Delivery Service [1-800-342-9678, 9:00 a.m. - 5:00 p.m. (EST). E-mail address: getinfo@haworth.com].

except for a short period during the turbulent years immediately following World War II. There was another gradual increase in divorces in the 1960s, while the marriage rate during the past 20 years has shown a moderate decrease. In Japan, the most frequently cited reasons for divorce were incompatibility for males and financial problems for females.

Recently, the number of children affected by divorce has increased because of the gradual rise in the frequency of divorces once again. Many of these children are reared in a single-parent lifestyle situation headed by women who usually are economically vulnerable. The Japanese government provides several programs targeted at this group, but not enough has been done. In the future, Japan needs to make stronger efforts for developing more extensive social benefits and services to meet the many and varied needs of single-mother families.

HISTORY OF JAPANESE DIVORCE TRENDS

Historical trends concerning divorce in Japan can be divided into two major stages: the periods before and after World War II. In the pre-World War II stage, there are three significant periods: the years from 1882–the earliest year for which statistics are available–to 1897–the period which registered the highest recorded divorce rate ever in Japanese history; the year 1898 to 1899, when the Meiji Civil Code was enacted, forcing a sharp decline in the divorce rate; and, the years from 1900 to 1943, which saw a continuous, moderate decrease. That 61 year period saw a reversal of trends, starting with a very high divorce rate, followed by an abrupt drop, and finally a continuous decline (see Table 1).

The primary reason for the high divorce rate during the years 1882 to 1897 (ranging from 3.39 per 1,000 at the highest to 2.62 per 1,000 at the lowest, with an average of 2.82 per 1,000), as reported by various writers (Yuzawa, 1974; Sodei, 1980; Kumagai, 1983), was the unfair, one-sided divorce custom which favored the husband's family. The husband had the privilege of expelling a wife who was infertile, was not compatible with family tradition or rules, or was not obedient to her in-laws.

Yuzawa (1974) and Kumagai (1983) also pointed to several other causes for this high divorce rate: forced arranged marriage; marriage at a young age and the consequent immaturity of the partners; and matrilineal marriage in farming and fishing regions of Japan, especially in Hokkaido, Tohoku, and Kyushu where the marital relationship would be easily terminated whenever an employment contract between the bride's family and the groom turned out to be unsatisfactory. The lack of a life-long commitment in these types of marriages was expected, and the ideas of the partnership marriage were not a feature of this period.

In general, the casual attitude toward marriage, divorce, and remarriage that existed at that time contributed to this high divorce rate in Japan, where divorce and remarriage were much less stigmatized than in the West. However, it should be noted that this attitude was more commonly observed among ordinary Japanese than among the upper strata.

Japan witnessed an abrupt drop in the divorce rate during the years 1898 to 1899. As Table 1 shows, the divorce rate in 1898, 2.27 per 1,000, declined to 1.50 per 1,000 in 1899. Yuzawa (1974) and Kumagai (1983) contend that a possible reason for this drop is due to the enactment of the Meiji Civil Code, which involved changes in registration procedures for marriages and divorces.

These changes required reports of marriage and divorce to be validated, and also required the submission of a formal written paper explaining the reasons for divorce. Goode (1963) was also interested in the drop in divorces during those years. However, he questions the statistical validity of the divorce rate for the period.

Although there is no definitive explanation available for this sharp drop in the divorce rate, it can be concluded that Japan, in general, became more conscious and deliberate about marriages and divorces.

Two factors contributed to the further gradual decline in the divorce rate: from 1.46 per 1,000 population in 1900 to 0.68 per 1,000 in 1943. As Yuzawa (1974) indicated, forced divorce initiated by the husband's family gradually became much less common due to Japanese exposure to egalitarian or democratic ideas and social behavior from western countries. Kumagai (1983) observes that this has usually led to increasing divorce rates, as in the other industrialized countries, but, on the contrary, this led to a reduction in the divorce rate in Japan. She (Kumagai, 1983) concludes that "the hypothesis of a positive correlation between the level of industrialization and the rate of divorce cannot be confirmed in Japan during this period, perhaps because of the nature of the Japanese family and society."

Sodei (1980) advances an additional cause for the declining trend in the divorce rate: Confucian education and principles, which emphasize the importance of family tradition, respect for the authority of the family head and husband, and the value of a good wife being considerate and wisely submissive to the family tradition, became much more familiar as they were disseminated among the common people, rather than only among the upper social strata, as formerly practiced. Attitudes toward divorce changed, and the climate of opinion became highly critical. Women, especially those who were divorced, were considered disgraced. Divorce was

TABLE 1. Marriage and Divorce Rates in Japan for Selected Years: 1888-1986

	Marriage		Divorce	
	Number	Per 1,000	Number	Per 1,000
1888	330,246	8.3	109,175	2.76
1889	340,445	8.5	107,408	2.68
1890	325,141	8.0	109,088	2.70
1895	365,633	8.7	110,883	2.62
1898	471,298	10.8	99,464	2.27
1899	294,935	6.7	65,845	1.50
1900	346,528	7.9	63,828	1.46
1905	350,898	7.5	60,061	1.29
1910	441,222	9.0	59,432	1.21
1915	445,210	8.4	59,943	1.14
1920	546,207	9.8	55,511	0.99
1925	521,438	8.7	51,687	0.87
1930	506,674	7.9	51,259	0.80
1935	556,730	8.0	48,528	0.70
1940	666,575	9.3	48,556	0.68
1943	743,842	10.2	49,705	0.68
1947	934,170	12.0	79,551	1.02
1950	715,081	8.6	83,698	1.01
1955	714,861	8.0	75,267	0.84
1960	866,115	9.3	69,410	0.74
1965	954,852	9.7	77,195	0.79
1970	1,029,405	10.0	95,937	0.93
1975	941,628	8.5	119,135	1.07
1980	774,702	6.7	141,689	1.22
1981	776,531	6.6	154,221	1.32
1982	781,252	6.6	163,980	1.39
1983	762,552	6.4	179,150	1.51
1984	739,991	6.2	178,746	1.50
1985	735,850	6.1	166,640	1.39
1986	710,962	5.9	166,054	1.37

Source: Kokumin Seikatsu Senta (Center for Citizen's Life), 1988.

considered the shame, not only of individuals, but also of their parents, family, and relatives.

The second stage of this study's divorce trend started immediately following World War II. The divorce rate during the years between 1944 and 1946 are unavailable because of the turmoil arising from the conclusion of the War. The most critical periods, however, are the years from 1947 to 1950, 1951 to 1964, and 1965 to 1983.

According to Kumagai (1983), Japan witnessed an increase in the divorce rate just after World War II. Comparing the rate of 0.68 per 1,000 in 1943 with 1.02 per 1,000 in 1947, she indicates several reasons for this increase during the turbulent years after the War: "the state of confusion caused by radical social change and the legal policies of the occupation after the defeat of World War II; the postponed marital dissolutions which were at last actualised; and the termination of remarriages due to the discovery that former husbands had not been killed in the war."

After the turmoil of the last year of the war and the immediate post-war period, however, the divorce rate, starting in 1947, began decreasing again. Among the common people, who had by now generally adopted the view of divorce heretofore prevalent only among the upper strata, divorce was still considered a disgrace. This decreasing trend continued until 1964.

The years from 1965 to 1983 saw a significant increase in the divorce rate, with an almost doubling of the ratio from 0.79 per 1,000 in 1965 to 1.51 per 1,000 in 1983. During this period various factors emerged in Japan that were similar to those experienced in many other industrialized countries: economic growth, spread of individualism, women's increasing level of education, women's economic independence, and the spread of attitudes which placed a premium on seeking personal happiness. Recently, the divorce rate has again started decreasing: 1.39 per 1,000 in 1985; 1.37 in 1986; and 1.30 in 1987. Although it is too soon to identify this decrease as a trend, a possible explanation of the source for these numbers would be the decline in the number of potential divorces from the generation of so-called "baby boomers," born in the late 1940s. However, it remains to be seen whether this decline will establish itself as a trend or whether it will turn out only to be a fluctuation in a generally rising rate of divorce.

MARRIAGE AND ITS DURATION IN JAPAN TODAY

Major features of Japanese marriage were changed by the introduction of the new Civil Code of 1947 which set forth the democratic or egalitarian model for marriage. A marriage becomes valid by agreement of both parties, male and female, and an official registration in the family records or the *Koseki* at the city or town office. The minimum legal marriage age for males is 18 years, and 16 years old for females.

In 1986, the total number of marriages reported was 710,962, and the marriage rate was 5.9 per 1,000 population. However, looking at the marriage rate in Japan during the past 40 years, as indicated in Table 1, the last 20 years have shown a decrease. The Statistical Report of Marriages by the Ministry of Health and Welfare in 1987 (Kosei-sho Daijin-kanbo Tokei Joho-bu, 1987) indicates a modest trend towards postponement of marriage among young people. The marriage age has increased by nearly two years over the past 30 years. The average ages of people when first married has increased as follows: 1955: 26.6 for males, 23.8 for females; 1965: 27.2 for males, 24.5 for females; 1975: 27.0 for males, 24.7 for females; 1985: 28.2 for males, 25.5 for females. Overall, the slight tendency to postpone marriage is growing.

Two major marriage types are commonly practiced in Japan: love marriage and marriage through go-betweens. According to the 1987 official report of Ministry of Health and Welfare (Kosei-sho Daijin-kanbo Tokei Joho-bu, 1987), the rate of love marriage has been increasing and is now the dominant type: 49.5 percent for marriage through go-between, 50.5 for love marriage in 1966; 37.2 for marriage through go-between, 62.8 for love marriage in 1973; 29.3 for marriage through go-between, 70.7 for love marriage in 1982.

The average duration of a marriage was 8.1 years in 1978 (1970: 7 years). In recent years, the duration of marriages has changed: the proportion of people with less than a five year marriage has dropped from 65.3 percent in 1950, to 51.8 percent in 1970, to 42.2 percent in 1978. On the other hand, the proportion of people married for five or more years has increased from 34.7 percent in 1950, to 48.2 percent in 1970, to 57.8 percent in 1978 (Kumagai, 1983). Kumagai notes that this trend is different from that of other industrialized countries. In Japan, couples married longer experience more divorce than younger couples, a situation which leads to more complicated divorce issues, such as child custody as well as other legal problems.

MARITAL DISSOLUTION

The divorce system in Japan has been regulated by legal authorities since enactment of the Meiji Civil Code in 1898. Further, the new Civil Code of 1947 emphasized the importance of equality between both sexes.

Based on the Civil Code of 1947, the Domestic Relations Law, and other related laws, four general categories of divorce exist in Japan: divorce by agreement of both parties, divorce by arbitration, divorce by judgment, and divorce by judicial decision. The last three types of divorce involve either a family court, a local court, or a higher court.

In Japan, divorce by agreement has always been the dominant type. However, this trend has been gradually changing. The percentage of divorces by mutual agreement has dropped from 98.2 percent in 1948, through 91.2 percent in 1960, to 90.4 percent in 1982. The proportion of the other three types, which involve a legal process in family court, has been continuously increasing, from 1.8 percent in 1948, to 8.8 percent in 1960, to 9.6 percent in 1982 (Koseisho Daijin-Kanbo Tokei Joho-bu, 1984). The increasing occurrence of divorce litigation has been a growing occurrence starting in the 1950s through the '60s and '70s to today. Although the proportion of this type of divorce is still low, attitudes among the Japanese people toward divorce litigation have recently begun to become moderate, and it is less taboo than in the past.

REASONS FOR DIVORCE

In Japan, a higher number of females than males tend to seek a divorce, even though women generally have to face more difficulties after divorce. In 1978, 55.3 percent of wives, 35.2 percent of husbands, and 9.5 percent of others, initiated divorce (Tamura & Tamura, 1988). Based on the Vital Statistics on Divorce in 1978 reported by the Ministry of Health and Welfare, scholars (Sodei, 1980; Kumagai, 1983; Atsumi, 1987; Tamura & Tamura, 1988) have identified various reasons for divorce.

The most frequently cited reasons husbands sought a divorce were: incompatibility (31.2%); adultery (27.5%); and financial problems (14.2%). For wives, the most frequently cited reasons were: financial problems (26.4%); incompatibility (25.1%); and adultery (19.5%). From this data it can be concluded that incompatibility is an extremely important factor in marital dissatisfaction.

Kumagai (1983) presents an interesting observation. She comments that "with the decline in the traditional *ie* system (family system), the conjugal tie has become more crucial in Japan." The expectation within marriage has become more focused on the maintenance of shared ideas and mutual understanding among both sexes in Japan, as in the U.S. (Kumagai, 1983).

The females who divorce most frequently mention financial dissatisfaction as being very significant. Among Japanese females who ultimately divorce, it must be noted that economic problems during their marriage are a larger concern for them than for their non-divorced sisters.

A comparison of the incomes of divorced and non-divorced males in 1978 finds that divorced males were 16.3 percent more likely to have a lower income than non-divorced males. The divorced males were 14.2 percent less likely to have a high income than non-divorced males. Looking at the age group of 35 to 39 years old, who are considered to be the most likely to get divorced, the males who were divorced had a 27.2 percent more likely chance to have a lower income than non-divorced males (Tamura & Tamura, 1988).

According to Tamura and Tamura (1988), in 1978 the income of divorced husbands was lower than that of non-divorced husbands except for the 20-24 age group of males. Female divorcees tended to have been disappointed in their husband's financial ability, and to have experienced marital dissatisfaction due to the financial instability of the household. In fact, according to the 1978 report of the Ministry of Health and Welfare, the average monthly income of divorced couples was 134,398 yen ($1,075), while that of non-divorced couples was 181,773 yen ($1,454) (Kumagai, 1983).

In addition to this, those who divorce are more likely to be educationally disadvantaged. Comparing the level of education between divorced and non-divorced persons of both sexes, there were twice as many in the divorced group who finished only compulsory education than in the non-divorced group. The proportion of the divorced group which completed junior college was about one-half the proportion of the non-divorced group (Tamura & Tamura, 1988). As in the U.S., lower levels of education among divorced couples in Japan was also associated with lower incomes.

Divorced women were more likely to have worked than those who remained married; 52.9 percent of divorced wives worked while only 25.5 percent of wives in stable marriages did (Kumagai, 1983). According to Kumagai (1983), women's employment creating financial independence from their husbands is an important element contributing to the tendency to divorce in Japan, as well as in the U.S. (However, it is also possible that in Japan, as in the U.S., women in unsatisfactory marriages may enter the labor force to protect themselves against the risk of divorce).

Tamura and Tamura (1988) and Kumagai (1983) also indicated another possible influence on divorce. Couples who resided with the parents of one of the partners were more inclined to end their marriage than were couples who had their own home. Thirty-five percent of wives and 31 percent of husbands among the divorced couples surveyed in 1978 resided with their parents, while only 19 percent of intact couples did. Conflicts between parents and daughters-in-law or sons-in-law concerning various family roles, attitudes toward marriage, and education and values, contribute to the development of conflicts between young couples, resulting in marital dissatisfaction or marital instability.

CHILDREN AND THEIR PARENTS' DIVORCE

Under the Japanese legal system there are two categories of responsibilities for taking care of children after their parents divorce. The first involves parental authority over the children, and legal advocacy for their rights. The second is guardianship with child custody and child-rearing responsibilities. Usually, a person with parental authority also has guardianship.

The numbers of children affected by divorce has been increasing. Various scholars have begun to pay attention to this problem. Based on the 1984 report of the Ministry of Health and Welfare and on other sources of information (Noda, 1980; Kumagai, 1983; Atsumi, 1987; Tamura & Tamura, 1988), the proportion of the divorces which involve children under 20 years of age has climbed from 57.3 percent of the total in 1950, involving 80,481 children, to 70 percent of total in 1983, involving 226,000 children (see Table 2).

According to Atsumi (1987), opting for a divorce to end an unsatisfactory marriage, even if children are involved, has just emerged as an acceptable alternative. Married couples with children are now more likely than

TABLE 2. Number of Children Involved in Their Parents' Divorce

	Number of divorces	Percentage of divorces involving children	Number of children involved parents' divorce
1950	83,689	57.3	80,481
1960	69,410	58.3	71,339
1970	95,937	59.1	89,687
1980	141,689	67.6	166,096
1985	166,640	68.2	202,000

Sources: Kosei-sho Daijin-kanbo Tokei Joho-bu, 1984; Tamura & Tamura, 1988.

earlier to pursue divorces for their own personal happiness than to remain together for the sake of the children. Most court cases surrounding divorce now involve children. Eighty-seven percent of all cases dealt with in family court in 1985 involved a fight over child custody or other family financial issues (Atsumi, 1987).

As Table 3 indicates (Kosei-sho Daijin-Kanbo Tokei Joho-bu, 1984; Tamura & Tamura, 1988), the proportion of custodial mothers and fathers has also changed. The fathers (45.2%) were more likely to gain authority of their children after divorce than mothers (44.9%) through 1965. This ratio began to reverse itself in 1966 with 47.2 percent of divorced mothers gaining parental authority while only 43.6 percent of the fathers did. In 1985, it was 71.6 percent for mothers, 22.1 percent for fathers, and 6.3 percent for others. Improvements in the areas of education, job opportunities, and financial condition of Japanese women during these years contributed to the increase in the number of custodial mothers.

Referring to the 1978 report of the Ministry of Health and Welfare on divorce in Japan (Tamura & Tamura, 1988), only 50.7 percent of husbands in divorce cases paid compensation or property allocation to their wives at the time of divorce. Among wives in the same divorce cases, 54.6 percent were paid less than 1,000,000 yen ($8,000) and only 27 percent were paid over 2,000,000 yen ($16,000). Substantial numbers of husbands also did not contribute to child support: only 22.4 percent of all husbands paid child support, while 54.8 percent of all wives did, and 6.7 percent of both parties contributed child support money together. Tamura and Tamura

TABLE 3. Percentage of Parental Authority Over Children Held by Fathers and Mothers

	Fathers	Mothers	Others	Total
1955	46.2	40.6	13.1	100.0
1960	46.8	41.7	11.5	100.0
1965	45.2	44.9	9.9	100.0
1966	43.6	47.2	9.2	100.0
1970	40.2	51.0	8.8	100.0
1975	33.7	57.9	8.4	100.0
1980	25.7	67.2	7.1	100.0
1985	22.1	71.6	6.3	100.0

Sources: Kosei-sho Daijin-kanbo Tokei Joho-bu, 1984; Tamura & Tamura, 1988.

(1988) were critical of the irresponsible attitudes of husbands, and suggested legal involvement to force husbands to pay child support.

CONCLUSION

Following a divorce, children experience a restructuring of the family system, and many have been faced with various interpersonal difficulties with custodial and non-custodial parents alike. In Japan as in the U.S., divorce means for children an abrupt discontinuity of interpersonal relationships with family members, especially with non-custodial parents.

The key issue in the "Easy Divorce" system, or mutual divorce agreement by both parties, in Japan is that women who have children are most likely not to gain a clear agreement about financial support from ex-husbands. An increased amount of the child-rearing burden falls on divorced single mothers. This is the salient result. In Japan today, new divorce regulations need to be carefully developed, especially for women who have children, in order to assure child support, alimony, and other financial support from the former husband.

REFERENCES

Atsumi, M (1987). *Rikon no hon (A book for divorce).* Tokyo: Fujin Gaho.

Goode, W.J. (1963). *World Revolution and Family Patterns.* New York: The Free Press.

Kokumin Seikatsu Senta (Center for Citizen's Life). (1988). *Kurashi no tokei '88 (A life statistic in 1988).* Tokyo: Okura-sho (Ministry of Finance).

Kosei-sho Daijin-kanbo Tokei Joho-bu (Statistics and Information Department of Minister's Secretariat in Ministry of Health and Welfare). (1984). *Rikon tokei (Divorce statistics).* Tokyo: Author.

Kosei-sho Daijin-kanbo Tokei Joho-bu (Statistics and Information Department of Minister's Secretariat in Ministry of Health and Welfare). (1987). *Konin tokei (Marriage statistics).* Tokyo: Author.

Kumagai, F. (1983). Changing divorce in Japan. *Journal of Family History,* Spring, 85-108.

Sodei, T. (1980). Rikon no genjo to shorai (Divorce: present and future). In A. Noda (Ed.), *Rikon o kangaeru (Think about divorce)* (pp. 34-58). Tokyo: Yuhikaku.

Tamura, K., & Tamura, M. (1988). *Rikon no ningen gaku (Study of divorce).* Tokyo: Shisutemu faibu.

Yuzawa, Y. (1974). Nihon no rikon no jittai (Realities of divorce in Japan). In M. Aoyama, Y. Takeda, T. Arichi, I. Emori, & H. Matsubara (Eds.), *Kazoku: koninno kaisho (Family: Dissolution of Marriage)* (pp. 331-350). Tokyo: Kobundo.

Stepfamily Lifestyles
and Adolescent Well-Being
in The Netherlands

Ed Spruijt

SUMMARY. Stepfamilies function in different ways: some prefer traditional family forms, while others opt for more nontraditional lifestyles, in line with modern individualistic and egalitarian gender values in society. What are the effects of different lifestyles on the well-being of youngsters? We tested the hypothesis that the physical, psychological and relational well-being of adolescents from stepfamilies with a nontraditional lifestyle is better than the well-being of adolescents from more traditional stepfamilies. We report on a preliminary investigation into 269 stepchildren and a national study into adolescent development including 114 step-adolescents. The hypothesis is rejected and some possible practical implications are discussed. *[Article copies available for a fee from The Haworth Document Delivery Service: 1-800-342-9678. E-mail address: getinfo@haworth.com]*

Ed Spruijt is Associate Professor, Department of Youth, Family and the Life Course, Faculty of Social Sciences, Utrecht University, Heidelberglaan 2, P.O. Box 80.140, 3508 TC, Utrecht, The Netherlands. E-mail SPRUIJT@FSW.RUU.NL

[Haworth co-indexing entry note]: "Stepfamily Lifestyles and Adolescent Well-Being in The Netherlands." Spruijt, Ed. Co-published simultaneously in *Journal of Divorce & Remarriage* (The Haworth Press, Inc.) Vol. 26, No. 3/4, 1997, pp. 137-153; and: *Divorce and Remarriage: International Studies* (ed: Craig A. Everett) The Haworth Press, Inc., 1997, pp. 137-153. Single or multiple copies of this article are available for a fee from The Haworth Document Delivery Service [1-800-342-9678, 9:00 a.m. - 5:00 p.m. (EST). E-mail address: getinfo@haworth.com].

Since the eighties a number of surveys on the effects of living in stepfamilies have appeared (Pasley & Ihinger-Tallman, 1987; Hetherington & Arasteh, 1988; Ganong & Coleman, 1994). Most research comparing adjustment and health problems in adolescents from stepfamilies versus other family structures has found lower educational expectations, and lower general well-being in adolescents in stepfamilies (Furstenberg, 1987; Hetherington, 1993; Dronkers, 1993; Spruijt & Hendrickx, 1995). However, those differences tend to be rather small (Ganong & Coleman, 1987; Amato & Keith, 1991), which suggests that across-group differences are not as conceptually meaningful as within-group differences. Therefore, it is important to examine why some children of divorce, and in this study children of remarriage after divorce, fare better than other children in the same situation.

Generally, the differences studied within stepfamilies are the more structural characteristics: remarried couples compared with cohabiting couples; stepmothers and stepfathers; simple stepfamilies (only one adult has children from a previous marriage) and complex stepfamilies (both adults have brought children into the marriage); remarriages with residential children and remarriages with non-residential children (Cherlin, 1978; Pasley & Ihinger-Tallman, 1987; Hetherington & Arasteh, 1988; Vemer, Coleman, Ganong & Cooper, 1989; Fine & Kurdek, 1992). More recently, research on stepfamilies has focused on stepparental behaviour and stepparenting style (Fine, Voydanoff, & Donnelly, 1993; Crosbie-Burnett & Giles-Sims, 1994). Clinical literature concentrates more on the meaning of the complexity of stepfamilies, specific characteristics of stepfamilies such as different histories of the family members, the open boundaries to other family systems and, according to Cherlin (1978), the lack of institutionalized societal support (Visher & Visher, 1988; Pasley & Ihinger-Tallman, 1987).

In our study we try to define different models of stepfamily life based on the ideas of uniqueness and postmodernity of stepfamily life in connection with, in particular, the work of Fitzpatrick (1984), Burgoyne and Clark (1984), and Scanzoni (1983, 1987). Fitzpatrick has developed a marital typology, based on a number of items, for instance, traditionalism, autonomy and conflict avoidance. Scanzoni (1983) has described how the family has developed from a conventional, traditional form of life into a progressive, modern one. In the modern family there is more opportunity for the autonomy of the children, and there is an interchangeable division of roles and tasks between husband and wife. In their study of contemporary family relations, including stepfamilies, Scanzoni, Polonko, Teachman and Thompson (1994) advise focusing more on process and change than on structure and stability. This view seems to be in accordance with

McLanahan's (1981) typology of divorced women, where a distinction is made between changers and stabilizers. Burgoyne and Clark (1984) categorized stepfamilies into progressive families and ordinary families. In our study we attempt, according to these views, to distinguish the different lifestyles of stepfamilies and the consequences of those lifestyles for adolescent well-being. Our underlying assumption is that in a modern, individualistic society, adolescent well-being in stepfamilies will be higher in the modern, open, nontraditional families. Of course the terminology is problematic. Lavee and Olson (1993) distinguished seven types of couples, including traditional, conflicting, harmonious and vitalized ones. Booth and Amato (1994) distinguished between traditional and nontraditional families, based on the division of labour between mother and father, and the attitudes of both parents toward gender roles. In our study we decided to use a traditional (closed) lifestyle, a nontraditional (open) lifestyle, and a divided (conflicting) lifestyle. We define nontraditional stepfamilies as those in which there is acknowledgement of the specific step-situation, open communication including the former family situation, and the parents hold egalitarian views toward gender roles.

We control for the following background variables of the stepfamily: social class, time since stepfamily formation, stepfather or stepmother family, frequency of contact with the nonresident parent, and the following personal characteristics of the stepchildren: age, sex and educational level. We want to know the effects on the physical, emotional and relational well-being of older stepchildren living in stepfamilies with a different degree of traditionalism.

STEPFAMILY LIFESTYLES

Most stepfamily studies stress the importance for the developing adolescent of open communication, acknowledgement of the step-situation and consideration of the previous family situation (Furstenberg & Cherlin, 1991; Ganong & Coleman, 1994). Most clinical studies (Visher & Visher, 1989) report a positive relation between children's well-being and a nontraditional, open way of stepfamily life and most literature stresses the importance of both mothers and fathers in children's socialization (Lamb, 1987). In nontraditional stepfamilies the communication and contact with the non-custodial parent is mostly maintained and for this reason nontraditional stepfamily life, with enduring communication between children and the non-custodial parent, may be the least problematic for children. A number of experts have stressed the importance of continuing open relationships with both biological parents, yet recent research findings are inconsistent (Furstenberg & Cherlin, 1991; Wallerstein, 1991). Wallerstein (1991) concluded that we do not know the potentialities or limitations of the role of the visiting parent in the psychological, social and moral development of the child. Furstenberg (1988) concluded that children without contact with their father in the last five years appeared in many instances to be doing better on a range of behavioral and academic measures than children with contact. Booth and Amato (1994) concluded in their study into the effects of living in two-parent, traditional and nontraditional families, that there were hardly any effects on children's well-being. We therefore need more information about the effects of living in nontraditional, open stepfamilies on adolescent well-being.

Apart from the possible effects of the nontraditional, open stepfamily situation on the physical and psychological well-being of youngsters, the question as to how the stepfamily situation affects their relational well-being is also important. Other studies report the effects of parental relationships on one's own partner and marital relationship (Glenn & Kramer, 1987; Lee, 1995). Is it true that the children's experiences with divorce and differences in stepfamily life have led them to adopt a different view on relations? In their study about men, women and children ten years after divorce, Wallerstein and Blakeslee (1989) concluded that many young people from divorced families did finally seem able to establish relationships satisfactorily, but that entering adulthood for all the respondents is a critical threshold. McLanahan and Bumpass (1988) also found that children of divorced parents do not enter adulthood in a carefree way. In contrast, other studies have found no overall relation between a nontraditional, open lifestyle and children's well-being (see, for example, Kalter, Kloner, Schreier, & Okla, 1989; Furstenberg & Cherlin, 1991; Spruijt & Hendrickx, 1995). There are an increasing number of studies reporting no lesser degree of well-being for children from more traditional stepfamilies. These conflicting findings led to the following question:

> *Have step-youngsters from stepfamilies with a nontraditional lifestyle a higher degree of physical, psychological and relational well-being than step-youngsters from stepfamilies with a more traditional lifestyle?*

PRELIMINARY INVESTIGATION

Method

Our first study was an exploratory investigation into 269 stepfamilies after divorce in The Netherlands. In each family, three members (parent, stepparent and one child 10 through 17 years old) were interviewed. The investigation consisted of two parts. The qualitative (and most intensive) oral part was composed of semi-structured interviews with 40 parents, 40 stepparents and 40 children. The quantitative, written part of the study consisted of questionnaires filled in by 229 parents, 229 stepparents and 229 stepchildren. The selection of the respondent families took place in a random way by means of a complex selection procedure using 24 registry offices in towns and villages spread throughout The Netherlands. The three selection criteria for the stepfamilies were: (1) they had to comprise two adults and at least one child, (2) the divorce of the residential parent must have been granted at least one year before, and (3) the stepfamily must have lived together for at least one year.

A calculation was made of the extent to which the response of 269 families was similar to or different from the full sample. The response was 33%. This is relatively high when one takes into consideration that three members of a family had to be willing to take part. However, the response was not sufficient to draw any general conclusions, which is why we consider this study as a preliminary investigation.

Independent Variables

In order to measure differences in lifestyles in stepfamilies, we have developed a set of twenty 5-point items. Indicators have been derived from the literature (Olson et al., 1983; Scanzoni, 1983; Fitzpatrick, 1984; Burgoyne & Clark, 1984) and from the qualitative, oral interviews with parents and stepparents. The scalability of the selected items was subsequently tested using factor analysis. The following items met our criteria (factor loading > .50, Cronbach's alpha > .60):

1. Do the children visit their other parent? (never to very often)
2. Do you talk to others about your stepfamily situation every now and then? (never to very often)
3. Do you like it if others know that you are part of a stepfamily? (not at all to very much)
4. Do you talk to family members of your/your partner's ex-husband/ wife every now and then? (never to very often)
5. Looking after a family is more important for a woman than work outside the home (strongly agree to strongly disagree)
6. A mother with young children should not work outside the home (see item 5)
7. It is logical that a man has fewer duties in the household than a woman (see item 5)

8. Quarrels in a family should be prevented as much as possible (see item 5)

The scale formed using these items is called the degree of traditionalism of the stepfamily lifestyle (range 5-40, Cronbach's alpha is .69 for parents and .67 for stepparents; low score on the items 1-4 means traditionalism, high score on the items 5-8 means traditionalism). The score of parent and stepparent as a couple results from adding up their individual scores. The score of a couple can be similar (six or fewer points difference between the partners) or divided (seven or more points difference between the partners). We therefore distinguish four stepfamily lifestyles:

1. Stepfamilies with a traditional family lifestyle (19%).
2. Stepfamilies with a semi-traditional family lifestyle (24%).
3. Stepfamilies with a nontraditional family lifestyle (29%).
4. Stepfamilies with a divided family lifestyle (28%) n = 269.

Background Variables

In this study the following background variables were included in the investigation: parental education and occupation, family income, social class, religion, previous relationships of the partners, length of the single-parent period and courtship period, housing at the start of living together, stepfather or stepmother-family, family composition, length of time living together, marital status and present place of residence.

Dependent Variables

In order to gain insight into the well-being of the youngsters, a number of positive and negative experiences were presented to them in the quantitative part of the study on a 5-point scale. These statements had often been mentioned in the qualitative part of the research project. Six positive statements (for example: doing something pleasant alone with the stepparent, and: being satisfied about how the family gets on) and seven negative statements (for example: a lot of tension occurs in the family, and: sometimes feeling lonely in the family) were selected. Only those statements to which (almost) all stepchildren responded were included in the study.

Main Results

The traditional stepfamily lifestyle is characterized by a relatively low social class: income, educational and occupational levels of men and women are low. Few of the women have paid work outside the home. The families are often religious. For nearly half of the stepparents this is their first relationship. The parents have, of course, been married before, and their single-parent period was relatively short. When starting to live together, the parent and stepparent often choose new housing. A mutual child is often born and the families are more likely to live in the country rather than an urban area.

Stepfamilies with a nontraditional, open family lifestyle are characterized by a relatively high social class. Income, educational and occupational levels of men and women are high. The wife often has paid work outside the home. The families are generally not religious. The relationship history of the stepparent is complex: for almost 80% of the stepparents the present relationship is their second or third. The families usually live in cities. Most of the stepmother families have a nontraditional lifestyle.

Stepfamilies with a divided lifestyle occupy a middle position with respect to social class: higher than the traditional families, but lower than the families with a more open, nontraditional lifestyle. The relationship history of the stepparent is not complex: for 35% of them the present relationship is their first one. Few mutual children have been born in these families.

A large majority of the youngsters from the families with a traditional as well as a nontraditional lifestyle are satisfied with their family life, but the level of satisfaction among the children from families with a divided lifestyle is significantly lower. The occurrence of tension and quarrels, not getting enough time and attention, and sometimes feeling lonely, are the most frequently mentioned negative experiences. The global picture shows that the children from families with a divided family lifestyle are the least satisfied, whereas the children from the traditional families are slightly more satisfied than the children from the nontraditional families.

THE MAIN STUDY

Sample

In our main study we made use of the dataset (wave 1) of the Utrecht Study of Adolescent Development (USAD). USAD is a longitudinal panel study, based on a representative national sample of 3393 young people from 12 to 24 years of age. One of the parents of the adolescents concerned was also interviewed. The random selection was based on statistics on households and young persons living independently, from the National

Script Panel and the National Mini Census. The percentage of refusals was 26.1%. Control calculations indicate that the random selection of young people deviates only slightly from information known about young people based on other sources. However, there is one important area of deviation: the percentage of those of different racial background are hardly represented at all. Data from wave 2 will be available at the end of 1995 and data from wave 3 at the end of 1998. We used the data on the 114 youngsters from stepfamilies after divorce in the sample. The panel survey gathers its information from face-to-face interviews and questionnaires (both of which take about one hour).

Independent Variables

In this second study we developed a set of 27 5-point items derived from our first study, the literature (Olson et al., 1983; Scanzoni, 1983; Fitzpatrick, 1984) and from a pilot study belonging to the USAD project (USAD, 1991). The scalability of the selected items was subsequently tested by means of factor analysis (principal components analysis, one factor 45% of the variance). The following items met the criteria (factor loading > .58, Cronbach's alpha > .75).

1. Stepfamilies fare better living like a first nuclear family.
2. After divorce it is better to forget the past.
3. The best family form is still two first married partners and their children.
4. Quarrels in a family should be prevented as much as possible.
5. Looking after a family is more important for a woman than work outside the home.
6. A mother with young children should not work outside the home.
7. It is logical that a man has fewer duties in the household than a woman.

The scale formed by means of these items is called the degree of traditionalism of the stepfamily situation (Cronbach's alpha is .78; a high score on the items means a high degree of traditionalism). The total score on this scale results from adding up the seven item scores (range 7-35). We distinguished three types of stepfamily lifestyles:

1. stepfamilies with a more traditional family lifestyle (32%),
2. stepfamilies with a semi-traditional family lifestyle (34%), and
3. stepfamilies with a nontraditional family lifestyle (34%, n = 114).

A traditional stepfamily lifestyle is defined as that in which there is denying of the specific step-situation, no communication about the former family situation, and the parents hold traditional views toward gender roles. In study 2 no stepfamilies with a different view on the family pattern of the parent and stepparent were distinguished, because only one of the parents was a respondent.

Background Variables

In study 2 we measured: family characteristics (time since stepfamily formation, gender of stepparent, social class of stepfamily, religious involvement, political view, place of residence), and personal characteristics of the youngsters (age, gender, educational level, religious involvement, political attitude) and frequency of contact with the nonresident parent.

Dependent Variables

Physical well-being. A standardized scale (General Health Questionnaire, Joosten & Drop, 1987) was used to measure physical well-being (e.g., Do you sometimes have headaches? Do you often get up tired in the morning? Do you sometimes feel dizzy? Is your stomach often upset?) It is a checklist for general physical ill-health and measures complaints in a number of relevant physical areas. Dutch surveys often use this method. Possible answers: 1 = yes/2 = no. The physical well-being scale (Cronbach's alpha = 0.74) involves 13 items and ranges from 13 to 26 (26 = healthy).

Psychological well-being. We used three indicators for the operationalization:

1. The Cantril ladder (Cantril, 1965), measuring *mental health*: We would like to know how you are feeling? (0 = very bad, 10 = very good).
2. The number of thoughts about *suicide* in the past 12 months (Kienhorst, 1988). Have you thought about suicide in the past 12 months? (1 = never to 4 = often).
3. The Goldberg scale (Goldberg, 1978), measuring *psychological stress* (e.g., Do you feel as if you have been under pressure all the time during the last four weeks? or: Did you feel unhappy and depressed during the last four weeks?) Possible answers: 1 = not at all to 5 = much more than usual. The scale (Cronbach's alpha = 0.92) consists of 10 items and ranges from 10 to 50 (50 = high stress level).

Relational well-being. We discern two different aspects of relational well-being: having a best friend and/or partner at the moment, and wishing to have (more) children or not. The intention to have children in the future is regarded as an indication of positive relational well-being and comprises a single question.

RESULTS

Stepfamily Lifestyles and Background Variables

Traditional stepfamilies are situated in the lower social class significantly more often, and the family income of these families is relatively low. The income level in the nontraditional stepfamilies is relatively high. Traditional families often have conservative political views. No relation with stepfamily lifestyle has been found with the period since formation of the stepfamily, stepfather/stepmother family, or with the degree of contact with the nonresident parent. Finally, family size is the lowest in nontraditional stepfamilies, but the differences are not significant (see Table 1).

The youngsters from the different stepfamilies do not differ in age or sex. The educational level of youngsters from nontraditional stepfamilies is the highest, and they often have no religious attitude.

Well-Being of the Adolescents

Table 2 gives the results of the differences between the well-being variables of the youngsters from the three different stepfamilies. The conclusion is clear: there are no significant differences between the scores on the well-being variables of the three groups of youngsters.

Table 3 presents the results of the OLS regression analysis of the connection between the lifestyle of stepfamily and the physical, psychological and relational well-being of youngsters, controlled for seven background characteristics.

The first line in Table 3 gives information about the central hypothesis. The relations are not significant. This means rejecting our central hypothesis: Youngsters from stepfamilies with a more nontraditional lifestyle do not have a higher degree of physical, psychological or relational well-being compared with youngsters from stepfamilies with a more traditional lifestyle.

Time since separation and formal remarriage do not seem to be important predictors for the well-being of youngsters. Moreover, the gender of

TABLE 1. Mean Scores on Background Variables by Stepfamily Lifestyle (N = 114)[2]

	a. traditional stepfamily lifestyle	b. semi-traditional stepfamily lifestyle	c. non-traditional stepfamily lifestyle	F value	p value	significant contrasts
Characteristics of the stepfamilies						
1. time since stepfamily formation (1-4)	3.17	3.13	3.13	$F_{(2,111)} = .016$	p = .98	
2. stepfather/stepmother family (1-2)	1.16	1.12	1.11	$F_{(2,111)} = .332$	p = .72	
3. contact nonresident parent (1-3)	1.92	1.85	1.98	$F_{(2,111)} = .381$	p = .68	
4. social class stepfamily (1-5)	2.64	3.21	3.39	$F_{(2,111)} = 4.872$	p = .01**	a-c
5. family income (1-12)	6.11	6.97	8.28	$F_{(2,111)} = 4.566$	p = .01**	a-c
6. family size (1-6)	4.25	4.00	3.82	$F_{(2,111)} = .843$	p = .43	
7. religious attitude (1 = yes, 2 = no)	1.42	1.51	1.62	$F_{(2,111)} = 1.483$	p = .23	
8. political attitude (1 = conservative)	4.17	4.59	5.34	$F_{(2,111)} = 8.051$	p = .00**	a,b-c
Characteristics of the youngsters						
1. age youngsters	18.1	18.2	18.3	$F_{(2,111)} = .022$	p = .98	
2. sex (1 = boy, 2 = girl)	1.44	1.56	1.44	$F_{(2,111)} = .784$	p = .46	
3. education (1-4)	1.86	2.28	2.39	$F_{(2,111)} = 3.385$	p = .03*	a-c
4. religious attitude (1 = yes, 2 = no)	1.53	1.56	1.87	$F_{(2,111)} = 6.627$	p = .00**	a,b-c

*significant at the .05 level or better. **significant at the .01 level or better.
[2]Use has been made of the Scheffé analysis to check which of the categories of youngsters differ significantly. For example a,b-c means that there is no significant mutual difference between the types a and b. However, there is a significant difference between type c and other types.

147

TABLE 2. Mean Scores of the Youngsters on the Well-Being Variables by Stepfamily Lifestyle (N = 114)

	a. traditional stepfamily lifestyle	b. semi-traditional stepfamily lifestyle	c. non-traditional stepfamily lifestyle	F value	p value
Physical well-being					
1. physical health (1-10)	7.17	6.90	7.31	$F_{(2,111)} = .292$	p = .75
Psychological well-being					
2. mental health (1-10)	7.86	7.95	7.69	$F_{(2,111)} = .475$	p = .62
3. no psychological stress (1-10)	7.53	7.64	8.79	$F_{(2,111)} = .685$	p = .51
4. no thoughts of suicide (1-10)	7.83	7.70	7.60	$F_{(2,111)} = .436$	p = .65
Relational well-being					
5. having friends and partner (1-5)	3.31	3.64	3.54	$F_{(2,111)} = 1.030$	p = .36
6. planning to have a child (1-5)	3.78	3.72	3.53	$F_{(2,111)} = .585$	p = .56

Note: No significant p values.

148

TABLE 3. Results of OLS Regression Analysis on Well-Being Variables of Youngsters (Betas) (N = 114)

Independent variables	Dependent variables					
	physical well-being	psychological well-being			relational well-being	well-being
	physical well-being	mental health	no thoughts of suicide	psycho-logical stress	having best friend and/or partner	want to have (more) children
- stepfamily lifestyle (0 = traditional to 10 = nontraditional)	.08	-.01	-.11	.03	.19*	-.13
- time since (step)family formation	.12	-.14	-.06	-.06	.02	-.02
- stepfather/stepmother family	.05	.08	-.12	-.05	.07	.02
- freq. contact nonresident parent	-.02	-.08	-.02	-.12	.05	-.11
- social class stepfamily	-.03	-.10	-.02	.12	-.19	.12
- age	-.03	-.10	-.05	-.05	.40**	.12
- boys/girls	-.29**	-.15*	-.17*	-.35**	.33	-.07
- educational level	.11	.06	.07	.10	-.15	-.07
F	1.927	.857	.632	2.108	4.439	.767
Significance	.063	.555	.749	.041	.000	.632
Multiple R	.358	.248	.214	.383	.502	.235

*significant at the .05 level or better   **significant at the .01 level or better

149

the stepparent has no significant influence on the well-being of the young-sters. Connections of very low significance can be demonstrated between educational level and well-being variables. Gender is an important characteristic with respect to the variables physical well-being and psychological well-being. Age is an important characteristic with respect to one aspect of relational well-being (logical considering our operationalization of this concept), but not with respect to the other aspect.

DISCUSSION

Questions about the long-term effects of differences in stepfamily life on the physical, psychological and relational well-being of young people are central to this article. This issue is important with respect to the future, apart from anything else. What is the state of well-being of the increasing number of children of remarried parents in different situations? Our data have demonstrated that the physical, psychological and relational well-being of youngsters from stepfamilies with an open, nontraditional lifestyle is no better than for a closed, traditional lifestyle. It is important that we draw this conclusion based on the answers of the youngsters themselves and not on those of their custodial parents. The well-being of the step-youngsters from families with a traditional lifestyle is as good as the situation in nontraditional families.

The traditional lifestyle is definitely not a lifestyle that agrees with the general social developments of modernity, individualization and egalitarian attitudes toward sex roles. What then might explain the considerable satisfaction level in families with a traditional, closed stepfamily lifestyle? On further consideration we do not think that the relative success of the traditional stepfamily may be seen as a general appreciation of tradition. The good functioning of this stepfamily lifestyle does not necessarily imply that non-stepfamilies with a comparable lifestyle will also function well. We assume that this stepfamily lifestyle functions so well just because it is a stepfamily. The preliminary investigation discovered that the members of this family lifestyle have often experienced a less than easy divorce. Custodial parents and children often mentioned that the divorce was accompanied by vehement quarrels, fights and fierce emotions. The children of this family lifestyle often reported being relieved at the departure of the nonresident parent (mostly the father). The arrival of the stepfather made the family (in any case outwardly) complete again. Considering a past history of this nature, it is easier to understand why traditional stepfamilies are fairly satisfied with their new family situation. Lastly, in considering families with a nontraditional lifestyle, it must be said that, in a certain sense, they have a harder time than the traditional ones. Nontraditional stepfamilies have to operate in a more complex situation, in which room has to be made for the former family situation, including the nonresidential parent, possibly with his or her new family.

Of all the stepfamilies investigated in these research projects, 40% admit to having needed help and advice. Two-thirds have actually called upon the social and health services. Their experiences with these services were, in a number of cases, rather disappointing. A possible explanation for the disappointment of the clients concerned might be found in the fact that counsellors and psychotherapists are not sufficiently conscious of the fact that there are many different possible variants of stepfamily life. These investigations show that stepfamilies arrange their family life in various ways and that there are no significant differences between the scores on the well-being variables of the different groups of adolescents.

REFERENCES

Amato, P.R., & Keith, B. (1991). Parental divorce and adult well-being: a meta-analysis. *Journal of Marriage and the Family, 53*, 43-58.

Booth, A., & Amato, P.R. (1994). Parental Gender Role Nontraditionalism and Offspring Outcomes. *Journal of Marriage and the Family, 56*, 865-877.

Burgoyne, J., & Clark, D. (1984). *Making a go of it: A study of stepfamilies in Sheffield*. Boston: Routledge and Paul Kegan.

Cantril, H. (1965). *The pattern of human concerns*. Fredericton, New Brunswick, Canada: Rutgers University Press.

Cherlin, A.J. (1978). Remarriage as an incomplete institution. *American Journal of Sociology, 48*, 634-650.

Crosbie-Burnett, M., & Giles-Sims, J. (1994). Adolescent adjustment and stepparenting styles. *Family Relations, 43*, 394-399.

Dronkers, J. (1993). Zullen wij voor de kinderen bij elkaar blijven? (Staying together because of the children?). *Mens en Maatschappij (Men and Society) 67*, 23-44.

Fine, M.A., & Kurdek, L.A. (1992). The adjustment of adolescents in stepfather and stepmother families. *Journal of Marriage and the Family, 54*, 725-736.

Fine, M.A., Voydanoff, P., & Donnelly, B. (1993). Relations between parental control and warmth and child well-being in stepfamilies. *Journal of Family Psychology, 7*, 222-232.

Fitzpatrick, M.A. (1984). A typological approach to marital interaction: recent theory and research. In: L. Berkowitz (ed.), *Advances in Experimental Social Psychology*. New York: Academic Press.

Furstenberg, F.F. (1987). The new extended family: the experience of parents and children after remarriage. In: K. Pasley & M. Ihinger-Tallman (Eds.), *Remarriage and Stepparenting* (pp. 42-61). New York, London: Guilford Press.

Furstenberg, F.F. (1988). Child care after divorce and remarriage. In: E.M. Hetherington & J.D. Arasteh (Eds.), *Impact of divorce, single parenting and stepparenting on children* (pp. 245-261). Hillsdale, New Jersey: Lawrence Erlbaum Associates.

Furstenberg, F.F., & Cherlin, A. (1991). *Divided families.* Cambridge, M.A.: Harvard University Press.

Ganong, L.H., & Coleman, M. (1987). Effects of Parental Remarriage on Children: An Updated Comparison of Theories, Methods, and Findings from Clinical and Empirical Research. In K. Pasley & M. Ihinger-Tallman, *Remarriage and Stepparenting.* New York, London: Guilford Press.

Ganong, L.H., & Coleman, M. (1994). *Remarried Family Relationships.* Thousand Oaks, London, New Delhi: Sage Publications.

Glenn, N.D., & Kramer, K.B. (1987). The marriages and divorces of the children of divorce. *Journal of Marriage and the Family, 49,* 811-825.

Goldberg, D.P. (1978). *Manual of the general health questionnaire.* Horsham: General Practice Research Unit.

Hetherington, E.M., & Arasteh, J.D. (1988). *Impact of divorce, single parenting, and stepparenting on children.* Hillsdale, New Jersey: Lawrence Erlbaum Associates.

Hetherington, E.M. (1993). An overview of the Virginia longitudinal study of divorce and remarriage with a focus on early adolescence. *Journal of Family Psychology, 7,* 39-56.

Joosten, J., & Drop, M. (1987). De betrouwbaarheid en vergelijkbaarheid van drie versies van de VOEG (Reliability and comparability of three versions of the GHQ). *Gedrag & Gezondheid (Behaviour and Health) 8,* 251-265.

Kalter, N., Kloner, A., Schreier, S., & Okla, K. (1989). Predictors of children's postdivorce adjustment. *American Journal of Orthopsychiatry, 59,* 605-618.

Kienhorst, I. (1988). *Suicidaal gedrag bij jongeren (Adolescent Suicide).* Baarn: Ambo.

Lamb, M. (1987). The emergent American father. In M. Lamb (Ed.), *The father's role: cross-cultural perspectives* (pp. 3-25). Hillsdale, New Jersey: Lawrence Erlbaum Associates.

Lavee, Y., & Olson, D.H. (1993). Seven types of marriage: empirical typology. *Journal of Marital and Family Therapy, 19,* 325-340.

Lee, M. (1995). Are There Long Term Effects of Parental Marital Conflict on Children's Marital Relationships?: A Study of Hong Kong Couples. *International Journal of Sociology of the Family, 25,* 13-31.

McLanahan, S.S., Wedemeyer, N.V., & Adelberg, T. (1981). Network structure, social support, and psychological well-being in the single parent family. *Journal of Marriage and the Family, 43,* 601-612.

McLanahan, S.S., & Bumpass, L. (1988). Intergenerational consequences of family disruption. *American Journal of Sociology, 94,* 130-152.

Olson, D., McCubbin, H., Barnes, H., Larsen, A., & Wilson, M. (1983). *Families: What makes them work?* Beverly Hills, CA: Sage.

Pasley, K., & Ihinger-Tallman, M. (1987). *Remarriage and Stepparenting*. New York, London: Guilford Press.

Scanzoni, J. (1983). *Shaping tomorrow's family: Theory and policy for the 21st century*. Newbury Park, California: Sage.

Scanzoni, J. (1987). Families in the 1980s: time to refocus our thinking. *Journal of Family Issues, 8,* 394-421.

Scanzoni, J., Polonko, K., Teachman, J., & Thompson, L. (1994). *The sexual bond. Rethinking families and close relationships*. Newbury Park, London, New Delhi: Sage Publications.

Spruijt, A.P., & Hendrickx, J.J.P. (1995). A typology of stepfamilies in the Netherlands. In F. Deven (Ed.), *Research on reconstituted families in Europe*. Dordrecht, Boston, London: Kluwer Academic Publishers.

Spruijt, A.P. (in press). Adolescents from stepfamilies, single-parent families and (in)stable intact families in The Netherlands. *Journal of Divorce & Remarriage*.

Vemer, E., Coleman, M., Ganong, L.H., & Cooper, H. (1989). Marital Satisfaction in Remarriage: a Meta-analysis. *Journal of Marriage and the Family, 51,* 713-725.

Visher, E.B., & Visher, J.S. (1989). Parenting coalitions after remarriage: Dynamics and therapeutic guidelines. *Family Relations, 38,* 65-71.

Visher, E.B., & Visher, J.S. (1990). Dynamics of successful stepfamilies. *Journal of Divorce & Remarriage, 14,* 3-12.

Wallerstein, J.S., & Blakeslee, S. (1989). *Second chances*. New York: Ticknor and Fields.

Wallerstein, J.S. (1991). The long-term effects of divorce on children: a review. *Journal of American Academic Child and Adolescence Psychiatry, 30,* 349-360.

Marital Dissolution as a Stressor: Some Evidence on Psychological, Physical, and Behavioral Changes in the Pre-Separation Period

Arne Mastekaasa

Arne Mastekaasa is on the faculty, Department of Sociology, University of Oslo, P.O. Box 1096 Blindern, N-0317, Oslo, Norway and the Institute for Social Research, Oslo.

The data analyzed here were collected as part of a medical screening carried out by the Norwegian National Health Screening Service. Principal investigators for the psycho-social part of the study were Torbjørn Moum, Siri Næss, and Tom Sørensen. I am grateful to the National Health Screening Service and to the original investigators for allowing me to use these data.

Previous version presented at the 89th Annual Meeting of the American Sociological Association, August 5-9, 1994. Author's address: Department of Sociology, University of Oslo, P.O. Box 1096 Blindern, N-0317 Oslo, Norway.

[Haworth co-indexing entry note]: "Marital Dissolution as a Stressor: Some Evidence on Psychological, Physical, and Behavioral Changes in the Pre-Separation Period." Mastekaasa, Arne. Co-published simultaneously in *Journal of Divorce & Remarriage* (The Haworth Press, Inc.) Vol. 26, No. 3/4, 1997, pp. 155-183; and: *Divorce and Remarriage: International Studies* (ed: Craig A. Everett) The Haworth Press, Inc., 1997, pp. 155-183. Single or multiple copies of this article are available for a fee from The Haworth Document Delivery Service [1-800-342-9678, 9:00 a.m. - 5:00 p.m. (EST). E-mail address: getinfo@haworth.com].

155

INTRODUCTION

Marital dissolution is generally assumed to be a highly stressful event which has considerable negative effects for the individual. Compared not only to the currently married but also to never married persons, the divorced and separated are generally found to have more psychological and health problems and to be more likely to commit suicide. On many indicators the divorced are also worse off than the widowed (see e.g., Gove, Style & Hughes, 1990; Mergenhagen, Lee, & Gove, 1985).

Cross-sectional differences between the divorced and separated on the one hand and the married on the other are not conclusive evidence that marital dissolution is a major stressor. Such differences could be due to more *permanent strains* associated with the separated and divorced roles (see Avison & Turner, 1988). They could also be due to differential selection for divorce, or *differential selection* for remarriage among the divorced (Kelly & Conley, 1987; Mastekaasa, 1992, 1994; Spanier & Furstenberg, 1982). If the less healthy or happy are more likely to separate or divorce and/or less likely to remarry after divorce, they will be over-represented in the population of separated or divorced persons. What longitudinal evidence there is, however, suggests that selection is at best only a partial explanation of the unfavorable position of the separated and divorced (see, e.g., Booth & Amato, 1991; Doherty, Sue, & Needle, 1989; Mastekaasa, 1994; Menaghan, 1985; Menaghan & Lieberman, 1986).

To the extent that marital dissolution has serious negative consequences, an important question is how these consequences develop over time and how enduring they are. According to a *stress or crisis model*, one would expect the negative effects of the dissolution process to increase and reach a maximum about the time of the separation, but then gradually to decrease over time as people adjust to the new situation (Booth & Amato, 1991). Some studies have examined adjustment in the *post-separation* or post-divorce period. Although these studies generally indicate that the negative effects of marital dissolution decline over time, it is less clear how quickly people recover and how complete the adjustment is (Bloom et al., 1985; Booth & Amato, 1991; Kitson, Babri, Roach, & Placidi, 1989; Wertlieb et al. 1984).

Very little evidence is available on the *pre-separation* period. Most longitudinal studies of marital dissolution are based on samples drawn from public records of filings for divorce. In that case, only retrospective data on the pre-separation period are obtained, and such data have obvious weaknesses. Prospective studies of marital dissolution are clearly difficult to carry out, since the proportion of married people separating within a few years is (still) relatively low. As a result the few panel studies that have been reported in the literature suffer from small samples of separating persons and fairly low statistical precision (Booth & Amato, 1991; Kurdek, 1993).

The lack of information on the pre-separation period is serious. The actual break-up of the family unit may well take place several months or even years before the formal separation. Some retrospective data indicate that the period immediately preceding the final decision about whether to divorce or not is perceived as the most difficult (Kitson, Graham, & Schmidt, 1982). It has also been suggested that the pre-separation period may be more problematic for women while the post-separation period is more difficult for men (Bloom & Caldwell, 1981; Hagestad & Smyer, 1982; Moxnes, 1985). If only studies of the post-separation period are available, a highly partial and even misleading impression of the total impact of marital dissolution may result.

The aim of the present study, therefore, is to provide information on men's and women's experience of the pre-separation period. Cross-sectional survey data are combined with prospective information about subsequent changes in marital status during a 2-4 year period. With a comparatively large sample of more than 1,000 individuals separating during the 2-4 year period (and 35,000 who do not separate), it is possible to examine in considerable detail differences between people who are at different stages of the dissolution process.

The next section reviews previous studies and suggests some hypotheses. Data and methods are described in section 3. Results are presented in section 4, and section 5 summarizes and discusses the main findings.

PREVIOUS RESEARCH AND HYPOTHESES

Early research on stressful events tended to assume that the *amount of life change* associated with an event was the major determinant of its stressfulness (see Selye, 1982). Later research indicates that only *negative* events lead to marked increases in stress. A further conceptual distinction may be made between events that are negative because they are *unwanted* by the individual, and events that are culturally defined as negative or *non-normative*. Other dimensions of events assumed to influence stressfulness include *predictability* and *control*; events are assumed to be more stressful to the extent that they are unexpected and uncontrollable for the individual (Thoits, 1983).

Marital separations are generally associated with considerable changes in people's lives. Considerable variation in the degree of acceptance of divorce notwithstanding, marital separation is also generally a non-normative event. Moreover, marital separations will often be unexpected for at least one of the spouses and neither party is likely to be in complete control of the separation process (Hagestad & Smyer, 1982).

On the other hand, marital separation will in general be wanted by at least one of the spouses. Related to the wanted-unwanted dimension, Wheaton (1990) has suggested that the stressfulness of a role transition such as a marital separation is likely to depend on an individual's *role history*, that is, the accumulated experiences in the role that is altered by the transition. For some the beneficial effects of escaping from a chronically stressful marriage may more than outweigh other, negative effects of the separation process. (Cf. Avison & Turner's (1988) distinction between permanent conditions and discrete events as sources of stress.)

Some positive effects notwithstanding, marital separations can be expected to be generally stressful. It also seems reasonable to regard marital dissolution as a *process* rather than as a discrete event (Hagestad & Smyer, 1982). Considerable changes should therefore occur even before the formal separation. The following hypothesis is therefore suggested:

The amount of stress increases monotonically throughout the pre-separation period.

This hypothesis also seems well in line with previous empirical studies of the relationship between marital dissolution on the one hand and mental health, subjective well-being and several other indicators of stress on the other. The major exception is a study by Menaghan (1985), which showed that at the start of a 4-year period the average depression score of those who divorced during that period did not differ from that of the stably married.

Consistent with the hypothesis, Booth and Amato (1991) found that persons who later divorced or separated were more distressed and less happy than the stably married. Kurdek (1993) reports evidence of pre-separation increases in neuroticism, conscientiousness (men only), and faith in marriage (women only), and decreases in marital satisfaction. Doherty, Sue, and Needle (1989) report that 12 months (on average) before separation, those who separated had lower psychological well-being than those who remained married. No difference was found, however, for feelings of self-esteem, mastery, or for substance abuse. Wertlieb et al. (1984) found that in the six months preceding the separation people contacted physicians and other medical personnel significantly more often than did the stably married. The difference was very large for mental health contacts, but there was a difference even for other contacts. In a comparison of four small cross-sectional studies, Bloom and Caldwell (1981) found that women reported more severe psychological problems than men in the immediate pre-separation period, whereas men seemed to be more severely affected after separation.

With two exceptions these studies had only one wave of pre-separation observations. The ability to provide an adequate account of the pre-separation period is therefore obviously limited. Using panel data with two pre-separation waves, however, Booth and Amato (1991) found that persons who divorced or separated between 1983 and 1988 were more distressed and less happy than the stably married in 1983, but not in 1980. This study also suggests that people who divorce within a 3-5 year period experience more psychological problems *before* than after that period, although that difference may not be statistically significant. In Kurdek's (1993) study a sample of newlywed couples were followed up annually for 5 years. At the first interview, only those who separated or divorced within one year seemed to differ markedly from the stably married. Thus, there is evidence of increased stress in connection with marital dissolution, but not until the year immediately preceding the separation or the divorce.

Based on retrospective data, Kitson, Graham and Schmidt (1983) report that most respondents found the period immediately preceding the final decision to divorce to be most distressing. Also using retrospective data, Hagestad and Smyer (1982) and Moxnes (1985, 1990) found that most women felt that the pre-separation period was the most difficult; men, however, were more likely to find the post-separation period particularly problematic.

Kurdek (1993) found little evidence of *gender differences*. Considerable similarity between men and women prior to separation is also reported by Doherty et al. (1989). Bloom and Caldwell (1983), Hagestad and Smyer (1982) and Moxnes (1985), on the other hand, all suggest that there are important gender differences in that the pre-separation period is relatively more difficult for women and the post-separation period more difficult for men (for opposite findings on the post-separation period, see Riessman & Gerstel, 1985).

Although the empirical evidence is not unanimous there are a number of theoretical reasons for expecting the separation process to be different for men and women. Several authors have suggested that women are more vulnerable to marital problems than men (Gove 1972; Hagestad & Smyer 1982; Kurdek 1980; McRae & Brody, 1989). In view of Wheaton's argument mentioned above, one would therefore expect the separation process to be on average less negative (or more positive) for women than for men. Consistent with this, there is also considerable evidence that women more often than men want a marital separation and take the initiative in obtaining one (Moxnes, 1990; Zeiss, Zeiss, & Johnson, 1980).

If women are more sensitive to marital problems and more likely to take the initiative in obtaining a marital separation, they should also be more prepared for it and, as a consequence, in a better position to control the separation process. Retrospective studies of the separation process provide some support for these assumptions (Hagestad & Smyer 1982; Moxnes 1990).

Based on these considerations the following hypothesis is suggested:

The amount of stress associated with the process of marital dissolution increases more rapidly over time for men than for women.

Note that this hypothesis deals only with the degree of *change* during the pre-separation period. If women are more strongly affected by enduring marital problems, the overall *level* of stressfulness of the pre-separation period may well be equally high or higher for women than for men.

Hypotheses 1 and 2 implicitly assume that the formal separation is the most crucial single event of the separation process, and that there is a continuous increase in stress until that point. This seems reasonable in view of the literature cited above (see also Albrecht, 1980). The formal separation does not, however, coincide perfectly in time with the 'actual' separation, that is, the actual dissolution of the common household. In the empirical analyses that follow I attempt to disentangle the effect of living separate from the spouse from the general effect of the separation process.

So far I have only discussed the general stressfulness of the separation process. Stress is not directly measurable, however, and empirical studies have to rely on measuring possible *outcomes of stress*, like psychological problems, alcohol abuse, or poor role functioning. But differences on such outcome measures between, say, men and women do not necessarily reflect similar gender differences in the stressfulness of the event. For one thing, the outcomes of stressful events will also depend on the individual's social and psychological *coping resources*. If, say, women seem to experience more problems than men, this is not necessarily due to a higher level of stress, but could also be a result of inferior coping resources (Kessler & McLeod, 1984).

Another problem is that people may have different *modes of manifesting stress* (Pearlin, 1989). Again gender differences may be expected. Alcohol use, for instance, probably is a less unacceptable way of reacting to stress for men than for women. On the other hand, women may be more prone to react with an increased level of depressive symptoms. For this reason, Pearlin (1989) underscores the importance of multiple outcome measures.

In the present study I am not able to deal with these problems in a completely satisfactory way. As suggested by Pearlin, however, I do include a quite broad range of possible outcomes, with measures of both psychological and physiological states and of behaviors. More specifically, there are measures of subjective well-being, distress, feelings of loneliness, self-assessed health, body weight, alcohol use, and smoking.

METHODS

Sample and study design. The data were collected as part of a medical screening of the entire adult population of one of Norway's 19 counties. The county of Nord-Trøndelag is comparatively rural and sparsely populated (6 people per km^2), with a total population of 127,000 (including children). Nineteen percent of the occupationally active population is employed in agriculture and fisheries, 28 percent in other manufacturing, and 53 percent in the service sector; comparable numbers for Norway as a whole are 8, 30, and 62. The county's divorce rate is quite low; 6.2 divorces per 1,000 married couples in 1985, compared to 8.9 for the country as a whole.

During the period January 1984-February 1986 all adults 20 years old and above were invited to participate in a screening for hypertension, diabetes and lung disease. On arrival at the screening, participants were asked to hand in a one-page self-administered questionnaire which had been distributed by mail as a part of the invitation to participate in the screening (Questionnaire I). Participants were given a second questionnaire (Questionnaire II) when they left the screening, and were asked to return it by mail to the investigators.

The subpopulation of interest is people who are married at the time of the screening. I also exclude people above 70 since extremely few separations occur beyond that age. The total number responding to both questionnaires is about 38,000 (due to missing data on individual variables the effective sample size in most analyses is slightly lower). The mean age was 47 years. Eleven percent had at least some college or university education, 32 percent had secondary education (10th to 12th grade), and the remaining 57 percent had only compulsory education (9 years or less).

The questionnaire data provide information about the various dependent and independent variables at one specific time point (body weight was measured as part of the medical examination). Information about subsequent separations and the timing of these separations for the years

1984 to 1987 are taken from public marriage registers. (In the vast majority of cases a divorce is preceded by a separation. When speaking of separations here, I include, however, those few cases where divorces were effected without prior separation.) Since the screening itself was carried out during the period January 1984 to February 1986, there are data on subsequent changes in marital status for a period varying between 22 and 47 months, depending on when a particular individual was screened.

Dependent variables. There are three indicators of psychological problems. *Subjective well-being* is a composite measure of four items, two identical seven-point overall life satisfaction items and two semantic differential items, in which the respondent rates his or her life on seven-point scales (very strong and fit versus very tired and rundown, and very depressed-very happy). The composite score is the arithmetic average of the responses on the four items. Cronbach's α for the summated scale is .82. *Loneliness* is a single 5-point item, ranging from "very often" (scored 5) to "never" (scored 1). *Distress* is a summated scale of four 4-point items asking how often during the past month the respondent has (1) felt calm and comfortable, (2) restless or nervous, (3) had sleeping problems, and (4) has used tranquilizers or sleeping pills. Cronbach's α is .74.

Two measures are expected to capture mainly physical effects of the dissolution process: self-assessed health and body weight. *Self-assessed health* is a single-item 5-point measure with response alternatives ranging from "very good" (scored 5) to "very poor" (1). Although more detailed health measures would certainly have been desirable, there is some evidence that this type of simple overall assessment has surprisingly high validity (Moum, 1992).[1] It should be noted, however, that self-assessed health is not an objective physiological measure, but a subjective evaluation. As such it is similar to the more psychologically oriented measures mentioned above.

Body weight is measured is kilograms. In medical studies, weight is often corrected for variations in height, e.g., by computing so-called "body mass" which is defined as weight divided by height squared. Weight is used in the present analyses, since that makes the coefficients more easily interpretable. To check the robustness of the results, however, the analysis is also performed with body mass as the dependent variable.

There are two behavioral measures: alcohol use and cigarette smoking. *Alcohol use* is a composite score of two items, one a 5-point scale of frequency of alcohol use (with response alternatives ranging from "never drink alcohol" to "more than 10 times" during the past two weeks), and the other a dichotomous measure of intensity (whether the respondent has felt intoxicated during the past two weeks). The two items were standardized and averaged. Cronbach's α is .53. The fairly low α suggests that frequency and intensity of alcohol use may be differentially related to the independent variables. I therefore also perform additional analyses of these indicators separately. *Cigarette smoking* is measured as number of cigarettes per day.

Independent variables. Time before the separation is measured as the time between the screening and the date of the formal separation.[2] Respondents were asked whether they *lived together with spouse or cohabitor* or not (coded 1 and 0, respectively). Thus, this measure does not distinguish between people living together with their spouses, and those who have established a relationship of cohabitation with a new partner. Previous studies of the present data have shown that people who live together with a cohabitor shortly *after* the formal separation report very high levels of subjective well-being, whereas those who live alone are very unhappy (Mastekaasa, 1993). A likely consequence of grouping together cohabitors and people living together with their spouses therefore is that the situation of the latter may appear to be overly positive. It should be kept in mind, however, that the vast majority of those who report living together with spouse or cohabitor have not yet left their spouse.

The analyses control for children, age, education, and employment status. The presence of *children* is measured by asking respondents whether they are living together with children or not. This measure thus does not distinguish between persons living apart from their children and those who do not have children at all. Since most mothers live together with their children during the pre-separation period, this is not likely to be a major problem for the interpretation of findings for women. For men, however, the failure to distinguish between childless persons and fathers who live apart from their children may attenuate the effects of this variable.

For definitions of age, education, and employment status, see Table 1.

Statistical procedures. The present data are basically cross-sectional, but a time dimension is added since it is known whether people separate within 2-4 years after the survey data were collected, and if so, the date of separation. I analyze these data by estimating separate regression models for the separating and the stably married. For the separating the model has the following form:

$$Y_j = a + b_1[\ln(4)-\ln(T)] + b_2[\ln(4)-\ln(T)]^2 + cS + \Sigma d_i X_i + e_1 S[\ln(4)-\ln(T)] + e_2 S[\ln(4)-\ln(T)]^2 + \Sigma g_i SX_i + U \qquad (1)$$

TABLE 1. Descriptive Statistics by Gender and Separation Status

	Men		Women	
	Sepa-rating	Stably married	Sepa-rating	Stably married
Subjective well-being (min. = 1, max. = 7)	4.933	5.167	4.963	5.175
	(.946)	(.802)	(.899)	(.813)
Distress (min. = 1, max. = 4)	1.683	1.460	1.772	1.580
	(.597)	(.496)	(.646)	(.581)
Loneliness (min. = 1, max. = 5)	2.331	1.696	2.567	1.989
	(1.082)	(.792)	(1.087)	(.931)
Self-assessed health	2.952	2.895	2.993	2.901
(very poor = 1, very good = 5)	(.654)	(.649)	(.643)	(.643)
Body weight (kilograms)	78.368	79.570	63.145	66.933
	(10.706)	(10.471)	(10.682)	(11.661)
Alcohol use (Z-scores)	.569	.250	.039	−.195
	(1.025)	(.968)	(.836)	(.650)
Smoking (no. of cigarettes per day)	8.918	4.467	7.282	3.351
	(9.260)	(7.153)	(7.557)	(5.580)
Age (years)	39.466	47.975	36.352	45.964
	(9.692)	(12.458)	(8.905)	(12.790)
Education (years beyond compulsory)	1.898	1.710	1.795	1.386
	(2.106)	(2.159)	(1.805)	(1.729)
Not employed (= 1, employed = 0)	.121	.151	.305	.422
	(.327)	(.359)	(.461)	(.494)
Children ≤ 15 yrs.	.542	.471	.649	.457
(one or more = 1, else = 0)	(.499)	(.499)	(.478)	(.498)
Time until separation (years)	1.280	—	1.273	—
	(.895)	—	(.862)	—
Living alone (yes = 1, no = 0)	.221	—	.225	—
	(.415)	—	(.418)	—

The Y_j are the various dependent variables described above, S is sex, T is time measured in years (fractions of years are represented by decimals), and the X_i are the remaining independent variables described above, including the dummies for children and living alone. U is an error term. The logarithmic transformation of the time variable is used to take into account that the rate of change in the various dependent variables is assumed to increase throughout the pre-separation period (as suggested by Kurdek's (1993) results). The subtraction of ln(T) from ln(4) means that the origin of the logarithmic time scale is the date of separation, and time is measured backwards until the date of the screening. To allow for deviations from the hypothesized relationship between time and the dependent variables (thus making it easier to reject the hypotheses), the square of the $[\ln(4)-\ln(T)]$ term is also included. If not significant at the .05 level, however, this quadratic term is dropped from the final equation.[3]

By means of product terms all independent variables are initially allowed to have different coefficients for men and women. However, interaction terms that are not significant at the .05 level are dropped from the final equation.

For the married the time and living alone variables are not defined, and these terms are dropped from the equation. Otherwise the equation for married people is identical to (1).[4]

Since the Y values of each respondent are measured only once *individual level* changes in these values can not be examined. The b_1 and b_2 parameters of equation (1) show, however, how the expected levels of the dependent variables vary during the four years preceding the formal separation. *Average* differences between people who are at different stages in the dissolution process thus can be assessed. The relationship between each dependent variable and time can be interpreted as *net* changes in these variables. It should be underscored, however, that this model is strictly descriptive. Using time until the dissolution as the independent variable does not imply an assumption that the marital dissolution is in a strict sense the cause of the estimated changes in, e.g., alcohol consumption. Increases in alcohol consumption may also, for instance, exacerbate tensions between the spouses and thus increase the likelihood of separation.

Questions may also be raised about the adequacy of linear regression methods for several of the dependent variables. For some of the variables logistic or tobit regression may be strictly more appropriate. Due to the quite large number of dependent variables, and to the desirability of making comparisons across dependent variables, however, linear regression is used as an approximation in all analyses. Additional analyses not presented indicate that the main results are not very sensitive to the choice of the ordinary linear regression model.[5]

RESULTS

Descriptive results. Table 1 presents descriptive statistics for the dependent and independent variables used in the analyses. Means and standard deviations are given separately for men and women and for the separating and those who remain married.

The separating differ considerably from the stably married on the psychological measures, on alcohol use, and cigarette smoking. They are also somewhat younger and more likely to have children below 15 years of age. The differences in education and employment status are quite small.

Slightly above 20 percent of those who separate during the 2-4 year period live alone. As noted earlier, this number underestimates the proportion who have left their spouses, since men and women who live together with new partners are not included. The proportion living alone also varies over time, increasing strongly as the date of the formal separation approaches. Using a simple logistic regression model with time, time squared, age and age squared as independent variables, the estimated probability of living alone for a 40 year old person is .03 four years before the separation, .10 at two years, .22 at one year, .37 at six months, and .60 one month before the separation (results not shown).

Psychological outcomes. The main results for the psychological variables are presented in Table 2. Significant relationships between the dependent variables and time until the formal separation are also displayed graphically in Figures 1 to 3.

Table 2 and Figure 1 show that the results for *subjective well-being* are well in line with hypothesis 1: Subjective well-being seems to decline over the pre-separation period. But the relationship between time and well-being is very similar for both men and women; the gender with time interaction was clearly not significant and was dropped from the final model presented here. Thus there is no support for hypothesis 2.

It may also be worth noting that living alone or not during the pre-separation period does not seem to make any difference, but persons with children have lower well-being than persons without children. Lack of employment is very strongly associated with lower well-being for men, but not for women. The relationship between employment and well-being is much stronger for separating than for stably married men.

The relationship between time and *distress* is significantly different for men and women. For men the relationship between these variables is very much a mirror image of the corresponding relationship between time and well-being (compare Figures 1 and 2). Subjective well-being declines monotonically over time and distress increases. For women the relationship between time and distress is more complex. Women who later separate are much higher on distress than the stably married even 4 years before the formal separation. Women's level of distress then seems to decline slightly over time, but increases strongly again in the months immediately preceding the separation. Similar to the findings for subjective well-being, whether the spouses live together or not during the pre-separation period does not seem

TABLE 2. Regression of Psychological Measures on Characteristics of the Pre-Separation Period and Background Variables

	Subjective well-being		Distress		Loneliness	
	Sep.	Mar.	Sep.	Mar.	Sep.	Mar.
Constant	5.161***	5.267***	*1.806***	*1.526***	*2.358***	*1.979***
	(.074)	(.011)	(.080)	(.007)	(0.95)	(.011)
Sex	.028	−.040***	−.301***	−.049***	−.407***	−.220***
	(.069)	(.012)	(.109)	(.008)	(.115)	(.010)
Age	−.225***	−.127***	.153***	.082***	.048	−.013
	(.043)	(.008)	(.029)	(.005)	(.037)	(.007)
Age * Sex	.051	−.028*	−.119**	−.042***	—	—
	(.060)	(.011)	(.041)	(.007)		
Age squared	.025	.040***	−.045*	−.022***	−.049*	−.024***
	(.027)	(.004)	(.019)	(.003)	(.022)	(.003)
Age squared * Sex	.073	.030***	.001	−.016***	—	—
	(.038)	(.006)	(.026)	(.004)		
Education	.017	.019***	−.027**	−.009***	−.043**	−.002
	(.014)	(.002)	(.009)	(.002)	(.017)	(.003)
Education * Sex	—	—	—	—	—	—
Not employed	−.067	−.184***	.218***	.136***	.356***	.240***
	(.085)	(.013)	(.058)	(.009)	(.084)	(.012)
Not employed * Sex	−.984***	−.328***	.449***	.161***	—	—
	(.151)	(.024)	(.103)	(.016)		
Children	−.222***	−.014	.048	−.028***	−.013	−.078***
	(.060)	(.012)	(.041)	(.008)	(.071)	(.013)
Children * Sex	—	—	—	—	—	—
In (Time)	−.077*	—	−.170	—	.029	—
	(.032)	—	(.098)	—	(.053)	—
In (Time) * Sex	—	—	.294*	—	.173*	—
	—	—	(.137)	—	(.071)	—
In (Time) squared	—	—	.068*	—	—	—
	—	—	(.027)	—	—	—
In (Time) squared * Sex	—	—	−.086*	—	—	—
	—	—	(.037)	—	—	—
Living alone	−.058	—	−.001	—	.514***	—
	(.071)	—	(.048)	—	(.084)	—
Living alone * Sex	—	—	—	—	—	—
R^2	.117	.054	.118	.053	.110	.041
N	1046	35726	1040	35411	1039	35244

Note: Regression coefficients with standard errors in parentheses
Sep. = Persons who separate within a 2-4 year period after data collection
Mar. = Persons who remain married for a 2-4 year period
Significance probabilities (two-tailed): ***p < .001; **p < .01; * p < .05
Coefficients significantly different (.05 level) for the separating and the stably married are in *italics*

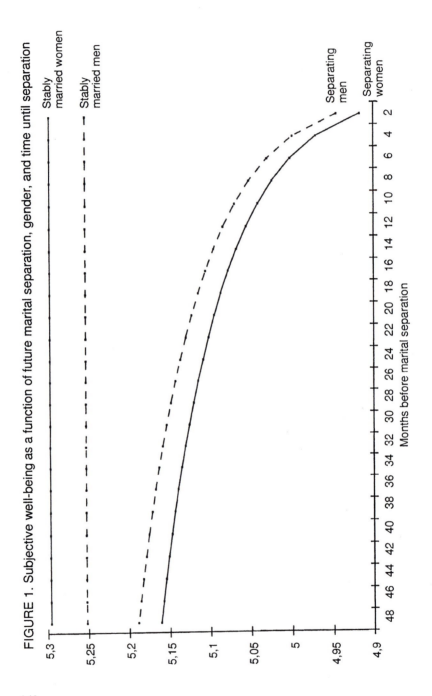

FIGURE 1. Subjective well-being as a function of future marital separation, gender, and time until separation

Stably married women

Stably married men

Separating men

Separating women

Months before marital separation

FIGURE 2. Distress as a function of marital separation, gender, and time until separation

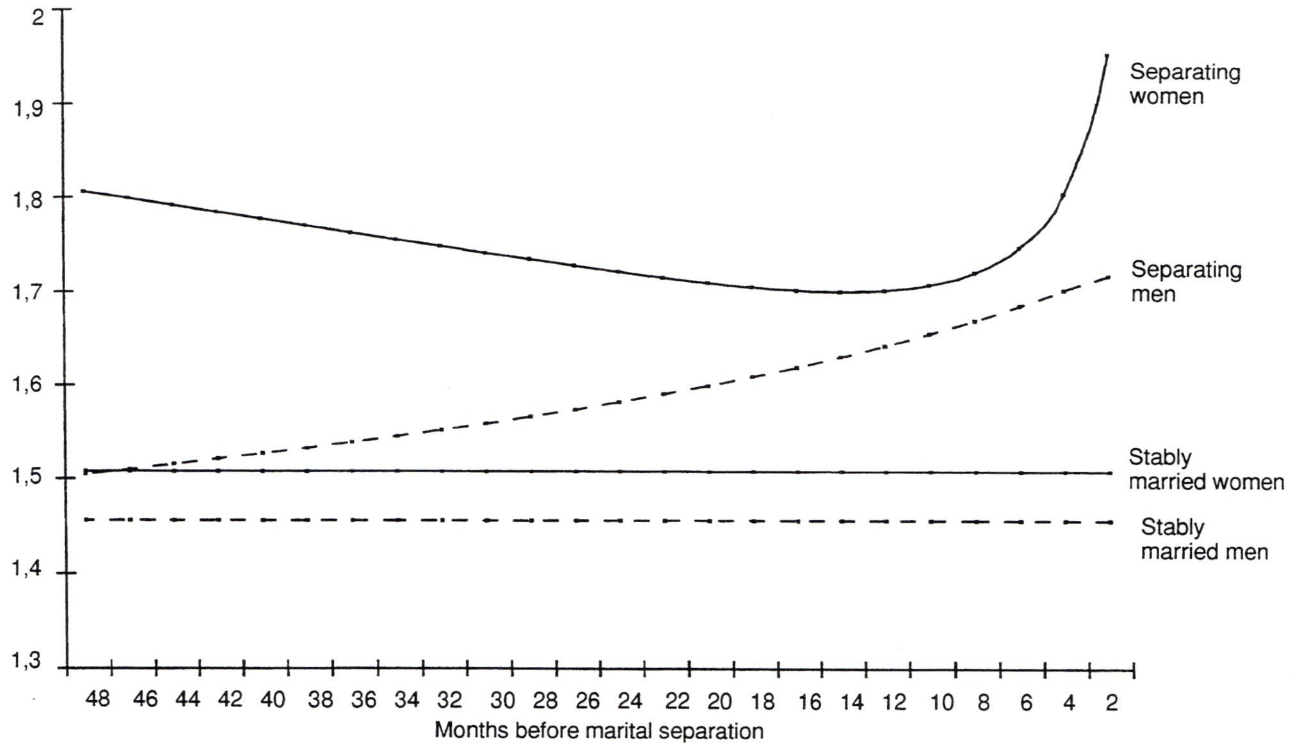

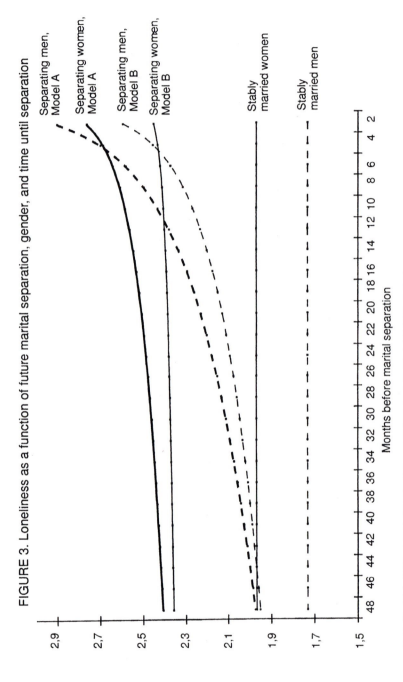

FIGURE 3. Loneliness as a function of future marital separation, gender, and time until separation

Months before marital separation

Note: Model A: Without controlling for living apart from spouse. Model B: With control

Separating men, Model A

Separating women, Model A

Separating men, Model B

Separating women, Model B

Stably married women

Stably married men

to have any systematic effect. Again there is a large difference between the employed and the not employed, particularly for men.

With regard to feelings of *loneliness*, living arrangements do seem to make a difference. Those who live without a spouse or cohabitor during the pre-separation period report much higher levels of loneliness. On the other hand, children do not seem to alleviate feelings of loneliness.

Whether or not one controls for living alone or together with spouse or cohabitant also has considerable impact on the estimated relationship between time and loneliness. In addition to showing the relationship as estimated in Table 2 (model B in Figure 3), I therefore also show the relationship between time and loneliness when estimated without controlling for living alone (model A). The model A results show that feelings of loneliness increase monotonically over time, although the relationship is significant only for men. The significant gender with time interaction supports hypothesis 2. Controlling for living alone clearly reduces the relationship between time and loneliness for both genders; for women the level of loneliness is now approximately constant during the pre-separation period. Together these results show that feelings of loneliness do increase over time, but this is to a large extent due to the fact that many spouses cease living together during the pre-separation period.

It is interesting to note that four years before the separation, men who later separate differ only minimally from stably married men, whereas separating women feel clearly more lonely than women who remain married. This conforms well with the results for subjective well-being and distress: Several years before separation there is little difference between separating and non-separating men, while there are quite large differences between separating and non-separating women. Although marital dissolution seems to be an important stressor, these more enduring differences suggest that the low subjective well-being of separating women is also due to other factors.

Physiological outcomes. Results for *self-assessed health* and body weight are shown in Table 3. None of the hypotheses suggested above receive any support. Although not significant, one may nevertheless note that the coefficient for the time variable has the expected negative sign, indicating declining health during the pre-separation period. Again employment is found to be a very strong predictor, particularly for men. Men who are not employed rate their health much more negatively than the employed.

In the analysis of *weight loss*, the coefficient for the time variable is not quite significant at the .05 level if a two-tailed probability is computed. But if living alone is dropped from the model (yielding what was referred to as model A in the analysis of loneliness above), the coefficient for time

TABLE 3. Regression of Physiological Measures on Characteristics of the Pre-Separation Period and Background Variables

	Self-assessed health		Body weight	
	Sep.	Mar.	Sep.	Mar.
Constant	3.031***	3.027***	65.253***	66.499***
	(.050)	(.008)	(.853)	(.143)
Sex	−.019	.012	*14.719****	*12.817****
	(.042)	(.008)	(.672)	(.125)
Age	−.193***	−.175***	*1.378****	*.201****
	(.022)	(.005)	(.374)	(.009)
Age * Sex	—	—	—	—
Age squared	.040**	.032***	−.887***	−.731***
	(.013)	(.002)	(.229)	(.043)
Age squared * Sex	—	—	—	—
Education	.034***	.036	−.050	−.136***
	(.010)	(.002)	(.168)	(.032)
Education * Sex	—	—	—	—
Not employed	−.117*	−.157***	−.146	1.398***
	(.058)	(.009)	(.851)	(.149)
Not employed * Sex	−.368***	−.295***	—	—
	(.103)	(.016)		
Children	−.031	.007	.033	.042
	(.041)	(.009)	(.719)	(.162)
Children * Sex	—	—	—	—
ln (Time)	−.027	—	−.642	—
	(.022)	—	(.384)	—
ln (Time) * Sex	—	—	—	—
ln (Time) squared	—	—	—	—
ln (Time) squared * Sex	—	—	—	—
Living alone	.006	—	−.845	—
	(.049)	—	(.854)	—
Living alone * Sex	—	—	—	—
R^2	.125	.168	.359	.264
N	1045	35779	1043	35776

Note: Regression coefficients with standard errors in parentheses
Sep. = Persons who separate within a 2-4 year period after data collection
Mar. = Persons who remain married for a 2-4 year period
Significance probabilities (two-tailed): ***p < .001; **p < .01; * p < .05
Coefficients significantly different (.05 level) for the separating and the stably married are in *italics*

does become significant. A reasonable interpretation is that some weight loss does occur during the pre-separation period, but one can not conclude that there is a weight loss which is independent of changes in living arrangements. Some support for hypothesis 1 thus is provided, but there is no evidence of a time by gender interaction (hypothesis 2).[6] See Figure 4.

Behavioral outcomes. With regard to *alcohol consumption,* the most striking finding clearly is the strong gender by time interaction. As shown in Figure 5, the relationship between time and alcohol use is very different for men and women. For men, alcohol consumption seems to increase almost linearly over time. Separating women, on the other hand, seem to differ strongly from those who remain married several years before the separation. The level of alcohol consumption seems to decrease over time, but to increase very strongly during the months immediately preceding the separation.

As noted above, the measure of alcohol consumption is a composite of one question about frequency of use and another about intensity (whether or not intoxicated during the past two weeks). Separate analyses of the two items show that the relationship with time is roughly similar for both items, but it is significant only for intensity.[7]

Since both men and women show evidence of a net increase in alcohol consumption over time, the results are partially consistent with hypothesis 1. But for women the increase is not monotonic. The findings are definitely inconsistent with hypothesis 2; the changes are more dramatic for women than for men.

Harking back to Figure 2, the relationship between time and women's alcohol use is seen to be very similar to that between time and distress. Women's distress scores, too, showed a decline during the first part of the pre-separation period, but a strong increase immediately prior to the formal separation.

The coefficient for children is negative, but not significant. The relationship between living alone and use of alcohol is positive, indicating that those who live alone drink more, but it is not significant.

The relationship between time and *smoking* also is significantly different for men and women (see Table 4).[8] As shown in Figure 6, separating men smoke more than women in the early pre-separation period, but the difference disappears over time. The estimated relationships between time and smoking are negative for men and positive for women, but when considered separately, none of them are significantly different from zero. To the extent that the pre-separation period is associated with more smoking, however, that effect seems to be limited to women. The results thus provide weak

FIGURE 4. Body weight (kilograms) as a function of future marital separation, gender, and time until separation

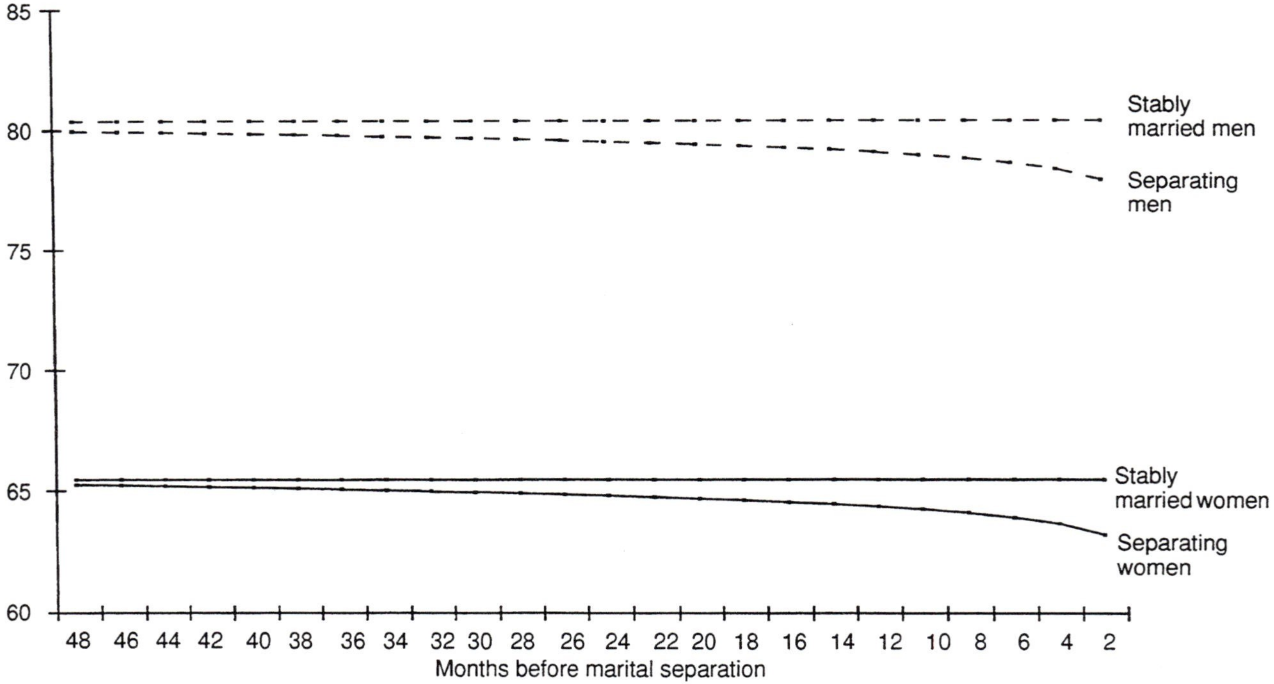

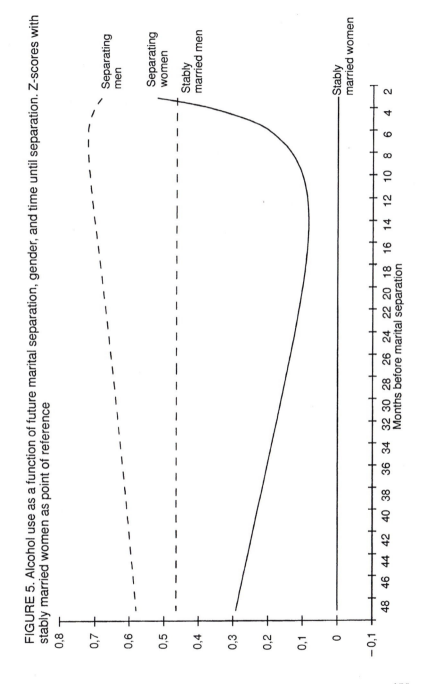

FIGURE 5. Alcohol use as a function of future marital separation, gender, and time until separation. Z-scores with stably married women as point of reference

TABLE 4. Regression of Behavioral Measures on Characteristics of the Pre-Separation Period and Background Variables

	Alcohol use		Smoking	
	Sep.	Mar.	Sep.	Mar.
Constant	.229***	− .050***	7.654***	4.302***
	(.124)	(.011)	(.791)	(.087)
Sex	.288	.471***	2.708**	1.241***
	(.163)	(.010)	(.972)	(.082)
Age	− .093**	− .099***	− .745*	− .551***
	(.034)	(.006)	(.305)	(.050)
Age * Sex	—	—	—	—
Age squared	.045*	− .017***	− .640**	− .346***
	(.021)	(.003)	(.199)	(.025)
Age squared * Sex	—	—	—	—
Education	− .007	.002	− .509***	− .391***
	(.015)	(.002)	(.135)	(.018)
Education * Sex	—	—	—	—
Not employed	− .091	− .039**	.030	− .026
	(.090)	(.013)	(.815)	(.099)
Not employed * Sex	.328*	− .032	5.304***	1.251***
	(.159)	(.018)	(1.438)	(.174)
Children	− .074	− .085***	− .941	− .429***
	(.065)	(.012)	(.581)	(.094)
Children * Sex	—	—	—	—
ln (Time)	− .320*	—	.442	—
	(.154)	—	(.428)	—
ln (Time) * Sex	.457*	—	− 1.196*	—
	(.215)	—	(.579)	—
ln (Time) squared	.124**	—	—	—
	(.042)	—	—	—
ln (Time) squared * Sex	− .156**	—	—	—
	(.058)	—	—	—
Living alone	.091	—	− .025	—
	(.076)	—	(.690)	—
Living alone * Sex	—	—	—	—
R²	.104	.099	.058	.044
N	1034	35331	1013	34363

Note: Regression coefficients with standard errors in parentheses
Sep. = Persons who separate within a 2-4 year period after data collection
Mar. = Persons who remain married for a 2-4 year period
Significance probabilities (two-tailed): ***p < .001; **p < .01; * p < .05
Coefficients significantly different (.05 level) for the separating and the stably married are in *italics*

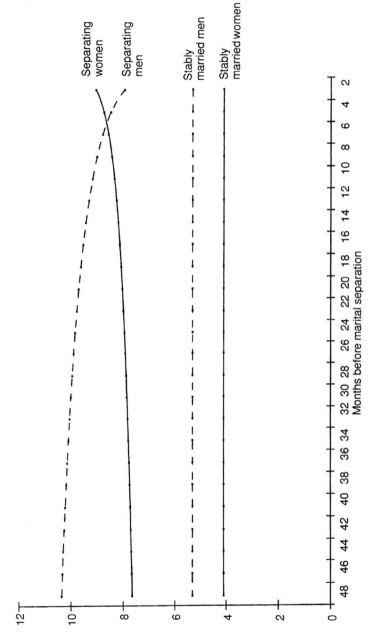

FIGURE 6. Smoking (cigarettes per day) as function of future marital separation, gender, and time until separation

support for hypothesis 1 and are clearly inconsistent with hypothesis 2. Also there is no indication that living alone has any impact on smoking.

Compared to the stably married of the same age and education, both separating men and separating women smoke considerably more throughout the entire pre-separation period. The interactions of not employed with gender show that non-employed men smoke particularly much, particularly if they are also separating.

SUMMARY AND DISCUSSION

In general terms, the present results confirm that the process of marital dissolution is highly stressful. As the time of the formal separation approaches, there is a strong decline in subjective well-being and corresponding increases in loneliness, distress, and use of alcohol. These changes are also manifested physically in the form of weight loss. Although no significant relationship was found between time and self-assessed health, *hypothesis 1* is generally supported.

Hypothesis 2, predicting more negative change for men than for women during the pre-separation period, is, however, generally rejected. Loneliness was the only outcome measure for which this pattern was evident. For subjective well-being and weight loss there is no significant gender difference. For smoking there is a weak indication of an increase for women, but not for men. The findings on smoking are consistent with an earlier Norwegian study of divorce (Moxnes, 1990). The patterns of change in distress and alcohol consumption, which are very similar, are surprising. Separating women are much more distressed and drink more alcohol than stably married women four years before the separation. They then tend to become somewhat less distressed and to drink less until the months immediately preceding the formal separation; at this point there is a sharp increase. Men seem to experience a more monotonic and almost linear increase in distress and alcohol use, but the relationship between time and alcohol use is weak for men. The results do show that both stably married and separating men drink more alcohol than women (and a precise measure of quantity consumed would probably have yielded a larger gender difference), but it is nevertheless surprising that the relative increase in alcohol consumption during the pre-separation period is larger for women.

Although most outcome measures show considerable variation during the pre-separation period, and particularly in the months immediately preceding the formal separation, the separating also often seem to differ strongly from the stably married several years before the formal separation. Such seemingly long-standing differences are most clearly found for both men's and women's smoking and for women's distress, loneliness, and alcohol consumption. Several years before the separation, separating women thus seem to differ more from stably married women than separating men differ from stably married men.

This gender difference can be explained in at least two ways. One interpretation is that women are more strongly affected by long-standing marital problems. Another possible explanation is that more permanent differences between the stably married and the separating are due to differential selection for marital dissolution, and that this selection is stronger for women. Women's feelings of distress or behavior like smoking and alcohol consumption (or personality characteristics associated with these) might have a stronger impact on the probability of marital dissolution than similar feelings or behavior on the part of men. The present analysis does not make it possible to choose between these explanations. In view of the previous studies cited earlier (e.g., McRae & Brody, 1989), an explanation in terms of gender differences in the experience of marital problems seems most likely. Whatever explanation is preferred, however, the results do indicate that at least for men the low well-being of the separated and divorced is not due to differential selection for marital dissolution.

Neither subjective feelings nor the behavioral outcomes considered here seem to depend strongly on whether or not persons who separate have small children. The only outcome measure found to be significantly related to the presence of children is subjective well-being. As noted above, an interpretational problem may arise to some extent since it is not possible to distinguish between childless persons and persons who are at the time of the survey living apart from their children. However, this should largely be a problem in interpreting the results for men. If the parents split up during the pre-separation period, children generally stay with their mothers. For none of the dependent variables, however, is there a significant children with gender interaction.

The analyses indicate that actual living arrangements during the pre-separation period also do not on average seem to have strong effects. It is still possible and even likely that for many individuals moving out of the common household is a very negative and stressful experience. For the population as a whole these negative effects seem to be counterbalanced by the positive effects of escaping from a difficult relationship.

Lack of employment is associated with more psychological problems and poorer self-assessed health for both the separating and the stably married. This relationship is generally much stronger for men than for women, and particularly for separating men. For men the combination of non-employment and being in a pre-separation phase is also strongly associated with higher consumption of alcohol and (particularly) tobacco. These findings may indicate that the two stressors (lack of employment and marital separation) have multiplicative rather than additive effects, but men who are both non-employed and in a pre-separation phase may also be negatively selected.

Although the pre-separation changes in the outcome variables examined here are somewhat more dramatic for women than for men, the results for men are in general more consistent with the stress model. For men all significant relationships between time and the outcome variables are largely monotonic. Also, men who later separate most often differ little from the stably married four years before the formal separation. For women, changes during the pre-separation period are more often non-monotonic, and there seem to be more enduring differences between the separating and the stably married. The problems reported by men during the pre-separation period thus are more easily interpreted within the context of the stress model.

The findings for the psychological measures are more consistent with the stress model than are the results for the more physical and behavioral measures. This suggests that measures of well-being, loneliness and distress are quite direct and sensitive measures of the stresses associated with the dissolution process.

NOTES

1. Measures of blood pressure, blood sugar and heart rate are included in the data set, but were not believed to be relevant for the present study.

2. The exact date at which each individual respondent filled in the questionnaires is not known, only the time period during which the screening personnel visited a particular geographical area in the county. The midpoint of this period was used. This introduces some errors. Since the average screening period in each local area was 3.6 months, the average error can be assumed to be about 1.8 months. These errors can be assumed to be random and unrelated to the dependent as well as to other independent variables. It is well known that such errors tend to create some downward bias in the numerical magnitude of the coefficients. Since the present study deals with the pre-separation period, it is also desirable not to include a considerable number of people who answered the survey questions after the formal separation. Only persons with time values above one month were therefore included in the analyses.

3. In additional analyses not presented here I also estimate the equation using time and time squared as independent variables, i.e., without the logarithmic transformations. This had no impact on conclusions with regard to hypotheses 1 and 2.

4. Thus, only interactions that are significant in the separation sample are included. Due to the very large sample size, some additional interactions were significant in the stably married subsample. To facilitate comparison, and because most of them are of quite trivial magnitude, they are not included here.

5. An additional problem with the methods used here is that *censoring* is not taken into account; people are observed for unequal periods of time (from 2 to 4 years). This means that the "stably married" category includes an unknown number of people who do in fact separate 2 to 4 years after the screening, but this information is not available in our data. This problem can be handled by means of hazard rate methods (Mastekaasa, 1994). In order to keep the presentation simple, this is not done here. There is no reason to believe that the censoring problem leads to serious distortions of the results; the number of people who separate during a four year period is very low compared to the number who remain married. The censoring that occurs here also is exogenously determined (by the procedures used for matching the interview and the register data). Moreover, very few persons separate more than once during a four-year period (at least in the area studied here). This means that people who are separated within a two-year period should not differ systematically from those that separate within four years. The sample of separating persons in our study should therefore be an unbiased sample of all those who separate during a four-year period.

6. If body mass is used as the dependent variable, the results are very similar.

7. This analysis was also performed using logistic instead of OLS regression, with very similar results. In particular, the gender-specific relationships between time until the separation and intensity of alcohol use are similar and significant (a test of change in model fit by dropping the four time and time with gender terms gives a χ^2 of 10.80, corresponding to a p-value of .03).

8. Since the smoking variable is truncated from below, linear regression is not strictly appropriate. I therefore also estimated a tobit model with the same independent variables as in Table 4. All coefficients that were significant in the linear regression also were significant in the tobit model and with the same signs.

REFERENCES

Albrecht, E. L. (1980). Reactions and adjustments to divorce: differences in experiences of men and women. *Family Relations, 29,* 59-68.

Avison, W. R., & Turner, R. J. (1988). Stressful life events and depressive symptoms: Disaggregating the effects of acute stressors and chronic strains. *Journal of Health and Social Behavior, 29,* 253-264.

Bloom, B. L., Asher, S. J., & White, S. W. (1978). Marital disruption as a stressor: A review and analysis. *Psychological Bulletin, 85,* 867-894.

Bloom, B. L., & Caldwell, R. A. (1981). Sex differences in adjustment during the process of marital separation. *Journal of Marriage and the Family, 43,* 693-701.

Booth, A., & Amato, P. (1991). Divorce and psychological stress. *Journal of Health and Social Behavior, 32,* 396-407.

Doherty, W. J., Su, S., & Needle, R. (1989). Marital disruption and psychological well-being: A panel study. *Journal of Family Issues, 10*, 72-85.

Gove, W. R. (1972). The relationship between sex roles, marital status, and mental illness. *Social Forces, 51*, 34-44.

Gove, W. R., Style, C. B., & Hughes, M. (1990). The effect of marriage on the well-being of adults: A theoretical analysis. *Journal of Family Issues, 11*, 4-35.

Hagestad, G. O., & Smyer, M. A. (1982). Dissolving long-term relationships: Patterns of divorcing in middle age. In S. Duck (Ed.) *Personal Relationships, vol. 4: Dissolving Personal Relationships* (pp. 155-188). New York: Academic Press.

Kelly, E. L., & Conley, J. J. (1987). Personality and compatibility: A prospective analysis of marital stability and marital satisfaction. *Journal of Personality and Social Psychology, 52*, 27-40.

Kessler, R. C. & McLeod, J. D. (1984). Sex differences in vulnerability to undesirable life events. *American Sociological Review, 49*, 620-631.

Kitson, G. C., Babri, K. B., Roach, M. J., & Placidi, K.S. (1989). Adjustment to widowhood and divorce. *Journal of Family Issues, 10*, 5-32.

Kitson, G. C, Graham, A. V., & Schmidt, D.D. (1983). Troubled marriages and divorce: A prospective suburban study. *Journal of Family Practice, 17*, 249-258.

Kurdek, L. A. (1990). Divorce history and self-reported psychological distress in husbands and wives. *Journal of Marriage and the Family, 52*, 701-708.

Kurdek, L. A. (1993). Predicting marital dissolution: A 5-year prospective longitudinal study of newlywed couples. *Journal of Personality and Social Psychology, 64*, 221-242.

Mastekaasa, A. (1992). Marriage and psychological well-being: Some evidence on selection into marriage. *Journal of Marriage and the Family, 54*, 901-911.

Mastekaasa, A. (1994). The subjective well-being of the previously married: The importance of cohabitation and time since the marital dissolution. *Social Forces, 73*, 665-692.

Mastekaasa, A. (1994). Psychological well-being and marital dissolution: Selection effects? *Journal of Family Issues, 15*, 208-228.

McRae, J. A., Jr. & Brody, C. J. (1989). The differential importance of marital experiences for the well-being of women and men: A research note. *Social Science Research, 18*, 237-248.

Menaghan, E. (1985). Depressive affect and subsequent divorce. *Journal of Family Issues, 6*, 295-306.

Menaghan, E., & Lieberman, M. A. (1986). Changes in depression following divorce: A panel study. *Journal of Marriage and the Family, 48*, 319-328.

Mergenhagen, P. M., Lee, B. A., & Gove, W. R. (1985). Till death do us part: Recent changes in the relationship between marital status and mortality. *Sociology and Social Research, 70*, 53-56.

Moum, T. (1992). Self-assessed health among Norwegian adults. *Social Science and Medicine, 35*, 935-947.

Moxnes, K. (1985). Hans og hennes skilsmisse. *Tidsskrift for samfunnsforskning,* *26*, 419-436.

Moxnes, K. (1990). *Kjernesprengning i familien? Familieforandring ved samlivsbrudd og dannelse av nye samliv.* Oslo: Norwegian University Press.

Pearlin, L. I. (1989). The sociological study of stress. *Journal of Health and Social Behavior, 30*, 241-256.

Riessman, C. K., & Gerstel, N. (1985). Marital dissolution and health: Do males or females have greater risk? *Social Science and Medicine, 20*, 627-635.

Selye, Hans (1982). History and present status of the stress concept. In L. Goldberger & S. Breznitz (Eds.), *Handbook of Stress,* New York: Free Press.

Spanier, G. B., & Furstenberg, F. F. (1982). Remarriage after divorce: A longitudinal analysis of well-being. *Journal of Marriage and the Family, 44*, 709-720.

Thoits, P. A. (1983). Dimensions of life events that influence psychological distress: An evaluation and synthesis of the literature. In H.P. Kaplan (Ed.), *Psychological Stress: Trends in Theory and Research.* New York: Academic Press (pp. 33-103).

Wertlieb, D., Budman, S., Demby, A., & Randall, M. (1984). Marital separation and health: Stress and intervention. *Journal of Human Stress, 10*, 18-26.

Wheaton, B. (1990). Life transitions, role histories, and mental health. *American Sociological Review, 55*, 209-223.

Zeiss, A. M., Zeiss, R. A., & Johnson, S. M. (1980). Sex differences in initiation of and adjustment to divorce. *Journal of Divorce, 4*, 21-33.

UNITED KINGDOM

Infant-Mother Attachment
in Separated and Married Families

Cheryl Kier
Charlie Lewis

SUMMARY. Two contrasting predictions about the effects of parental marital separation on infants' attachment to their mothers are considered. The "early adversity" hypothesis suggests that infants will
be adversely affected by negative life events and thus will develop
anxious attachments to their mothers. The "protective" hypothesis
claims that infants are resistant to stressors because of their limited
cognitive ability, and therefore will be no more likely to develop
anxious attachments than other infants. Results from 76 mother-
child pairs in the "strange situation" procedure (assessing infant-

Cheryl Kier, PhD, is a Lecturer at the University of East London, Department
of Psychology, Romford Road, London E15 4LZ. Charlie Lewis, PhD, is a Senior
Lecturer at Lancaster University, Lancaster, UK.
The authors wish to thank Liz Meins for coding the tapes, the women who
served as strangers, the many people who helped us in recruiting, and the families
who participated.

[Haworth co-indexing entry note]: "Infant-Mother Attachment in Separated and Married Families."
Kier, Cheryl and Charlie Lewis. Co-published simultaneously in *Journal of Divorce & Remarriage* (The
Haworth Press, Inc.) Vol. 26, No. 3/4, 1997, pp. 185-194; and: *Divorce and Remarriage: International
Studies* (ed: Craig A. Everett) The Haworth Press, Inc., 1997, pp. 185-194. Single or multiple copies of
this article are available for a fee from The Haworth Document Delivery Service [1-800-342-9678, 9:00 a.m.
- 5:00 p.m. (EST). E-mail address: getinfo@haworth.com].

185

mother attachment) supported the "protective" hypothesis in that there were no significant differences between infants in two marital status groups. The role of marital status versus unfavorable life events in affecting children's development was discussed. *[Article copies available for a fee from The Haworth Document Delivery Service: 1-800-342-9678. E-mail address: getinfo@haworth.com]*

The general consensus in the divorce literature seems to be that the separation/divorce of their parents negatively influences children's development (e.g., Hetherington, Cox, & Cox, 1982). The effects are said to be greater if the breakup occurred before the child's fifth birthday (e.g., Allison & Furstenberg, 1989), and that boys are more affected than are girls (e.g., Hetherington et al., 1982; Rutter, 1971). Yet these conclusions have referred almost exclusively to children who have been examined at school-age or older. There is almost no attention devoted to children under the age of three.

Knowledge about the effects of divorce on children at such a young age remains speculative. Two major contentions are observable in the literature. One is that early adversity leads to current and long-lasting difficulties for the individual. The other suggests that due to their young age, infants are not greatly affected by events that occur during this time period (Rutter, 1989). The arguments for both points of view will be reviewed next.

Ethological attachment theory (e.g., Vaughn, Egeland, Sroufe, & Waters, 1979), which suggests that the failure to develop a secure attachment (with the mother) by 12 to 18 months results in less than optimal development for the child, concurs with the "early adversity" hypothesis. Ethologists claim that events which affect the quality of the mother-infant relationship may affect the attachment of the infant to the mother. Marital separation and divorce often result in an overburdened mother (Brandwein, Brown & Fox, 1974; Hetherington, Cox, & Cox, 1979a), and one who is self-absorbed (Rohrlich, Ranier, Berg-Cross, & Berg-Cross, 1977). Life in a one-parent family requires new negotiation of roles and necessitates a period of trial and error before a new equilibrium is reached (Hetherington, Cox, & Cox, 1976). These are not considered to be ideal circumstances for a mother to be sensitively responsive to her infant (Ainsworth, Bell, & Stayton, 1974). Research on mothers' parenting after divorce suggests that they are more punitive and controlling than mothers who are married (Hetherington et al., 1976; Wallerstein & Blakeslee, 1989). Thus it is likely that infant-mother relationships in divorced families may not be conducive to a child feeling secure in its attachment to mother. The above data may suggest that the disruptions of marital separation would affect the mother's sensitivity to the infant's needs and therefore disrupt the infant-mother attachment.

There is very little empirical evidence upon which to draw to assess the accuracy of this contention. Studies of lone-parent families investigating infant-mother attachment have been limited to samples of families at risk (poverty stricken, poorly educated mothers, unplanned pregnancies, unstable relationships, mental retardation, abusing/neglecting parents). Using these "high risk" samples, Crittenden (1985) and Egeland and Farber (1984) found no significant differences between infants from one- vs. two-parent families. However, Egeland and Farber found a tendency for boys from one-parent families to be the most likely group to show an anxious attachment. When Vaughn, Gove, and Egeland (1980) observed a subsample of the infants from the Egeland and Farber study six months later, they found a trend for more infants from non-intact families than from intact families to be anxiously attached to their mothers (65% of the anxiously attached group were from single-parent families). While the effect of parental marital separation on young infants' attachment is still equivocal, circumstantial evidence with slightly older children gives tentative support to the early adversity hypothesis. For example, Peretti and di-Vitorrio (1993) found that children aged between three and six reported the experience of guilt, low confidence, and feeling less sociable if their parents were divorced.

In contrast to the research on attachment, evidence from the literature on stress and children suggests that infants may in fact be protected from adverse events such as father absence and divorce due to their young age. Rutter (1989) argued that since infants under about six months of age have not yet formed attachments to others, and because they also lack the cognitive capacity to understand what was happening during times of stress, they suffered no lasting effects. It is possible that infants will have no recollection of any strife between parents and will be more adaptable than older children to new situations (such as living in a one-parent family or in a step-family) because they will not have recalled anything different (cf. Wallerstein & Blakeslee, 1989). The present study is one of the first empirical attempts to assess the effects of parental marital separation on children as young as one to two years of age. Using questionnaire data, Hodges, Landis, Day, and Oderberg (1991) found that mothers' reports of the quality of the relationships children (aged one to three years) had with their parents was related to the fathers' visitation patterns. The present study expands upon this by utilizing a standard laboratory observation procedure to assess the infant-mother attachment relationship. The aim of this paper is to assess whether infants from separated/divorced families are more likely to display an anxious pattern of attachment in contrast to a matched sample of infants from married-parent families. If the hypothesis that marital separation is necessarily harmful is correct (herein referred to as the "early adversity" hypothesis), marital separation will result in more anxious attachments among the infants in the separated sample. On the other hand, if Rutter's hypothesis about infancy being protective is correct (herein referred to as the "protective" hypothesis), there should be no differences in the number of securely attached infants in the two groups.

There have been some recent suggestions that the strange situation procedure may have different meanings for children from families that do not fit into the traditional mold of the middle-class, two-parent family with one breadwinner and one major caregiver who remains at home (e.g., Clarke-Stewart, 1989). However, given the strong record of the reliability and validity of the strange situation (e.g., Ainsworth, Blehar, Waters, & Wall, 1978) the method is worth employing as long as the interpretation of any group differences is conducted with caution.

METHOD

Subjects

Seventy-six infants and their mothers served as participants. Half of the mothers had separated from their husbands/partners on average 13.13 months (sd = 9.59) prior to the study. They had been living with their former partners for an average 4.96 years (sd = 3.44) prior to the breakup of the relationship. (Thus their weddings took place on average 6.3 years prior to the study.) The mean age of the infants in the separated group was 21.82 months (sd = 9.10).

The other half of the sample was still living with the father of their child. They had been living together an average of 7.64 years (sd = 3.25; their weddings took place approximately the same time as those of the separated families). The mean age of the infants in the married group was 20.08 months (sd = 7.13). There were 15 boys and 23 girls in each group, matched for age. Volunteers were recruited from health visitors (N = 24), mother/toddler groups, playgroups, and other parenting groups (N = 24), the local media (N = 8), the local courts (N = 3), and referrals from other participants (N = 16). In one separated family two children participated.

Attachment Assessments

All infants and mothers participated in the strange situation procedure as described by Ainsworth et al. (1978). The women who acted as the stranger were unaware of the aims of the study. A coder trained to classify infant patterns of attachment in the standard manner who was also blind to the hypotheses of the study scored all the videotaped sessions. Four patterns were coded, as described by Ainsworth et al. (1978) and Main, Kaplan, and Cassidy, (1985): secure (B), anxious-avoidant (A), anxious-resistant (C), and anxious-disorganized (D).

RESULTS

Table 1 shows the attachment classifications for the separated and married groups separately. For infants from separated mothers, 52.6% were securely attached, 21.1% showed the avoidant attachment pattern, 5.3% displayed the resistant attachment pattern, and 13.2% were classified as showing the disorganized pattern. In the married group, 68.4% of infants were classified as securely attached, 13.2% were scored as avoidant, 13.2% resistant, and 2.6% disorganized. The distribution of categories for each group is comparable to that obtained by other researchers in the field, who obtain roughly 66% secure (B) infants, 22% avoidant (A) infants, and 12% resistant (C) infants (e.g., Ainsworth et al., 1978). (Insufficient information exists thus far on the percentage of disorganized [D] infants to be expected in a sample.)

Because of the small numbers involved, infants rated as avoidant, resistant and disorganized were combined into one "anxious" category for

TABLE 1. Attachment Classifications for Children from the Separated and Married Families.

Group:	Separated		Married	
	n	%	n	%
A (Avoidant)	8	21.1	5	13.2
B (Secure)	20	52.6	26	68.4
C (Resistant)	2	5.3	5	13.2
D (Disorganized)	5	13.2	1	2.6
unclassified/ equipment failure	3	7.9	1	2.6
Total	38	100.1	38	100

data analysis. In order to assess the effects of parental marital status and the child's sex upon the infant-mother attachment category, two binary logistic models were fitted to the data (displayed in Table 2) using the GLIM package (Francis, Green, & Payne, 1993). First a model examining secure (i.e., B) vs. the other groups (A, C, & D) was fitted. There is no evidence at the 5% level of a significant difference in the proportion of B relationships in married families being different from those in the separated families (before fitting sex, Chi-Square [df = 1, N = 74] = 1.35; after fitting sex, Chi-Square [df = 1, N = 74] = 1.16; after fitting parental marital status, Chi-Square = 1.12). The same holds for the interaction between child sex and parental marital status (Chi-Square [df = 1, N = 74] = 2.17). Second, a model was fitted to compare D relationships with the others (A, B, & C). There was a trend to suggest that the proportion of D relationships is higher in separated families (Chi-Square [df = 1, N = 74] = 3.4, regardless of whether sex is fitted before or after). However, this analysis should be treated with caution as it was exploratory.

DISCUSSION

The results suggest that one year post-separation, infants are not harmed by the separation experience, as evidenced by their ability to develop secure attachments to their mothers as frequently as children from married-parent families. The lack of differences between the groups supports the "protection hypothesis" (cf. Rutter, 1989). This predicts that young infants will be shielded from negative experiences such as separa-

TABLE 2. Attachment Classifications for each Sex Within each Marital Status Group.

	Separated Girls		Separated Boys		Married Girls		Married Boys	
	n	%	n	%	n	%	n	%
Anxious	7	30.4	8	53.3	7	30.4	4	26.7
Secure	14	60.9	6	40.0	15	65.2	11	73.3
unclassified/ equipment failure	2	8.7	1	6.7	1	4.3	0	00.0
Total	23	100	15	100	23	99.9	15	100

tion because they have not yet formed attachments (i.e., to the father) and because their cognitive grasp of events is limited. It is possible that differences were not found in the behavior of the infants in the two types of families because the infants were so young at the time of the parental separation that they were not affected by it.

Although the "early adversity" hypothesis would predict that the infant-mother relationship would be negatively affected by maternal life stress (such as marital separation), it may be that separated mothers put extra energy into their relationship with the child once their marriages have broken down. Infants may not necessarily be at risk simply because their mothers are experiencing stress. Despite the hardships that may have ensued after a marital separation, mothers can still be adequate in their parenting roles. This ties in with the findings of Wynn and Bowering (1990), who reported that the homemaking practices of separated/divorced mothers of preschoolers were similar to those of married mothers. Despite the stresses facing the separated mothers, the authors found that they were able to make practical adjustments in order to cope with their circumstances.

Separated mothers may be attempting to compensate for the absence of a father and therefore expend more effort in caring for their children. Children may become more important to mothers after separation (Wallerstein & Blakeslee, 1989). Although this may mean that some separated mothers are perceived by professionals as "overprotective," these data suggest that without a partner some separated women have more freedom to devote themselves to their children at this point in time.

Alternatively, there may be a sleeper effect which will be revealed in later years. There is evidence of sleeper effects among children of depressed mothers, and a similar mechanism may operate among children with separated mothers. Ghodsian, Zajicek, and Wolkind (1984) found that there was no relationship between maternal depression and child behavior problems when both were measured when the child was 14 months old, but there was a relationship between maternal depression measured when the child was 14 months old and behavior problems when the child was 42 months old (even among mothers who were no longer depressed at 42 months). The preschool period may thus be a time when the effects of early environmental stress (such as parental separation) are manifested.

A final possibility to explain the lack of differences is that infants may be so difficult to care for in the first place that parenting is not greatly affected by marital separation. Although it has been found that divorced mothers may be less "effective" than married mothers (Hetherington et al., 1976; Wallerstein & Blakeslee, 1989), this research has been limited to older children. Married as well as separated mothers of infants may have so much to cope with that they are not affected by the presence or absence of a partner. The high rate of depression among mothers with infants and toddlers (New & David, 1985; Richman, 1976; 1977) and the large amount of stress these mothers report in their parenting role (Abidin, 1986) attest to this. Father involvement at this age is reported to be minimal (Gottfried & Gottfried, 1988; Oakley, 1979), thus even married mothers may have little support. This shared difficulty with motherhood may explain the lack of differences that were found between the two marital status groups.

The data are consistent with the notion that any long-term problems which children may face appear *not* to result from the experience of separation per se. School-aged children may experience difficulties due to events which occur *after* the separation. For example, conflict between the parents often increases over time despite the fact they are no longer living together (Hetherington et al., 1982; Westman, Cline, Swift, and Cramer, 1970), or the life circumstances of the one-parent family may continue to deteriorate (Weitzman, 1985). Environmental changes associated with the divorce process may negatively affect children (Stolberg & Anker, 1983). The adjustment of school-age children may depend on the level of cooperation or style of conflict between the parents (Camara & Resnick, 1988), which may require time to become established. Researchers (e.g., Cherlin, Furstenberg, Chase-Lansdale, Kiernan, Robins, Morrison, & Teitler, 1991; Emery, 1982) have increasingly suggested that conflict in marriage may be the cause of later difficulties for children post-divorce. However, conflict prior to the separation does not explain the fact that infants are adjusting adequately 13 months post-separation. If problems arise at pre-school or school age, this cannot be attributed solely to pre-divorce conflict.

The results from this study present a less gloomy picture than that of many other studies of children from separated/divorced families. It seems that despite unfortunate circumstances for the mother, one- to two-year old children can develop adequately, at least during the first year after separation. Although long-term effects of parental separation on infants may well occur, results from the present study suggest that short term effects are minimal.

REFERENCES

Abidin, R.R. (1986) *Parenting Stress Index*. Charlottesville, Virginia: Pediatric Psychology Press.

Ainsworth, M.D.S., Bell, S.M., & Stayton, D.J. (1974) Infant-mother attachment and social development: "Socialization" as a product of reciprocal responsiveness to signals. In M.P. Richards (Ed.) *The integration of the child into a social world*. London: Cambridge University Press.

Ainsworth, M.D.S., Blehar, M.C., Waters, E., & Wall, S. (1978) *Patterns of attachment*. Hillsdale, New Jersey: Lawrence Erlbaum Associates.

Allison, P.D., & Furstenberg, F.F. Jr. (1989) How marital dissolution affects children: Variations by age and sex. *Developmental Psychology*, 25, 540-549.

Brandwein, R.A., Brown, C.A., Fox, E.M. (1974) Women and children last: The social situation of divorced mothers and their families. *Journal of Marriage and the Family*, 36, 498-514.

Camara, K.A., & Resnick, G. (1988) Interparental conflict and cooperation: Factors moderating children's post-divorce adjustment. In E.M. Hetherington & J.D. Arasteh (Eds.) *Impact of divorce, single parenting, and stepparenting on children*. Hillsdale, New Jersey: LEA.

Cherlin, A.J., Furstenberg, F.F. Jr., Chase-Lansdale, P.L., Kiernan, K.E., Robins, P.K., Morrison, D.R., & Teitler, J.O. (1991) Longitudinal studies of the effects of divorce on children in Great Britain and the United States. *Science*, 252, 1386-1389.

Clarke-Stewart, A. (1989) Infant daycare: Maligned or malignant? *American Psychologist*, 44, 266-273.

Crittenden, P.M. (1985) Social networks, quality of child rearing, and child development. *Child Development*, 56, 1299-1313.

Egeland, B., & Farber, E.A. (1984) Infant-mother attachment: Factors related to its development and changes over time. *Child Development*, 55, 753-771.

Emery, R.E. (1982) Interparental conflict and the children of discord and divorce. *Psychological Bulletin*, 92, 310-330.

Francis, B.J., Green, M., & Payne, C. (1993) *The GLIM system Release 4 Manual*. Oxford: Oxford University Press.

Ghodsian, M., Zajicek, E., & Wolkind, S. (1984) A longitudinal study of maternal depression and child behavior problems. *Journal of Child Psychology and Psychiatry*, 25, 91-109.

Gottfried, A.E., & Gottfried, A.W. (1988) *Maternal employment and children's development*. New York: Plenum Press.

Hetherington, E.M., Cox, M., & Cox, R. (1976) Divorced fathers. *Family Coordinator*, 25, 417-428.

Hetherington, E.M., Cox, M., & Cox, R. (1979) The development of children in mother-headed families. In D. Reiss and H.A. Hoffman (Eds.) *The American family: Dying or developing*. New York: Plenum Press.

Hetherington, E.M., Cox, M., & Cox, R. (1982) Effects of divorce on parents and children. In M.E. Lamb (Ed.) *Nontraditional families: Parenting and child development*. Hillsdale, New Jersey: Lawrence Erlbaum Associates.

Hodges, W.F., Landis, T., Day, E., & Oderberg, N. (1991) Infants and toddlers and post divorce parental access: An initial exploration. *Journal of Divorce & Remarriage*, 16, 239-252.

Main, M., Kaplan, N., & Cassidy, J. (1985) Security in infancy, childhood, and adulthood: A move to the level of representation. In I. Bretherton and E. Waters (Eds.) *Monographs of the Society for Research in Child Development*, 50, Serial No. 209, 147-166.

New, C., & David, M. (1985) *For the children's sake.* Harmonsworth: Pelican.

Oakley, A. (1979) *Becoming a mother.* Oxford: Martin Robertson & Co. Ltd.

Peretti, P.O., & di-Vitorrio, A. (1993) Effect of loss of father through divorce on personality of the preschool child. *Journal of Social Behavior and Personality,* 21, 33-38.

Richman, N. (1976) Depression in mothers of preschool children. *Journal of Child Psychology and Psychiatry,* 17, 75-78.

Richman, N. (1977) Behaviour problems in pre-school children: Family and social factors. *British Journal of Psychiatry,* 131, 523-527.

Rohrlich, J.A., Ranier, R., Berg-Cross, L., & Berg-Cross, G. (1977) The effects of divorce: A research review with a developmental perspective. *Journal of Clinical Child Psychology,* 6, 15-20.

Rutter, M. (1971) Parent-child separation: Psychological effects on the children. *Journal of Child Psychology and Psychiatry,* 12, 233-260.

Rutter, M. (1989) Pathways from childhood to adult life. *Journal of Child Psychology and Psychiatry,* 30, 23-51.

Stolberg, A.L., & Anker, J.M. (1983) Cognitive and behavioral changes in children resulting from parental divorce and consequent environmental changes. *Journal of Divorce,* 7, 23-41.

Vaughn, B., Egeland, B., Sroufe, L., & Waters, E. (1979) Individual differences in infant-mother attachment at 12 and 18 months: Stability and change in families under stress. *Child Development,* 50, 971-975.

Vaughn, B., Gove, F., & Egeland, B. (1980) The relationship between out-of-home care and the quality of infant-mother attachment in an economically disadvantaged sample. *Child Development,* 51, 1203-1214.

Wallerstein, J.S., & Blakeslee, S. (1989) *Second chances.* London: Corgi Books.

Weitzman, L.J. (1985) *The divorce revolution: The unexpected social and economic consequences for women and children in America.* New York: The Free Press.

Westman, J.C., Cline, D.W., Swift, W.J., & Kramer, D.A. (1970) Role of child psychiatry in divorce. *Archives of General Psychiatry,* 23, 416-420.

Wynn, R.L., & Bowering, J. (1990) Homemaking practices and evening meals in married and separated families with young children. *Journal of Divorce & Remarriage,* 14, 107-123.

The Relationship Between Marital Disruption and Adolescent Values: A Study Among 13-15 Year Olds

Leslie J. Francis

Thomas E. Evans

SUMMARY. A sample of 16,411 year nine and year ten pupils throughout England and Wales completed a detailed inventory of values. The responses of those whose parents have experienced separation or divorce are compared with those whose parents have not experienced this form of family disruption. Significant differences are found

The Revd. Professor Leslie J. Francis is the D J James Professor of Pastoral Theology and Mansel Jones Fellow at Trinity College, Carmarthen, Dyfed Wales SA31 3EP and University of Wales, Lampeter. The Revd. Thomas E. Evans is Senior Lecturer in Theology and Religious Studies at Trinity College, Carmarthen.

This analysis is part of the Teenage Religion and Values project at the Centre for Theology and Education at Trinity College, Carmarthen. Aspects of this project have been sponsored by Crusaders, Rank Foundation, Hockerill Education Foundation, All Saints' Educational Trust and Friends First Day Schools Fund.

[Haworth co-indexing entry note]: "The Relationship Between Marital Disruption and Adolescent Values: A Study Among 13-15 Year Olds." Francis, Leslie J. and Thomas E. Evans. Co-published simultaneously in *Journal of Divorce & Remarriage* (The Haworth Press, Inc.) Vol. 26, No. 3/4, 1997, pp. 195-213; and: *Divorce and Remarriage: International Studies* (ed: Craig A. Everett) The Haworth Press, Inc., 1997, pp. 195-213. Single or multiple copies of this article are available for a fee from The Haworth Document Delivery Service [1-800-342-9678, 9:00 a.m. - 5:00 p.m. (EST). E-mail address: getinfo@ haworth.com].

195

in all fourteen value areas included in the survey. In summary marital disruption is associated with lower personal wellbeing, and more radical or less socially conformist attitudes. *[Article copies available for a fee from The Haworth Document Delivery Service: 1-800-342-9678. E-mail address: getinfo@haworth.com]*

INTRODUCTION

Data provided by the Office of Population Censuses and Surveys (1990, 1993) demonstrate the rising divorce rate in England and Wales since the mid-1960s. According to Haskey (1990) by the time they are 16 years old, one in four children are now likely to have experienced parental divorce. In her review of lone parenthood and family disruption, Burghes (1994) argues that, as more and more children experience family change, research into the impact of family disruption on children will be increasingly important.

At present sound empirically based knowledge regarding the influence of marital disruption on children is restricted by a number of problems associated with research in this area (Kanoy and Cunningham, 1984; Demo and Acock, 1988; Demo, 1993). These include reservations about the representativeness of some of the samples studied, as well as the restrictions placed on both longitudinal and cross-sectional studies. There are significant difficulties in synthesising the findings of research generated in different cultures and at different points in history. What is shown to be the case in North America may not necessarily be the case in Britain. What was shown to be the case in Britain in the 1970s may not necessarily be the case in Britain in the 1990s. Recent research concerned with attitudes towards divorce and marital disruption clearly indicates both significant shifts over time and significant differences between countries and cultures (Harding, Phillips and Fogarty, 1986; Jowell, Brook and Dowds, 1993) or even within different parts of the UK (Jowell, Witherspoon and Brook, 1988). Moreover, while it is relatively straightforward to demonstrate a relationship between marital disruption and specific features of the young person's experience, it is much less easy to prove the *causal* nature of such relationships.

To date three main groups of studies have explored the relationship between marital disruption and a range of social and psychological outcomes during childhood, adolescence and adulthood.

One group of studies has looked at the relationship between parental divorce and differences in young people's behaviour, attitude or achievement during the school years. For example, Douglas (1970) studied bed-wetting among 15 year olds. He reported that adolescents whose parents had either separated or divorced during their first five years of life were twice as likely to be bed-wetting as those whose parents were together.

Ferri (1976) looked at school behaviour among 11 year olds. His analysis of the National Child Development Study data found that children whose parents had divorced had poorer behaviour at school and were considered less well adjusted, although this relationship disappeared after controlling for other indices of deprivation.

Cherlin, Furstenberg, Chase-Lansdale, Kiernan, Robins, Morrison and Teitler (1991) looked at behaviour scales completed by teachers and parents, reporting on 11 year olds in both the USA and the UK. The findings varied in the two cultures and were different for boys and for girls.

Elliott and Richards (1991) explored disruptive behaviour and self-reported worry and unhappiness among sixteen year olds in the National Child Development Study. Their data show two findings. Children whose parents divorced between the ages of 7 and 16 had higher scores of unhappiness and worry and displayed more disruptive behaviour at the age of 16. They also scored higher on both indices at the age of 7, before their parents divorced.

Both Ferri (1976) and Elliott and Richards (1991) also looked at the relationship between marital disruption and educational achievement in math and reading at the ages of 11 and 16 respectively. Again significant differences among those whose parents have divorced and those continuing to live in intact families are reduced by controlling for other background variables.

Clark and Barber (1994) compared adolescent self-esteem in post-divorce, mother-headed families, and two-parent, always married families. No difference in self-esteem by family structure was found.

A second group of studies has looked at the relationship between parental divorce and differences in the behaviour, attitudes, personality or achievement of college students. For example, Crossman, Shea and Adams (1980) compared the level of ego development, locus of control, and identity achievement in 294 college students who came from intact, divorced, and divorced-remarriage family backgrounds. Divorce backgrounds were not predictive of lower scores on any of the three measures. Similarly, Parish (1981) examined the self-concept of 1,409 college students in the USA. He found no significant differences in self-concept between students from divorced families and students from intact families. Phillips and Asbury (1990) examined several indicators of self-concept and mental health among a sample of 900 Black freshmen students, of whom 356 came from divorced or separated backgrounds. They found no significant differences on any of the measures. Garber (1991) also failed to find a relationship between parental divorce and self-concept in his sample of 324 undergraduates. Heyer and Nelson (1993) found no difference in autonomy scores in a sample of 388 college students between those whose parents were divorced and those from intact families, although those from divorced backgrounds recorded higher confidence and sexual identity scores.

Vess, Schwebel and Moreland (1983) compared the sex role orientation and sex role preference of two groups of college students, 84 who had experienced parental divorce before the age of ten and 135 whose parents had never divorced or separated. No significant differences were found between the two groups.

Lopez, Campbell and Watkins (1988) examined aspects of adjustment to college among 255 students from intact homes and 112 students from non-intact homes in the USA. They found no significant differences between the two groups.

Gabardi and Rosén (1991) explored the relationship between several measures of adjustment and parental divorce among a sample of 500 college students in the USA. Multivariate analyses of variance indicated that students from divorced families had significantly more sexual partners and more negative attitudes towards marriage than students from intact families.

Jennings, Salts and Smith (1991) employed the Favourableness of Attitudes Towards Marriage Scale among 340 college freshmen, 67 of whom came from divorced families. They found a significantly less favourable attitude towards marriage among those whose parents had separated or divorced. Similarly, Greenberg and Nay (1982) studied attitudes towards divorce among college students. They found that those from broken homes were more favourable toward divorce than other young people. On the other hand, Livingston and Kordinak (1990) examined the relationship between parental divorce and marital role expectations among a sample of 80 college students. They found no simple relationship between these two variables.

A third group of studies has looked at the relationship between parental divorce and differences in the behaviour and attitudes of adult samples. For example, MacLean and Wadsworth (1988) examined educational qualifications, using the 1946 National Survey of Health and Development cohort. They concluded that those who experienced parental divorce during their school years were significantly more likely to have lower educational attainment, whatever the social class of their family origin. Similarly, Kuh and MacLean (1990) demonstrated that women whose parents had separated or divorced by the time they were 16 were significantly less likely to have any educational qualifications by the age of 26, compared with their contemporaries from intact families.

Kiernan (1992) found significant differences in the ages when 'transitions' were made into young adulthood, comparing those who had experienced family disruption by the age of 16 with those who had not experienced such disruption. The transitions reviewed included leaving school, leaving home, forming partnerships and having children. For example, girls were shown to leave home earlier following parental divorce than those living in intact families or who had experienced the death of a parent. These data also demonstrated that women whose parents had divorced were more likely to have been teenage brides than their contemporaries from intact families. By the age of 36 they were also more likely to have been separated or divorced and twice as likely to have been married more than once.

Wadsworth's (1984) analysis of the National Survey of Health and Development data at the age of 26 concluded that those who had experienced family disruption were more likely to have had stomach, peptic or duodenal ulcers or a psychiatric disorder, although they were no more likely to have suffered from epilepsy, migraine, asthma or psoriasis.

Using two national surveys of the American adult population to test for the influence of parental divorce on adult adjustment, Kulka and Weingarten (1979) conclude that coming from a non-intact family has some negative significance for adult wellbeing.

Estaugh and Power (1991) compared self-reported drinking at the age of 23, using the National Child Development study, between young adults who had and who had not experienced family disruption during childhood. They found that individuals from disrupted families were *not* especially prone to heavy drinking.

A group of studies has looked at the relationship between parental divorce and their offspring's courtship patterns and marriage. Kulka and Weingarton (1979) found that individuals from disrupted homes are less likely to marry. Mueller and Pope (1977) found that women whose parents had divorced scored lower on predictors of marital stability. Booth, Brinkerhoff and White (1984) found that parental divorce increases courtship activity among offspring. Using a combined sample of USA national data, for white respondents only, Keith and Finlay (1988) demonstrated that parental divorce is associated with lower educational attainment and earlier age at marriage for both sexes. Daughters of divorced parents have a higher probability of being divorced. For sons of divorced parents, the probability of ever marrying is lower and of divorce is higher among those of lower social class background.

In a meta analysis of 37 studies dealing with aspects of the long-term consequences of parental divorce for adult wellbeing, Amato and Keith (1991) concluded that mean effect sizes were significant and negative for all outcomes, indicating that adults who had experienced parental divorce exhibited lower levels of wellbeing than did adults whose parents were continuously married.

In her review of the relevant literature, Burghes (1994) suggests that the range of outcome variables so far employed in research concerned with the possible impact of marital disruption during childhood and adolescence has been unfortunately restricted. The aim of the present study, therefore, is to broaden the discussion by exploring the relationship between marital disruption and a wide range of personal, social, political and moral values among a large sample of 13-15 year olds. This analysis uses the Teenage Religion and Values database developed by Francis and Kay (1995).

METHOD

Sample

A sample of 16,301 year nine and year ten pupils from 89 schools throughout England and Wales completed a specially modified form of the *CENTYMCA Attitude Inventory.* The sample comprised 8,537 year nine pupils and 7,764 year ten pupils, 8,201 boys and 8,100 girls.

Instrument

The CENTYMCA Attitude Inventory was developed by Francis (1982a, 1982b, 1984a, 1984b) in a sequence of studies concerned with attitudes and values between the ages of 13 and 39 years. The present analysis draws information from two main sections of this instrument.

The first section of the inventory is composed largely of multiple choice questions exploring aspects of the respondents' background, including routinely collected data like age, sex and denomination. This section of the inventory included the direct dichotomous question, 'Have your parents been separated or divorced?'

The second section of the inventory is composed of 128 Likert type items, arranged for scoring on a five point scale, from *agree strongly,* through *agree, not certain* and *disagree,* to *disagree strongly.* These items were constructed to profile the respondents' attitudes towards fourteen issues: personal wellbeing, worries, counselling, school, work, religious beliefs, church and society, supernatural, politics, social concerns, sexual morality, substance use, right and wrong, and leisure. Space does not permit the use of all these items in the present analysis.

Data Analysis

The present analysis intends to display the differences and similarities between the two groups of adolescents, those who have experienced marital disruption and those who have not, in a direct and straightforward manner. In the following tables the column headed 'disrupted' presents data for those whose parents have separated or divorced and the column headed 'intact' presents data for those whose parents have never separated or divorced. The percentage figures presented in these tables represent the product of the *agree* and *agree strongly* responses. The statistical significance of the differences in the responses of the two groups have been tested by the chi square test, computed by the SPSS statistical package (SPSS Inc., 1988).

RESULTS

Overview

The data demonstrate that more than one in five of the respondents (21.4%) came from families whose parents have been separated or divorced. The older pupils in the sample were more likely to have experienced parental separation or divorce than the younger pupils. Thus marital disruption has affected 20.7% of the pupils in year nine and 22.3% of the pupils in year ten.

Social Class

Social class was calculated on the classification system proposed by the Office of Population, Censuses and Surveys (1980) applied to the pupils' reporting of paternal occupation. The data demonstrate that pupils whose fathers are employed in higher social class occupations are less likely to report parental separation or divorce. Separation or divorce is reported by 12.2% of pupils whose father is in class one or professional occupations, 15.0% in class two or semi-professional occupations, 18.6% in non-manual class three occupations, 21.7% in skilled manual class three occupations, 20.1% in semi-skilled manual class four occupations and 26.0% in unskilled manual class five occupations.

Denomination

Like social class, denominational membership is a powerful predictor of differences in parental divorce or separation. Among the pupils who claimed no denominational allegiance, 24.9% had parents who had experienced separation or divorce, compared with 18.5% of Anglicans, 18.6% of Catholics, 15.8% of Methodists, 17.6% of Baptists and 10.4% of Presbyterians.

Personal Wellbeing

Table 1 demonstrates that there is a significantly lower level of personal wellbeing among the young people whose parents have experienced separation or divorce. They are less likely to find life really worth living or to feel that their life has a sense of purpose. They are more likely to feel that they are not worth much as a person and to suffer from depression. They are more likely to have considered taking their own life.

Worries

Young people whose parents have experienced separation or divorce are slightly more anxious about their own personal relationships. According to Table 2 they are a little more likely to worry about how they get on with other people and about their attractiveness to the opposite sex. They are more worried about their sex life. They are not, however, generally more anxious. They display no more worry than their contemporaries

TABLE 1. Personal Wellbeing

	intact %	disrupted %	X^2	P <
I feel my life has a sense of purpose	57.2	52.3	27.1	.001
I find life really worth living	72.0	64.7	68.3	.001
I feel I am not worth much as a person	12.0	16.1	39.2	.001
I often feel depressed	51.6	60.2	80.3	.001
I have sometimes considered taking my own life	24.7	33.9	116.8	.001

TABLE 2. Worries

	intact %	disrupted %	X^2	P <
I am worried about my sex life	16.9	19.2	10.1	.001
I am worried about my attractiveness to the opposite sex	32.9	34.7	3.8	.05
I am worried about how I get on with other people	51.6	53.7	5.0	.05
I am worried about going out alone at night in my area	31.0	29.5	2.7	NS
I am worried about being bullied at school	25.6	25.7	0.0	NS
I am worried about my exams at school	74.0	73.8	0.0	NS

from intact families about issues like being bullied at school. They are no more worried about school exams or about going out alone at night.

Counselling

Young people whose parents have experienced separation or divorce experience a greater need to turn to others for advice. According to Table 3 they derive less help than other young people from talking with their fathers, and, possibly as a consequence, are more likely to turn to close friends or to a school teacher for help, advice and support. On the other hand, they are no more likely than young people from intact homes to want to turn to doctors or clergy.

School

Table 4 demonstrates that young people whose parents have experienced separation or divorce hold a less positive attitude towards school. They are more inclined to regard school as boring and to feel that they are not happy in their school. They are less inclined to feel that teachers do a good job, or that their school is helping to prepare them for life. They are more inclined to worry about their school work. On the other hand, they are no less inclined than their contemporaries from intact families to like the people with whom they go to school.

Work

Table 5 suggests that young people whose parents have experienced separation or divorce hold a slightly less positive attitude towards the

TABLE 3. Counselling

	intact %	disrupted %	X^2	P <
I often long for someone to turn to for advice	34.6	39.9	32.6	.001
I would be reluctant to discuss my problems with a school teacher	48.3	45.6	7.9	.01
I would be reluctant to discuss my problems with a doctor	33.2	34.6	2.4	NS
I would be reluctant to discuss my problems with a Christian minister/vicar/priest	42.8	41.8	1.2	NS
I find it helpful to talk about my problems with my mother	51.2	49.5	3.2	NS
I find it helpful to talk about my problems with my father	32.9	28.3	26.3	.001
I find it helpful to talk about my problems with close friends	62.1	64.8	8.5	.01

TABLE 4. School

	intact %	disrupted %	X^2	P <
School is boring	31.8	38.9	62.1	.001
I am happy in my school	73.3	65.9	74.6	.001
I like the people I go to school with	90.0	89.3	1.5	NS
My school is helping to prepare me for life	68.5	66.0	7.9	.01
I often worry about my school work	63.5	65.5	4.6	.05
Teachers do a good job	45.2	41.1	18.4	.001

world of work. They are slightly less inclined to think that it is important to work hard when they get a job. They hold a slightly more cavalier attitude towards the prospects of unemployment. They are slightly more inclined to think that they would rather be unemployed than get a job which they dislike. On the other hand, they are no less inclined to want to get to the top in their work than pupils from intact families.

Religious Beliefs

Young people whose parents have experienced separation or divorce are less inclined to subscribe to religious beliefs than young people from intact families. According to Table 6, they are less likely to believe in God or to believe that Jesus Christ really rose from the dead. They are less likely to believe the Genesis account of creation. On the other hand, they are slightly more inclined to believe in life after death.

Church and Society

Table 7 demonstrates that young people whose parents have experienced separation or divorce hold a less positive attitude towards the role of the churches in contemporary society. They are more inclined to think that the church and the Bible are irrelevant for life today. They are less inclined to consider that the clergy do a good job. They are less inclined to want to get married in church or to have their children baptised or christened in church than pupils from intact families.

Supernatural

Although young people whose parents have experienced separation or divorce are *less* inclined to believe in God, Table 8 demonstrates that they

TABLE 5. Work

	intact %	disrupted %	X^2	P <
A job gives you a sense of purpose	77.3	76.8	0.4	NS
I think it is important to work hard when I get a job	95.0	93.1	18.7	.001
I want to get to the top in my work when I get a job	86.7	85.5	3.3	NS
I would not like to be unemployed	87.0	84.5	14.1	.001
I would rather be unemployed on social security than get a job I don't like doing	17.2	19.8	13.0	.001

TABLE 6. Religious Beliefs

	intact %	disrupted %	X^2	P <
I believe in God	43.1	38.6	23.1	.001
I believe that Jesus really rose from the dead	33.1	29.5	16.0	.001
I believe in life after death	41.1	43.9	8.8	.01
I believe that God made the world in six days and rested on the seventh	18.0	15.8	9.7	.001

are *more* inclined to believe in a range of supernatural phenomena. Thus they are more likely to believe in their horoscope, or to believe that fortune-tellers can tell the future. They are more likely to believe in ghosts and that it is possible to contact the spirits of the dead. They are more likely to believe in black magic.

Politics

Two main conclusions emerge from Table 9 regarding the relationship between separation or divorce and adolescents' attitudes towards politics. First, young people whose parents have experienced separation or divorce hold a more cynical attitude towards politics. They are more inclined to feel that it makes no difference which political party is in power. Second, young people whose parents have experienced separation or divorce adopt a more left wing political stance. They are likely to have more confidence in the Labour party and less confidence in the Conservative party.

TABLE 7. Church and Society

	intact %	disrupted %	X^2	P <
The church seems irrelevant to life today	25.8	28.4	9.8	.001
The Bible seems irrelevant to life today	28.9	31.1	6.1	.05
I want my children to be baptised/christened in church	59.0	53.5	33.7	.001
I want to get married in church	78.4	73.8	33.5	.001
Church is boring	49.2	53.9	23.6	.001
Christian ministers/vicars/priests do a good job	39.0	34.5	22.7	.001

TABLE 8. Supernatural

	intact %	disrupted %	X^2	P <
I believe in my horoscope	31.6	39.9	83.7	.001
I believe in ghosts	34.4	42.4	72.5	.001
I believe in black magic	16.6	21.9	52.0	.001
I believe that fortune-tellers can tell the future	16.0	24.4	130.0	.001
I believe it is possible to contact the spirits of the dead	27.8	37.7	125.6	.001

Social Concerns

Just as young people whose parents have experienced separation or divorce hold a more cynical attitude towards politics, so they also hold a more cynical attitude towards the world's problems. According to Table 10 they are less inclined to feel that they can do anything to help solve the world's problems. Table 10 also demonstrates that they are less inclined to be concerned about global issues, like the risk of pollution to the environment and the poverty of the Third World. On the other hand, young people from disrupted families are neither more conservative nor more liberal than young people from intact families in their attitudes towards violence on television or pornography.

Sexual Morality

Table 11 demonstrates that there is a significantly more permissive attitude towards sexual morality among the young people whose parents

TABLE 9. Politics

	intact %	disrupted %	X^2	P <
It makes no difference which political party is in power	17.7	21.3	23.6	.001
I have confidence in the Conservative party	21.2	16.7	33.5	.001
I have confidence in the Labour party	16.6	20.1	22.0	.001
Private schools should be abolished	22.3	24.4	6.4	.05
Private medicine should be abolished	14.7	17.9	20.8	.001

TABLE 10. Social Concerns

	intact %	disrupted %	X^2	P <
There is too much violence on television	18.7	18.7	0.0	NS
Pornography is too readily available	31.5	32.5	1.2	NS
I am concerned about the risk of pollution to the environment	68.6	64.0	25.8	.001
I am concerned about the poverty of the Third World	63.9	58.0	40.4	.001
There is nothing I can do to help solve the world's problems	22.9	27.2	26.7	.001

have experienced separation or divorce. They are less likely to think that it is wrong to have sexual intercourse under the legal age or outside marriage. They are less likely to think that divorce is wrong. They are less likely to think that homosexuality is wrong. On the other hand, they are more likely than young people from intact families to think that abortion is wrong.

Substance Use

Just as young people whose parents have experienced separation or divorce hold a more liberal attitude towards sexual morality, so they also hold a more liberal attitude towards substance use. According to Table 12 they are more likely to condone smoking cigarettes and becoming drunk. They are more likely to condone the use of marijuana and heroin. They are more likely to condone glue sniffing, although not the sniffing of butane gas.

TABLE 11. Sexual Morality

	intact %	disrupted %	X^2	P <
It is wrong to have sexual intercourse outside marriage	14.7	11.7	20.5	.001
It is wrong to have sexual intercourse under the legal age (16 years)	25.0	21.0	23.5	.001
Homosexuality is wrong	39.7	37.7	4.6	.05
Abortion is wrong	34.8	39.2	22.4	.001
Divorce is wrong	20.9	18.7	7.9	.01

TABLE 12. Substance Use

	intact %	disrupted %	X^2	P <
It is wrong to smoke cigarettes	46.6	38.7	67.5	.001
It is wrong to become drunk	22.4	18.5	24.3	.001
It is wrong to use marijuana (hash or pot)	59.0	52.8	41.9	.001
It is wrong to use heroin	79.2	76.4	12.6	.001
It is wrong to sniff glue	80.8	78.6	8.4	.01
It is wrong to sniff butane gas	74.5	72.7	3.4	NS

Right and Wrong

According to Table 13 young people whose parents have experienced separation or divorce are less likely to think that there is anything wrong in a variety of anti-social or criminal activities. They are less likely to think that there is anything wrong in writing graffiti, playing truant, or cycling after dark without lights. They are more likely to condone travelling without a ticket or shoplifting.

Leisure

Two main conclusions emerge from Table 14 regarding the relationship between separation or divorce and adolescents' attitudes towards their

TABLE 13. Right and Wrong

	intact %	disrupted %	X^2	P <
There is nothing wrong in shop-lifting	6.0	8.9	37.2	.001
There is nothing wrong in travelling without a ticket	17.8	21.4	23.3	.001
There is nothing wrong in cycling after dark without lights	14.0	18.1	36.9	.001
There is nothing wrong in playing truant (wagging) from school	15.7	22.1	78.9	.001
There is nothing wrong in writing graffiti (tagging) wherever you like	14.1	17.8	22.6	.001

TABLE 14. Leisure

	intact %	disrupted %	X^2	P <
I often hang about with my friends doing nothing in particular	65.2	69.8	26.2	.001
I wish I had more things to do with my leisure time	55.5	60.8	31.6	.001
My Youth Centre is boring	31.9	35.1	12.3	.001
My parents allow me to do what I like in my leisure time	49.1	50.0	0.9	NS
My parents do not agree with most of the things that I do in my leisure time	25.3	33.9	101.3	.001

leisure. First, young people whose parents have experienced separation or divorce hold a less positive attitude towards their leisure. They are more likely to long for more things to do with their leisure time. They are more likely to hang about with their friends doing nothing in particular. They are more likely to be critical of their local youth centre. Second, young people whose parents have experienced separation or divorce tend to feel that their parents are more critical of the ways in which they spend their leisure time. On the other hand, they are neither more nor less aware of parental restrictions being placed on their leisure time than young people from intact families.

CONCLUSION

This analysis has profiled the relationship between separation or divorce and adolescent values over fourteen specific areas. The data make it clear that there are significant differences over all fourteen areas between those young people whose parents have experienced separation or divorce and those whose parents have not experienced such separation or divorce. It is important to be clear just what kind of conclusions can be drawn from these findings and what kinds of conclusions cannot be drawn from these findings. Two main observations need to be made.

First, it is possible on the basis of these data to conclude that as a group young people whose parents have experienced separation or divorce differ in significant ways from young people whose parents have not experienced separation or divorce. As a group they enjoy lower personal wellbeing, worry more about relationships, long more to be able to turn to others for advice, confide more in teachers, hold less positive attitudes towards school and towards work, are less likely to believe in conventional religion, but more likely to believe in superstitions, are more cynical about politics and issues of global concern, tend to prefer left wing political views, are more liberal in their attitudes towards sexual morality and substance use, are more inclined to condone anti-social behaviour, and are less satisfied with their leisure time.

Second, however, it is not possible on the basis of the present analysis to conclude that these very real differences are necessarily or wholly a consequence of parental separation or divorce. In a cross-sectional study of this nature there are a number of correlates, like social class and religious background, which need to be taken into consideration in exploring the adequacy of a causal account. The present findings, at least, confirm the value of undertaking such further analyses.

REFERENCES

Amato, P.R. and Keith, B. (1991), Parental divorce and adult well-being: a meta-analysis, *Journal of Marriage and the Family*, 53, 43-58.

Booth, A., Brinkerhoff, D.B. and White, L.K. (1984), The impact of parental divorce on courtship, *Journal of Marriage and the Family*, 46, 85-94.

Burghes, L. (1994), *Lone Parenthood and Family Disruption: the outcomes for children*, London, Family Policy Studies Centre.

Cherlin, A.J., Furstenberg, F.F., Chase-Lansdale, P.L., Kiernan, K.E., Robins, P.K., Morrison, D.R. and Teitler, J.O. (1991), Longitudinal studies of effects of divorce on children in Great Britain and the United States, *Science*, 252.

Clark, J. and Barber, B.L. (1994), Adolescents in post divorce and always-married families: self-esteem and perceptions of fathers' interest, *Journal of Marriage and the Family*, 56, 608-614.

Crossman, S.M., Shea, J.A. and Adams, G.R. (1980), Effects of parental divorce during early childhood on ego development and identity formation of college students, *Journal of Divorce*, 3, 263-272.

Demo, D.H. (1993), The relentless search for effects of divorce: forging new traits or tumbling down the beaten path, *Journal of Marriage and the Family*, 55.

Demo, D.H. and Acock, A.C. (1988), The impact of divorce on children, *Journal of Marriage and the Family*, 50, 619-648.

Douglas, J.W.B. (1970), Broken families and child behaviour, *Journal of the Royal College of Physicians*, 4, 203-210.

Elliott, B.J. and Richards, M.P.M. (1991), Children and divorce: educational performance and behaviour before and after parental separation, *International Journal of Law and the Family*, 5, 258-276.

Estaugh, V. and Power, C. (1991), Family disruption in early life and drinking in young adulthood, *Alcohol and Alcoholism*, 26, 639-644.

Ferri, E. (1976), *Growing Up in a One-Parent Family*, Slough, National Foundation for Educational Research.

Francis, L.J. (1982a), *Youth in Transit: a profile of 16-25 year olds*, Aldershot, Gower.

Francis, L.J. (1982b), *Experience of Adulthood: a profile of 26-39 year olds*, Aldershot, Gower.

Francis, L.J. (1984a), *Young and Unemployed*, Tonbridge Wells, Costello.

Francis, L.J. (1984b), *Teenagers and the Church: a profile of church-going youth in the 1980s*, London, Collins Liturgical Publications.

Francis, L.J. and Kay, W.K. (1995), *Teenage Religion and Values Today*, Leominster, Gracewing.

Gabardi, L. and Rosén, L.A. (1991), Differences between college students from divorced and intact families, *Journal of Divorce & Remarriage*, 15, 175-191.

Garber, R.J. (1991), Long-term effects of divorce on the self-esteem of young adults, *Journal of Divorce & Remarriage*, 17, 1, 131-137.

Greenberg, E. and Nay, W. (1982), The intergenerational transmission of marital instability reconsidered, *Journal of Marriage and the Family*, 44, 335-347.

Harding, S., Phillips, D. and Fogarty, M. (1986), *Contrasting Values in Western Europe: unity, diversity and change*, Basingstoke, Macmillan.

Haskey, J. (1990), Children in families broken by divorce, *Population Trends*, 61, 34-42.

Heyer, D.L. and Nelson, E.S. (1993), The relationship between parental marital status and the development of identity and emotional autonomy in college students, *Journal of College Student Development*, 34, 432-436.

Jennings, A.M., Salts, C.J. and Smith, T.A. Jr (1991), Attitudes toward marriage: effects of parental conflict, family structure, and gender, *Journal of Divorce & Remarriage*, 17, 1, 67-79.

Jowell, R., Brook, L. and Dowds, L. (1993), *International Social Attitudes: the 10th BSA report*, Aldershot, Dartmouth.

Jowell, R., Witherspoon, S. and Brook, L. (1988), *British Social Attitudes: the 5th report*, Aldershot, Gower.

Kanoy, K.W. and Cunningham, J.L. (1984), Consensus or confusion in research on children and divorce: conceptual and methodological issues, *Journal of Divorce*, 7, 4, 45-71.

Keith, V.M. and Finlay, B. (1988), The impact of parental divorce on children's educational attainment, marital timing, and likelihood of divorce, *Journal of Marriage and the Family*, 50, 797-809.

Kiernan, K.E. (1992), The impact of family disruption in childhood on transitions made in young adult life, *Population Studies*, 46, 213-234.

Kuh, D. and MacLean, M. (1990), Women's childhood experience of parental separation and their subsequent health and status in adulthood, *Journal of Biosocial Science*, 22, 121-135.

Kulka, R.A. and Weingarten, H. (1979), The long term effects of parental divorce in childhood on adult adjustment, *Journal of Social Issues*, 35, 4, 50-77.

Livingston, R.B. and Kordinak, S.T. (1990), The long term effect of parental divorce: marital role expectations, *Journal of Divorce & Remarriage*, 14, 2, 91-105.

Lopez, F.G., Campbell, V.L. and Watkins, C.E. Jr (1988), The relation of parental divorce to college student development, *Journal of Divorce*, 12, 1, 83-98.

MacLean, M. and Wadsworth, M.E.J. (1988), The interests of children after parental divorce: a long-term perspective, *International Journal of Law and the Family*, 2, 155-160.

Mueller, C. and Pope, H. (1977), Marital instability: a study of its transmission between generations, *Journal of Marriage and the Family*, 39, 83-93.

Office of Population Censuses and Surveys, (1980), *Classification of Occupations 1980*, London, HMSO.

Office of Population Censuses and Surveys, (1990), *Marriage and Divorce Statistics: England and Wales, 1837-1983*, London, HMSO.

Office of Population Censuses and Surveys, (1993), *Marriage and Divorce Statistics: England and Wales, 1990*, London, HMSO.

Parish, T.S. (1981), The impact of divorce on the family, *Adolescence*, 16, 577-580.

Phillips, C.P. and Asbury, C.A. (1990), Relationship of parental marital dissolution and sex to selected mental health and self concept indicators in a sample of black university freshmen, *Journal of Divorce*, 13, 3, 79-91.

SPSS Inc. (1988), *SPSSX User's Guide*, New York, McGraw-Hill.

Vess, J.D., Schwebel, A.I. and Moreland, J. (1983), The effects of early parental divorce on the sex role development of college students, *Journal of Divorce*, 7, 1, 83-95.

Wadsworth, M.E.J. (1984), Early stress and association with adult health behaviour and parenting, in N.R. Butler and B.D. Corner (eds), *Stress and Disability in Childhood*, pp 100-104, Bristol, John Wright and Sons.

Correlates of Worldwide Divorce Rates

David Lester

SUMMARY. A study of nations of the world in 1980 found that national divorce rates were predicted primarily by a cluster of variables measuring development. In contrast, national marriage rates were predicted by development, militarism, rapid economic growth and size. *[Article copies available for a fee from The Haworth Document Delivery Service: 1-800-342-9678. E-mail address: getinfo@haworth.com]*

Yang and Lester (1991) explored the correlations between a large set of social indicators for the states of America and divorce rates. A factor-analysis identified seven independent (orthogonal) clusters of social indicators. The divorce rate was associated with scores on only one of these clusters, a cluster which appeared to measure social instability (with high rates of suicide, interstate migration, alcohol consumption and the percentage born in-state, low rates of church attendance and strict gun control laws). Divorce rates were not associated with the clusters which, on the

David Lester is Executive Director of the Center for the Study of Suicide, RR41, 5 Stonegate Court, Blackwood, NJ 08012.

[Haworth co-indexing entry note]: "Correlates of Worldwide Divorce Rates." Lester, David. Co-published simultaneously in *Journal of Divorce & Remarriage* (The Haworth Press, Inc.) Vol. 26, No. 3/4, 1997, pp. 215-219; and: *Divorce and Remarriage: International Studies* (ed: Craig A. Everett) The Haworth Press, Inc., 1997, pp. 215-219. Single or multiple copies of this article are available for a fee from The Haworth Document Delivery Service [1-800-342-9678, 9:00 a.m. - 5:00 p.m. (EST). E-mail address: getinfo@haworth.com].

basis of those social indicators loading most highly on them, appeared to measure wealthy/urban, elder population, southern, unemployment, overall participation in the labor force or dense/eastern. Yang and Lester argued that such a study, using a large set of social indicators and a factor-analytic procedure, were preferable to single predictor variable studies or those selecting only two or three predictor variables, for the selection of predictor variables for regression analyses is arbitrary. In factor-analysis all relevant variables are included, which permits the identification of clusters of related variables thereby suggesting the underlying social characteristic at work more clearly–in the case of statewide divorce rates, general social instability.

An obvious question to ask next was whether the social correlates of divorce rates worldwide were similar or different to those for the states of America. A data set was available for nations of the world in 1980 (Lester, 1995), and this data set was used for the present study.

METHOD

The data set consisted of 78 social and economic variables for 72 nations with populations over one million. The large number of variables made a factor-analysis impossible, for factor-analysis requires the existence of many more subjects (in this case nations) than variables. In order to deal with this problem, a preliminary correlational analysis was carried out to identify the major correlates of national divorce rates.

There were two sources for 1980 divorce rates–the United Nations (annual) and Kurian (1984). The Pearson correlation between the two sets of divorce rates was 0.81, and between the two marriage rates 0.91. Variables were examined which correlated with divorce rates from both sources (see Table 1). (Incidentally, for purposes of comparison, variables which correlate with *marriage* rates from both sources were also noted.)

RESULTS

The correlates of both sets of divorce rates were: caloric intake, quality of life, life expectancy, percent urban, literacy, fertility, percent in agriculture, infant mortality, and population/hospital beds. It seems that divorce rates were higher in nations which were more economically developed. These nine social variables were subjected to a factor analysis, using SSPS^X, with a principal components extraction and varimax rotation.

TABLE 1. Simple Correlates of Divorce and Marriage Rates Over Nations of the World (Pearson r's)

	divorce		marriage	
	UN	Kurian	UN	Kurian
marriage			0.32*	0.09
suicide	0.33*	0.21	0.19	0.27*
homicide	−0.21	−0.15	−0.25	−0.37*
gnp/capita	0.66*	0.22	0.14	0.23
gdp/growth	−0.04	−0.35*	0.42*	0.51*
inflation rate	−0.20	−0.02	0.03	0.08
unemployment rate	0.07	−0.04	−0.05	0.05
land area	0.24	0.28*	0.35*	0.29*
population	0.24	0.20	0.33*	0.29*
population density	−0.11	−0.22	0.35*	0.24
population growth	−0.37*	−0.22	−0.10	−0.25
quality of life (Estes)	0.46*	0.35*	0.01	−0.01
quality of life (Kurian)	0.47*	−0.07	0.25*	0.35*
civil liberties	−0.24	0.02	0.23	0.12
death rate	−0.02	0.35*	−0.26*	−0.25*
infant mortality	−0.42*	−0.36*	−0.27*	−0.43*
life expectancy (World Bank)	0.45*	0.35*	0.19	0.40*
life expectancy (Kurian)	0.49*	−0.02	0.26*	0.35*
% urban	0.42*	0.29*	0.11	0.29*
urban growth	−0.44*	−0.14	−0.21	−0.31*
female labor force part.	0.45*	0.19	0.12	0.01
birth rate	−0.42*	−0.25	−0.17	−0.19
fertility rate	−0.52*	−0.29*	−0.22	−0.35*
% elderly	0.47*	0.21	0.03	0.16
% young	−0.58*	−0.22	−0.23	−0.32*
% illegitimate births	−0.31	−0.29	−0.40*	−0.45*
% Christians	0.30*	0.11	−0.28*	−0.09
% Roman Catholics	−0.11	−0.04	−0.23	−0.15
% Muslims	−0.16	−0.13	−0.05	−0.01
caloric intake	0.56*	0.28*	0.34*	0.48*
military part. ratio	0.04	0.02	0.38*	0.43*
% defense expenditures	−0.03	−0.02	0.33*	0.32*
% males	−0.21	0.01	−0.02	−0.09
alcohol consumption	0.38*	0.10	0.10	0.23
literacy	0.39*	0.34*	0.12	0.37*
% in agriculture	−0.52*	−0.42*	−0.26	−0.43*
% in industry	0.45*	0.20	0.40*	0.46*
population/hospital beds	−0.42*	−0.31*	−0.06	−0.08
dependency ratio	−0.51*	−0.23	−0.41*	−0.43*
children in labor force	−0.49*	−0.29	−0.28*	−0.46*

* two-tailed p < .05 or better

Only a single factor had an eigenvalue greater than unity. Thus, all of the social variables associated with divorce rates were strongly associated with one another.

The correlates of both sets of marriage rates were: growth rate of the gross domestic product per capita, percentage labor force in industry, the military participation ratio (the proportion of males in the military), area, caloric intake, population, percent gross national product for defense expenditures, life expectancy, the quality of life, the dependency ratio (the proportion of residents under the age of 15 or over the age of 65), the illegitimacy rate, employment of children, infant mortality, and the death rate.

When these social variables were subjected to a factor analysis, using SPSS^X, with a principal components extraction and varimax rotation, four factors were identified (see Table 2), which appeared to measure development, militarism, rapid growth, and size. It can be seen that all four (independent) factor scores were associated with marriage rates. Incidentally, only scores on the factor for developed and size were associated with divorce rates (see Table 2).

DISCUSSION

Stack (1994), in a broad review of divorce, suggested that national divorce rates were associated with religion, urbanization and level of economic development. The present study has indicated that divorce rates do not appear to be related to the religious orientation of the country (Christian versus Muslim or Protestant versus Roman Catholic). However, divorce rates were associated with urbanization and the level of development. Thus, the modern way of life does appear to be conducive to high divorce rates. Other factors suggested by Stack as possible determinants of high divorce rates, such as female labor force participation and social disintegration did not appear to play a large or consistent role in predicting national divorce rates. These variables may, however, play a larger role in predicting divorce rates of regions within a nation, as Yang and Lester (1991) found for America.

Interestingly, the predictors of national marriage rates were more complex, though the level of development did appear to be associated also with marriage rates as with divorce rates. However, other independent factors, including militarism, rapid economic growth and size also appeared to be associated with marriage rates.

TABLE 2. Factor Analysis of Social Correlates of Marriage Rates

	I	II	III	IV
population	−0.10	−0.02	−0.11	0.81*
infant mortality	−0.86*	0.04	−0.35	0.11
area	0.09	−0.11	0.14	0.80*
death rate	−0.56*	0.29	−0.62*	0.06
gdp growth rate	0.06	0.33	0.76*	0.07
dependency ratio	−0.89*	0.01	0.08	−0.17
child labor	−0.78*	−0.07	−0.34	0.04
quality of life	0.91*	−0.14	0.29	−0.06
military part. rate	0.26	0.85*	0.16	−0.13
% defense expend.	−0.14	0.93*	0.03	−0.04
life expect.	0.94*	−0.07	0.23	−0.06
% in industry	0.90*	0.14	−0.07	−0.04
caloric intake	0.89*	0.19	−0.04	0.04
% variance	47.8%	15.1%	10.0%	7.9%
Pearson r:				
marriage (UN)	0.30*	0.33*	0.27	0.37*
marriage (Kurian)	0.47*	0.36*	0.33*	0.33*
divorce (UN)	0.59*	0.08	−0.21	0.69*
divorce (Kurian)	0.43*	−0.01	−0.14	0.39*

Factor labels:
  I   developed
  II   militaristic
  III   rapid growth
  IV   size

REFERENCES

Estes, R. J. *The social progress of nations.* New York: Praeger, 1984.

Kurian, G. T. *The new book of world rankings.* New York: Facts on File, 1984.

Lester, D. *Patterns of suicide and homicide around the world*, Commack, NY: Nova, 1995.

Stack, S. Divorce. *Encyclopedia of Human Behavior*, 1994, 2, 153-163. San Diego: Academic Press.

United Nations. *Demographic Yearbook.* New York: United Nations, annual.

World Bank. *World Tables, 1991.* Washington, DC: World Bank, 1991.

Yang, B., & Lester, D. Correlates of statewide divorce rates. *Journal of Divorce & Remarriage*, 1991, 15, 219-223.

Index

Note: Page numbers followed by f indicate figures; page numbers followed by t indicate tables.

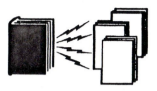

Haworth
DOCUMENT DELIVERY
SERVICE

This valuable service provides a single-article order form for any article from a Haworth journal.

- *Time Saving:* No running around from library to library to find a specific article.
- *Cost Effective:* All costs are kept down to a minimum.
- *Fast Delivery:* Choose from several options, including same-day FAX.
- *No Copyright Hassles:* You will be supplied by the original publisher.
- *Easy Payment:* Choose from several easy payment methods.

Open Accounts Welcome for . . .
- Library Interlibrary Loan Departments
- Library Network/Consortia Wishing to Provide Single-Article Services
- Indexing/Abstracting Services with Single Article Provision Services
- Document Provision Brokers and Freelance Information Service Providers

---

MAIL or *FAX* THIS ENTIRE ORDER FORM TO:

Haworth Document Delivery Service
The Haworth Press, Inc.
10 Alice Street
Binghamton, NY 13904-1580

or FAX: 1-800-895-0582
or CALL: 1-800-342-9678
9am-5pm EST

PLEASE SEND ME PHOTOCOPIES OF THE FOLLOWING SINGLE ARTICLES:

1) Journal Title: _____

   Vol/Issue/Year: _____ Starting & Ending Pages: _____

   Article Title: _____

2) Journal Title: _____

   Vol/Issue/Year: _____ Starting & Ending Pages: _____

   Article Title: _____

3) Journal Title: _____

   Vol/Issue/Year: _____ Starting & Ending Pages: _____

   Article Title: _____

4) Journal Title: _____

   Vol/Issue/Year: _____ Starting & Ending Pages: _____

   Article Title: _____

(See other side for Costs and Payment Information)

COSTS: Please figure your cost to order quality copies of an article.

1. Set-up charge per article: $8.00
   ($8.00 × number of separate articles) _____

2. Photocopying charge for each article:
   1-10 pages: $1.00 _____

   11-19 pages: $3.00 _____

   20-29 pages: $5.00 _____

   30+ pages: $2.00/10 pages _____

3. Flexicover (optional): $2.00/article _____

4. Postage & Handling: US: $1.00 for the first article/
   $.50 each additional article _____

   Federal Express: $25.00 _____

   Outside US: $2.00 for first article/
   $.50 each additional article _____

5. Same-day FAX service: $.35 per page _____

GRAND TOTAL: _____

METHOD OF PAYMENT: (please check one)

❑ Check enclosed   ❑ Please ship and bill. PO # _____
(sorry we can ship and bill to bookstores only! All others must pre-pay)

❑ Charge to my credit card: ❑ Visa;   ❑ MasterCard;   ❑ Discover;
   ❑ American Express;

Account Number: _____ Expiration date: _____

Signature: **✗** _____

Name: _____ Institution: _____

Address: _____

_____

City: _____ State: _____ Zip: _____

Phone Number: _____ FAX Number: _____

MAIL or *FAX* THIS ENTIRE ORDER FORM TO:

Haworth Document Delivery Service
The Haworth Press, Inc.
10 Alice Street
Binghamton, NY 13904-1580

or FAX: 1-800-895-0582
or CALL: 1-800-342-9678
9am-5pm EST)